A4

Making the
Perfect
Pitch

Making the Perfect Pitch

How to Catch a Literary Agent's Eye

edited by

KATHARINE SANDS

THE WRITER BOOKS

The Writer Books is an imprint of Kalmbach Trade Press, a division of Kalmbach Publishing Co. These books are distributed to the book trade by Watson-Guptill.

For all other inquiries, including individual orders or details on special quantity discounts for groups or conferences, contact:

Kalmbach Publishing Co.
21027 Crossroads Circle
Waukesha, WI 53187
(800) 533-6644

Visit our website at http://writermag.com.
Secure online ordering available.

For feedback on this or any other title by The Writer Books, contact us at this e-mail address: writerbooks@kalmbach.com.

Printed in Canada

03 04 05 06 07 08 09 10 11 12   10 9 8 7 6 5 4 3 2 1

Publisher's Cataloging-in-Publication

Making the perfect pitch : how to catch a literary agent's
   eye / [edited] by Katharine Sands.
   p. cm.
   Includes bibliographical references and index.
   ISBN 0-87116-206-7
   1. Authorship—Marketing. 2. Literary agents.
   I. Sands, Katharine.

PN161.M26 2004 070.5'2
                QBI03-200943

Text design by Mighty Media, Minneapolis
Cover design by Lisa Bergman

ACKNOWLEDGMENTS

It has been my great good fortune to know and work with so many talented writers and colleagues. This book and the agent who corralled it exist as a salute to Sarah Jane Freymann. A heart full of thanks to Sarah Jane, for bringing me into the world of books and for the privilege of being associated with the Sarah Jane Freymann Literary Agency. *Mahalo* for being mentoress nonpareil. I am deeply grateful. My favorite piece of your advice is so true of you: "When in doubt, always be majestic."

As an agent, it has been my privilege to work with clients whose works have turned me into a grandma with an accordion file of photos.

Group hug to all contributors to this book for sharing insights and collective wisdom. We have created a Rosetta Stone to unlock the mysteries of pitching. Kudos to all!

At The Writer Books, editor Phil Martin deserves many superlatives for being wonderful and fun to work with. But undoubtedly he would prefer to be thanked Midwestern style. "Yah, it wasn't so bad working together." And thanks for the able assistance from Amy Glander, whose helpful good cheer added to making this process a sheer pleasure. I am especially indebted to Elfrieda Abbe for her excellent editorial eye and warm encouragement of this project and indeed of all writers.

To my agents' culinary group, Tables of Content, thank you, Rita Rosenkranz, Sheree Bykofsky, and Lori Perkins, for making me feel like I am living on *Sex and the City*.

Thank you to my many best friends for being my nearest and dearest: best-loved best friend Erica Wexler, favorite best friend Kathy Hipple, longest-running best friend Laura Levin, newest best friend Toni Robino, most glamorous best friend Gretchen Kelly, along with Phoebe Collins, Tomislav Podreka, John Kildahl, Monica and Lydia Wellington, Beth Greenspan, and Andy Partridge. And thanks to Anthony Gaglione for all his help preparing the interview transcripts.

Finally, the book owes its life to inspirational editrix Donya Dickerson. Without Donya's developmental guidance and fairy godmothering, *Making the Perfect Pitch* would never have left the pitching stage to become the book, you, dear reader, are now holding.

CONTENTS

by Katharine Sands

Writing commercially has probably been a bane to writers since Pliny the Elder plied the trade. But, the truth is that today, writers can have the magical imagination of J. K. Rowling, the wit and wisdom of Frank McCourt, the perfect economy of Ernest Hemingway, and the ageless brilliance of (whoever really wrote) Shakespeare. But they still need to pitch, query, and propose before they can be published.

I've just returned home from a trip. A magical place of supreme beauty, Maui is home to the annual Maui Writers Conference. Each summer, the island event resonates with the love of all things literati. A hotbed of talented writers converge on the picture-perfect paradise to meet with agents from leading literary agencies and editors of top publishing houses.

Within days we are all filled with the spirit of Aloha, festooned with tropical leis, and clothed in bright beautiful Hawaiian floral prints. The dreams of wordsmiths waft around us like the scent of plumeria. We are all infused with hopes of returning home with great "finds" from writers who have come to pitch us.

For, you see, literary agents are lovers of words and the people who wield them. We happily serve as speakers and motivational teachers for writers' organizations, workshops, and publishing forums. We want to help writers to understand what they need to do to get their manuscripts published. And yes, we are always on the look-out for the next potential best seller.

Making the Perfect Pitch is what writers most need when they enter the literary arena: a hands-on guide to the nitty-gritty details of crafting a successful pitch. Each of the 40 articles in this book, all written by top agents and other authorities in the publishing field, provides insights and practical advice on how to make that perfect pitch. All of these experts offer a unique take on who and what gets published, viewed through the prism of the pitch. To a man or woman, these assembled notables share the dreams of writers. We are always in search of the *joie de livre* of a special book—writing that takes a fresh look, writing that is insightful, observant, funny, or urgent. Writing that is transporting. Writing that makes you want to turn the page.

How do you get agents excited about what is exciting to you? You can hire a caterer, a hit man, or a dominatrix. But you can't hire an agent. Literary agents must be enchanted, seduced, and won over to take you on as a client. They must want to devote their efforts to working on your behalf. This book was created to help you understand the ways we think, evaluate, and prognosticate. I am delighted to be agent provocateur for this book—corralling my colleagues into helping novice and veteran writers alike to navigate the "how to get published" landscape.

In today's Zeitgeist, pitching skills are crucial to the business of writing. Yet few writers know how to pitch. Showcasing the art of pitchcraft, this anthology is chock-full of query critiques, proposal examples, revelations of likes and dislikes of agents and editors, plus a sampling of best and worst pitching tales and big-break stories. *Making the Perfect Pitch* delves into a wide range of fiction and nonfiction subject areas— from literary fiction to genre thrillers, from children's books to octogenarian memoirs, from cookbooks to poetry—to bring writers wisdom on how to pitch with aplomb. You can study how to create plot and craft scenes, but without a strong, effective pitch, the chances of your talents showing up in a bookstore are minimal at best.

For the fledgling writer and the well-published professional, this is the everything-you-need-to-know guide to crafting pitches, queries, and proposals. You will discover how to blend passion with practicality to pitch your writing and sell your ideas. Explains Peter Rubie, "We have an enduring love affair not just with books, but with ideas."

Besides chapters on how top agents think, other articles here offer perspectives from related fields, like leading book-jacket copywriter Deb Babitt who offers tips on copywriting from her work with novels by John Grisham, Olivia Goldsmith, and Steven King. Laurie Horowitz shares insight into which books see film-rights action in Hollywood. Phoebe Collins reveals what strikes a chord on the other side of the desk as an experienced acquisitions editor. And consultant Tonianne Robino tells how to pitch a collaboration project to a famous person who might benefit from a little ghostwriting.

Mostly, the agents all share their best advice for how to catch their eye, from Esmond Harmsworth's courtship-ritual analogy to Joe Regal's search for the "providential diamond" of discovery. Sheree Bykofsky wants to "hear a diva do opera," while Sarah Jane Freymann is willing to be "moved, seduced, amazed, or inspired." Each agent shares a separate vision; each offers commonsense, industry-savvy advice.

In my New York City office—sounds of the Maui surf now a memory—the oceanic tide of manuscript submissions is a daily deluge. In the leaning tower of queries (often referred to as the "slush pile") are voices of every kind and description proposing books. Slush is mostly that: letters from prisoners proclaiming the story of their innocence, from people who think they are the Messiah or able to channel insights from unknown galaxies. The slush pile, testimony to human courage and survivorship, is filled with unsavory porn, memoirs of B-movie queens, has-beens, never-weres, and the people who loved them.

Wading deeper into the pile, I pull out a random sample; it's a shark expert with an idea for a series about a sexy ichthyologist who solves crimes. But maybe, just maybe, the voluminous voices of the mail will

IN THE LEANING TOWER OF QUERIES (OFTEN REFERRED TO AS THE "SLUSH PILE") ARE VOICES OF EVERY KIND AND DESCRIPTION.

yield something special. As Ellen Levine says, "You never know what's in the basket."

Inspiration is everywhere when you are a writer. The sidewalk plaque in front of the New York Public Library on Fifth Avenue reads, "The universe is made of stories, not atoms." One quote, and poet Muriel Rukeyser has made the perfect pitch, inspiring me to read her.

In my office, I am inspired daily by three placards hung over my desk:

"Imagination is more important than knowledge."
—Albert Einstein

"Words are the Voice of the Heart."
—unknown

"Imagination rules the world."
—Napoleon

Although Napoleon never achieved his dream to become a novelist . . . he might have if only he had known how to how to make the perfect pitch!

Publishing begins with a pitch. Literary agents and editors are forever on the lookout for writers who can bring new and interesting ideas to life. In a nutshell, pitching is about finding the right words and getting the right people to read them.

Use this eclectic collection as a treasure trove of our best ideas so you can make the perfect pitch for yours.

CHAPTER 1

A Morning in the Life of a Literary Agent

by James C. Vines

Imagine for a moment you're a literary agent. It's 11 a.m., and your assistant has just delivered the pile of query letters from today's mail. It's got to be at least 100 letters. This happens every day, and today you'll get over 100 new e-mail queries as well. You read 52,000 queries per year, and in all that material you're hoping to find a few good new projects.

Back in '98 you found and sold a record eleven first novels from the slush pile, but the average is much lower. You would rather reject a book that someone else might sell than take on something that feels "iffy" to you. You've got an hour set aside for this, and you're ready to go!

Thankfully, your assistant has already opened all the query letters with the SASE neatly clipped to each one. The first few don't do it for you. One puts you off by the rambling, sardonic tone of the letter; another is filled with irrelevant and unnecessary personal revelations in the opening sentences, making it clear this author doesn't know how to take advantage of the most important space on the page. And if the author can't use the most important space on the page of this letter in an effective and compelling manner, then what is the likelihood that she will in her manuscript?

The next one is printed on extremely fancy heavy linen paper with a flashy typeface and logo, which is unnecessary because it's the content that counts. Another one opens by reciting the astronomical sales figures of Rowling, Clancy, Grisham, and McMillan, and stating that he will best those numbers because he's got a great publicist (someone you've never heard of) and a burning desire to be the greatest author of all time. That's all well and good, but this goes on for 20 lines. It's only in the very last paragraph at the bottom of the page that he spends two sentences glossing over the briefest possible description of the novel, and summing up by saying the genre of his novel is "impossible to classify."

Well, if he can't classify it, how would Barnes & Noble figure out how to classify it? What this author doesn't know is that the best way to sell you on the novel is simply by presenting an enticing description of the story's main conflict and central characters. You set these aside for your assistant to reject with form letters.

Reviewing the first few has taken you less than a couple of minutes. Are you worried that you're not spending enough time carefully considering each novel? Do you feel that you really have to read three chapters of each of these novels to give them a fair shake? Do you feel that you should have a meeting to discuss each query letter and chapters with your colleagues? No. Happily, you are deluged with query letters every day. And after fourteen years in the business, you know that you are best off waiting for the right query letter to stir your interest and to simply reject all those that miss the mark for whatever reason.

In the next letter, the author has included a photo of herself, which is irrelevant. In the first paragraph she mentions she's written a nonfiction proposal for a dating book, so you quickly scan the rest of letter to find out what her "platform" is. Does she have a newsletter with 50,000 subscribers? Did she do 100 paid speaking engagements last year? Does she counsel movie stars on their love lives? Anything like that and she might have a winner.

She doesn't mention any such thing, but she does mention that she has a website. This is a mistake. It would be so much better if the author would just give you the information you need in the query letter rather than sending you on a hunt-and-peck mission on the computer to find out. Once her website finally loads, you find out she doesn't have a platform. This author does not understand that major publishers don't want to help an unknown author create a platform; publishers would rather wait until the platform is already established and then make a book deal at that time. Reject with form letter. Next.

You go through the rest of them quickly. A science-fiction novella of 45 pages with a storyline that spans 800 years. Impossible.

Yet another hackneyed P.I. novel. Next.

A self-published e-book on CD by someone who swears that every family member who read the novel loved it. Don't even want to go there.

A novel in which every word in every line of dialogue is phonetically spelled to imitate regional dialects. Nope.

MAJOR PUBLISHERS DON'T WANT TO HELP AN UNKNOWN AUTHOR CREATE A PLATFORM; PUBLISHERS WOULD RATHER WAIT UNTIL THE PLATFORM IS ALREADY ESTABLISHED.

It goes on like this for the remainder of the hour, and just when you are starting to think the whole batch is bad, a great one grabs your attention.

In this query letter, the author has her simple header at the top of the page with her name, address, telephone number, and e-mail address. But here is what grabs you: after the customary date and greeting, she just launches into the description of her novel. It's written like the flap copy you'd find in a published book.

The first sentence establishes the main character and the central conflict of the book. The next sentence reveals how the character is attempting to overcome this conflict, and this sentence also introduces the main character's love interest. From there, you learn about complications in the love story, and further complications in the conflict and plot. By the time you've reached the bottom of the page, even though the author doesn't give you the details of the resolution of the story, you are already e-mailing a message to her asking if she will send you the full manuscript for an exclusive read for five business days. You still realize that as good as the query letter is, it is only the first step. But you still can't help getting excited about it, because this is your job, and it's what you love to do.

Although it doesn't seem possible . . . the next one could be a winner, too. This query letter offers a nonfiction proposal on the future of the world's energy by a strongly credentialed journalist. As you read further, you see that not only has the author already interviewed numerous leading scientists for the book proposal, he believes he could even get one of the most important ones to co-author the book with him if that would be more appealing to publishers. This is definitely promising.

Since it's a policy book and not a how-to book, there's no need to worry about whether the author has a platform. For this kind of nonfiction proposal the credentials of the writer, the quality of the writing, and the importance of the subject are what matters. You are compelled to pick up the phone and call this author right away.

And that's it. Out of 100 queries, there are two possibilities. Not bad for an hour, and who knows, maybe you've just discovered the Next Big Thing.

And that's why you love what you do; the possibilities are endless.

JAMES C. VINES has been a literary agent in New York for 14 years. He started his career in 1989 at Raines & Raines, where he worked with such authors as James Dickey, Bruno Bettelheim, Cynthia Ozick, Winston Groom, and Roderick Thorp. In 1992 he moved to the Virginia Barber Literary Agency where he worked with bestselling authors Anne Rivers Siddons, Peter Mayle, and Anita Shreve.

In 1995 he founded the Vines Agency, Inc., which represents many award-winning and bestselling authors, including Koji Suzuki, Joe R. Lansdale, Don Winslow, Bernice L. McFadden, The Estate of Terry Southern, Snoop Dogg, Laura Doyle, Michael Stipe, Vickie M. Stringer, and Julia Spencer-Fleming.

CHAPTER 2

Five Questions to Ask Before Sending Your Query Letter

by Kristen Auclair

Everyone knows that agents are deluged with submissions, and my office is no exception. While I may take weeks to respond to most queries, I do try to look through my mail right away, quickly reading the query or cover letters to make sure that the pile isn't harboring any gems that will be snatched up by another agent who acts more quickly. A few of the letters are terrible, the majority of them are just fine—but a few stand out enough to compel me to contact the author immediately and ask for the proposal or manuscript, or throw the enclosed materials in my bag to read that night.

What do these few letters have that the others don't? It's a combination of several things. Of course, they include the necessary information such as a summary of the project and the author's credentials. But they're also professional, confident, and well-written. The authors display intelligence and knowledge about their subject matter and the market, and they've targeted me because they know my interests.

First things first: it's hard to make an amazing pitch if the project itself is a dud—so hone your writing skills, fine-tune the book's organization, and build your credentials. Make sure the manuscript (if it's fiction) or the proposal (if it's not) is ready and in pristine shape—and then craft the pitch.

As with any business correspondence, a query or pitch letter should contain a few key elements, including a brief summary of the project and the author's credentials or related experience. In general, the letter should only run one page long; very rarely should it exceed two pages.

Since I work primarily on nonfiction, author credentials are incredibly important to me. If it's a health or self-help book, I look for a doctor at the top of her field, or a journalist with access to the top experts, or the director of a respected health organization. For fiction, I love to see that the author has an M.F.A., or has published in some good literary journals and magazines. It varies from project to project and genre to genre, but in general I want an expert or an experienced writer—preferably both.

So. Your project is fantastic, your credentials are impeccable, and your letter has all the right elements. But as you read it again, you realize that it doesn't seem as impressive as it should. To determine what may be missing, make sure you can answer yes to these five questions:

1. Is it polished, error-free, and professional?
It seems ridiculous to mention, but don't forget to *proofread your letter*. I'm constantly surprised by the carelessness and breeziness of some letters and proposals I receive.

This is a business letter. Use stationery if you have it, and refrain from using "attention getters" like excessive exclamation points or stickers or pink ink or glitter. It's possible to be professional and lively without resorting to silliness. Here's a good example of a professional query letter that caught my eye:

Dear Ms. Auclair:
    Every year, 100,000 military wives and 38,000 women
in uniform are initiated into the crazy world of military life.
Nearly 200,000 military wives and women in uniform visit

CinCHouse.com every month desperate for information on how to relocate their household around the world, keep their marriage together during deployments, parent their children alone, and maintain their careers during multiple moves. Unlike the World War II-era military sweethearts everyone thinks of, these military women are predominantly career-oriented, 20-somethings, mothers of small children. They don't have the time or the inclination to learn about military life—or even their husbands' activities or whereabouts—from traditional spouse clubs, condescending command officials, or cranky books that focus on military protocol.

That's why CinCHouse.com came up with *Married to the Military: A Survival Guide for Military Wives, Girlfriends, and Women in Uniform*. Written in a lighthearted "Girlfriend's Guide" style, this orientation to military life focuses on the need-to-know information that is the top priority of visitors to our web-based magazine and community—we know because we track which sections and articles our visitors frequent most.

Best of all, *Married to the Military* has the backing of an established non-profit organization and the Internet's largest community of military women. And buyers of the book will go back to the community again and again, recommending it to "newbie" military wives, girlfriends, fiancées and servicemembers as their first step to getting a grip on military life.

I've enclosed for your review a book outline, the first three chapters, demographic and marketing information, and my personal qualifications as an author. If you are interested in this project, please contact me at [phone number] or [e-mail address] to discuss the proposal. Thank you for your consideration.

Best regards,

Meredith Leyva

Why does this pitch work? First, it draws the reader in by proving (with numbers, rather than just empty claims that "the audience is huge!") that there's a sizable market for this book, and tells me what I need to know about these potential readers.

Then, it explains how this book will appeal to that readership. It's going to be chock-full of information, yet also hip and friendlier than the other guides available.

Next, the author gives it a little punch with some enticing marketing information. And she closes her pitch with a description of what she enclosed and her contact information.

This letter is professional but still warm and inviting, hinting at the good stuff inside so that I'll want to read more. (And while Meredith couldn't have known this, my mom was a military wife, so the subject hit home for me—in addition to everything else, a little bit of luck never hurts.)

2. Does the tone of your query letter reflect the tone of your book?

Is your project a serious, analytical book about an important social issue? Or is it a lighthearted and funny take on pop culture? In either case, your voice should come across in the letter. Here's a good example:

> Dear Ms. Auclair:
>
> When my older brother Carter topped 400 pounds, I decided to save him. Actually, I felt like strangling him, but saving him seemed like a more reasonable option. What my brother needed, I felt, was a major kick in the butt. After twenty years of diets, he had given up trying to lose weight and get healthy. Everybody in the family was whispering behind closed doors, and nobody was doing anything about it. It was up to me to get Carter back on track.
>
> But how do you help a compulsive overeater? Force him to go on another diet? Encourage him? Confront him? Do an intervention? And how could I, the confrontation-coward of the universe, get my brother to face his problem and find the help he needed?
>
> *You Better Be Laughing, Too* is the true story of how I tried to save my brother from compulsive overeating. It was no joke—he was dying from obesity. But the story of trying to save Carter is a pretty funny one. For one thing, Carter did not want to be saved. That meant I had to trick him into getting healthy. For another,

I had problems of my own: My children's school secretary had it in for me, I was consuming Hostess Ho-Hos by the boxful, my 7-year-old announced he was "going mad," and my 9-year-old voiced a death wish every time he struck out in Little League. Besides all that, I was busy running a Bed and Breakfast, teaching a university course, and trying to finish an interminable freelance job. Squeezing in saving my brother was not going to be easy.

Little by little, drawing my reluctant family into the conspiracy, I made plans for the ultimate confrontation: an "intervention." But in the process, I was confronted by all manner of questions about addiction and the choices we make every day. Is addiction really a disease, or is it a choice? Is "denial" a psychological problem or a failure of courage? Does low self-esteem underlie the inability to recover from addiction? Or is it more simply an unwillingness to stay with the pain of facing one's demons? In point of fact, the question of facing one's demons goes beyond addiction. How many of us are ready and willing to face the truth about ourselves on a daily basis?

The scope of the story and timeliness of the topic make for a broad audience for this book. With the epidemic of obesity in America making national news, this very real danger is in our public consciousness like never before. But this book is more than a story about battling obesity. *You Better Be Laughing, Too* tells of a family's spiritual journey. It is the story of a family struggling to achieve health and balance amidst the ravages of addiction. It is a story about love and letting go, about the meaning of family, the limits of nurturing, and the point at which each person must take responsibility for who and what he has become.

I am a long-time journalist and medical writer whose publication credits include book chapters for *Courtroom Medicine* (Time/Warner Books), health articles for *Hudson Valley Magazine* and *Inside Health*; addiction-prevention educational materials for Scholastic, an assortment of chapters for Reader's Digest Books, and two books of poetry. I hold an M.F.A. in writing from

Columbia and an M.A. in English from NYU, where I also teach writing at NYU's Stern Graduate School of Business.

I would be happy to send you a chapter or two if you are interested. The completed manuscript is 75,000 words.

Sincerely,

C. L. Watson

C. L. accomplished a difficult task here—conveying the sometimes-humorous tone of the book while keeping the letter professional and showing me that the book covers some serious ground, too. I was eager to read this manuscript.

3. Are you sure that the agent you're pitching works on this type of project?

One only has to do minimal research to know that I don't work on children's books or genre fiction such as romance, horror, or science fiction. It's on our agency's website and in several guidebooks, and I mention my interests (and non-interests) every time I make a presentation at a writer's conference. Yet I'm frequently queried on projects in these genres. I'm not interested in them, don't know anything about them, and would not be a good agent for them.

It's impossible to know the details of what every agent is looking for, but you can at least do some preliminary research so that you don't waste your time pitching the wrong agents. Check out the agent's interests in the many guidebooks available, search online to find out if he or she has a website, and look at the acknowledgments pages of recently published books that are similar to yours to see who the author thanked.

4. Do you know your market?

I'm impressed by a writer who recognizes trends, but not by one who blindly follows them. (Besides, once the general reader spots a trend, it's already at least a year old—remember that most books don't get published until at least a year after they're sold.) To familiarize yourself with the market and current trends, spend some time in a bookstore and online, researching the competition or comparable books.

Many letters claim, "This is the only book on this subject," but when I do a quick check online, I find two or three that are quite comparable, and my confidence in the author's research abilities (or honesty) is deflated. Instead of making unsubstantiated claims, point out how your book will stand apart. Maybe it has a different approach, as Meredith's book does, or maybe it contains new research. Make comparisons, but not clichéd ones.

I'M IMPRESSED BY A WRITER WHO RECOGNIZES TRENDS, NOT BY ONE WHO BLINDLY FOLLOWS THEM.

5. Are you emphasizing the best aspects of your project?

If you've never published before, for goodness' sake there's no need to bring that to my attention. Make sure your letter focuses on the positive aspects of your project, whether it's the unique approach you take on the subject, your wonderful credentials, or the great marketing contacts you have.

This letter is shorter than most, but it caught my attention immediately because the author mentioned just the right things:

> Dear Kristen Auclair:
>
> I was given your name by [Agent]. My book is called *The Essential C-Section Guide* and I'm co-writing it with a former editor of mine from *Parenting* magazine. [Agent] was very kind and said that pregnancy/baby books aren't subject matters that interest her, but that you might consider our proposal.
>
> Can I e-mail the proposal to you, or would you prefer I mail it with writing samples? My work often appears in *Parenting* and *Self*; I have also written for *Glamour*, *Parents*, *Redbook*, *Shape*, and *Shape's Fit Pregnancy* (where I am also a contributing editor).
>
> I appreciate your time.
>
> Best,
>
> Dana Sullivan

What's right about this letter? Despite its brevity, it includes some key elements: Dana was referred by a trusted colleague (which makes the relative informality perfectly acceptable), and her writing credits include the best parenting and pregnancy magazines out there. That's important, because it means she has the contacts and the experience that editors like to see. She and her co-writer are seasoned health journalists who know how to research, write well, and meet deadlines.

Finally, don't pad your letter by telling me the audience is huge, that you're the perfect guest for Oprah, or that you're eager to promote your work. I've seen these claims so often that they no longer have any meaning for me. (And what author is not willing to promote his work?)

The truth is that there isn't one right way to pitch a book. So much depends upon the project, the author, and the whims of the agent on any particular day. But with research, care, and this five-point checklist, I think you'll be on the right track.

KRISTEN AUCLAIR is a literary agent with Graybill & English in Washington, DC. She represents varied categories and is especially interested in health, parenting, women's issues, travel, serious nonfiction, and literary fiction.

Recent projects include *The Mind-Body Diabetes Revolution* by Richard Surwit, Ph.D. (Free Press); *The Essential C-Section Guide* by Maureen Connolly and Dana Sullivan (Broadway); and *Growing Seasons* by Annie Spiegelman (Seal Press). Previously, Kristen was the publicist for The Lyons Press and an editor at HarperCollins. For more information, see the agency website at www.GraybillandEnglish.com.

CHAPTER 3

Notes to the New Writer

by Anna Ghosh

Most of us find it difficult to assume or affect a "salesman's" pluck, especially when selling ourselves. For a new writer, the process of querying an agent can become a frustrating and daunting task.

"What do they want me to say? . . . they just need to read the book!!"

"Given how thick these people are, what can I possibly point to in my work that they might be capable of understanding?"

Usually this sort of thinking leads nowhere. This is why it is so vital that the writer understand what really counts in a query letter. What can you do to seize the attention of an agent who is likely to be distracted, busy, and rather skeptical about you and your project?

Have Spirit

When the horse trader glances for the first time upon the stallion, he gauges first the spirit of the beast, not the gait, strength, speed, or agility. These qualities are only fully assessed later. And while gait, agility, and strength are analogous to the constituent parts of a good book—a good idea, stylish writing, organization—the spirit of the writer is often the thing first noticed and perhaps most telling.

An effective query letter is a distillation of the work's spirit or essence. It is not the place to impress with the minutiae of your research or to encapsulate all the twists in your novel. Rather than get bogged down by a synopsis or summary of your work, try to find that magical phrase or two that expresses its core idea, the key element that sets it apart. Show as much as possible of your voice, style, expertise, and ability to "arrange the furniture." A query letter must inform, but it must also enchant:

Example 1:

Our human bodies are inextricably tied to our individual identities and to our everyday living. Consider, then, the strange wonder of the opportunity to look inside ourselves at the foreign landscape which permits us to eat, sleep, and breathe, as well as skip rope, play a violin concerto, and shoot a three-pointer. *Body of Work: A Writer's Experience in the Human Anatomy Lab* offers a glimpse of this innermost world through the eyes of a first-year medical student who, as a poet, has been trained to describe and look closely at what she observes.

Example 2:

Both the collection of stories and the novel revolve around the theme of grief. In a way I believe I'm searching for the language of grief. Too, I want to speak for that minority that anyone can join at any time, the ill and the dying. I myself am diabetic, am partially blind, and I infuse my work with the notion of urgency in the face of a foreshortened life, yet with the patience and understanding that life is in the expanded individual moment.

Example 3:

> As the daughter of immigrants and the granddaughter of weavers, I have always believed in crossing the lines. In *Across the Black Waters*, I will cross international and generational borders to tell the story of a vast globalized people: the Indian diaspora.
>
> I will do so through the lens of my own sprawling family, setting our intimate dramas against the vivid backdrop of history. *Across the Black Waters* will portray in human terms, the social forces that swept millions of people out of India: eastward to East Asia and the Pacific, westward to England, Africa and North America.

Know Your Reader

Publishing—as opposed to writing—is a commercial endeavor and involves considerations quite removed from the writer's intellectual or aesthetic concerns. An agent has to sell the writer's project to a publisher. A publisher has to sell the finished books to booksellers. And finally a reader has to put down 25-odd dollars for their copy.

Because agents are the first link in the business, the writer's query must help them see the potential readership and demonstrate a sound understanding of the publishing landscape.

Again, the horse with the best hope of winning has not only honed her skill, but knows the terrain and competition. What are the books that are similar to yours? How successful have they been? Does your book fill a gap in the current literature on the subject?

> Short narrative books about scientific discoveries and technological breakthroughs have sold exceeding well as evidenced by *Longitude* and *Galileo's Daughter* by Dava Sobel, *The Map That Changed the World* by Simon Winchester, and *The Invention of Clouds* by Richard Hamblyn. The untold story about the invention of refrigeration and the profound impact it had on business, diet and society will appeal to this readership.

RATHER THAN GET BOGGED DOWN BY A SYNOPSIS OR SUMMARY OF YOUR WORK, TRY TO FIND THAT MAGICAL PHRASE OR TWO THAT EXPRESSES ITS CORE IDEA.

A query may point out a specific readership that an agent has not even considered:

> An estimated thirty-five million Americans live in interfaith households at present and the numbers are on the rise. There have been a few guides for Jewish-Christian weddings (see attached list) but *Interfaith Weddings* will be the first book to address the need for step-by-step guidance and inspiration for interfaith couples. Though the core audience for the book is interfaith couples, the book will also appeal to atheists, agnostics, and people who have no strong desire for a particular religious ceremony.

Prove That You're a Writer, Not a Dilettante

New writers are always a gamble for an agent. Agents don't get a penny until they sell the book to a publisher and actually receive the signing check. Before this happens, a great deal of time and effort may be expended. This is why agents will scour a query for concrete evidence of the writer's abilities. Talent can be found anywhere, but the writer with even modest credentials will appear vastly more committed and prepared to deliver a publishable book:

Example from an unpublished novelist:

> I am a recent graduate from the M.F.A. program at the University of Massachusetts. Last year Pulitzer Prize-winning author Carol Shields selected my story, [name of short story], for inclusion in the anthology *Scribner's Best of the Fiction Workshops*. My work has also appeared in *Quarterly West, Crab Orchard Review*, and is forthcoming in the *New Virginia Review*.

Example from a narrative nonfiction author:

> As a journalist and a poet, I believe I am uniquely qualified for both the intensive reporting and the lyrical writing that this story will require. I spent this past year as a fellow in the National Arts Journalism Program at Columbia University. For eight years, I

have been an editor and reporter at the *San Jose Mercury News*. My literary writing has been recognized through numerous publications and honors, including a Sundance Institute Writers Fellowship. I am a graduate of Stanford University.

Example from the author of the interfaith wedding guide:

> [The author] is an ordained Interfaith minister and a charismatic individual based in New York City who has officiated at numerous interfaith weddings across the country. Her keen understanding of interfaith issues and extraordinary ceremonies has mended deep rifts in families, brought tears to the eyes of participants, and earned her an overwhelming number of referrals and features in *Modern Bride, For the Bride*, and *Bridal Guide*.

For certain types of books, the author's credentials supersede all else. For example, a health book nearly always needs an author with an M.D.; a book of investment advice almost certainly won't sell if the author doesn't have a long track record in the financial field. You should understand early on whether you possess the necessary background to write your book or if there are any ways to compensate for the lack thereof.

At some point, all writers must contend with the impersonal rejection letter. The entire industry can seem like a soulless machine with a disappointing dependence on sales figures and marketing points. Is it possible to get a real human reaction to the work amid the crush to create bestsellers?

Fortunately, books, unlike the latest line of Nike shoes, are an extremely unruly product. Each book is unique in its essence, and so a mechanical approach to evaluating and selling them is insufficient. The attempts of publishers to repeat success with clones of former bestsellers repeatedly prove unsuccessful. And in every season there is a completely unexpected strong seller, hand-sold by one reader to the next.

Your book will not be for everyone, and the most irresistible query can fail if the agent has no interest in the subject. Plumb every available source of information, be it other writers, publishing guides, or the

Internet, to come up with the agents who are most likely to fully grasp the spirit and significance of your work. With a little bit of luck, your query will ignite the imagination of the agent perfect for you.

ANNA GHOSH has been an agent at Scovil Chichak Galen Literary Agency in New York City since 1995 where she represents a variety of adult fiction and nonfiction. She is especially interested in literary nonfiction, journalism, history and books on social and cultural issues. She also has a keen interest in international and Asian/African/Latino/Native-American writers and in scholars writing for a general audience.

Anna was educated at Woodstock International School, India, and at Hampshire College, Massachusetts, where she earned her B.A. in Cultural Anthropology and Literary Journalism.

Recent titles include: *Ambitious Brew: The Story of Beer in America* by Maureen Ogle (Harcourt); *A Radical Line: One Family's Century of Conscience* by Thai Stein Jones (Free Press); *Across the Black Waters* by Minal Hajratwala (Houghton Mifflin); *Reading Claudius: A Literary Memoir* by Caroline Heller (Dial); *The Memory Cure* by Dr. Majid Fotuhi (McGraw-Hill); *Queenmaker: A Novel of Kind David's Queen* by India Edghill (Picador); *Frida* by Barbara Mujica (Plume); and *Some People, Some Other Place* by J. California Cooper (Doubleday).

CHAPTER 4

I Am Willing to Be Seduced, Amazed, Charmed, or Moved

by Sarah Jane Freymann

I'm a literary agent who, truth be told, doesn't actually believe in "the pitch." My gut reaction to the question, "What is the perfect pitch?" is to answer, Zen-like, "The perfect pitch . . . is no pitch."

When Katharine asked me to write this piece, out of curiosity I looked up the word "pitch" in the dictionary—and this is what I found: "to put, set, or plant in a fixed or definite position; to deliver to serve to the batter; to determine the key or keynote of a melody; to attempt to sell or win approval for, promote, advertise, i.e. to pitch breakfast foods at a sales conference, politicians pitching on TV."

Maybe it's the breakfast-cereal and politicians-on-TV aspect of "pitching" that turns me off (although the concept of hitting the perfect note of a melody is intriguing).

While I am not interested in your selling me anything, per se, I *am* willing to be seduced, amazed, charmed, or moved. What I really want is for you to share your enthusiasm with me, your passion; to invite me along on a journey; to tell me something you, and you alone, know; to open my eyes to a truth that will enable me to see the world in a different way.

And, of course, to do so with beautiful writing.

As the unsolicited manuscripts and query letters pile up on my desk and computer screen, I am not so naïve, so high-minded, or so much a romantic to ignore that some clearly grab my attention—while others fall either flat or over-inflated on the page.

What is it about the approach that works? What are the elements of the successful pitch letter? First, let's face it—we're talking about writing. The importance of elegant, finely honed writing, even in the introductory "pitch" letter, cannot be overstated. Nor for that matter can all the other aspects of good professional writing such as spelling, punctuation, grammar, and so on.

And while there are no hard and fast rules, I have come, over the years, to the following preferences.

1. Write, don't call.

If you are introducing yourself to "pitch" an unsolicited work, do so with a query letter. A letter gives you the opportunity to organize your thoughts, list your credentials, and provide a flavor of your writing style. It also gives me the opportunity to digest, ponder, and re-read what you've written. If you insist on calling, introduce yourself, tell me what you do and how it relates to your book, and be prepared with a good story and a clear, succinct description of your book.

I represent quite a few spiritual book authors, and so get calls from people who say: "Hello, I've written the most amazing book about my spiritual experience." When I venture to ask what it's about, the answer I get is usually a variation on: "Umm, well, it's a new look at God, and human beings, and our relationship to the Universe."

There is someone, on the other hand, who calls me every few months—a lovely woman from somewhere down South—and she is forgiven. Because with a voice that sounds like Dolly Parton, she refers to me as "Miz Sarah" and while I have never formally taken her on as a client, I have read the revisions of her manuscript for going on three years now. And she never fails to tell me how she is praying for me and for the whole city of New York. And I do believe she is.

2. Do a little research first.

It doesn't hurt to do a little research on which categories agents prefer. For instance, if you read *Literary Market Place* or *Jeff Herman's Guide*, you'll see that I don't represent science fiction or category romances. You'll save yourself a lot of time by targeting the right agents for your work.

3. No gimmicks.

Please, don't under any circumstance resort to gimmicks like ostrich feathers, scented candles, cute stationery, aromatherapy (or snake) oil, wands, cat pawprints, dried flowers, or family photographs. All of which, and more, I have received. What those little enticements say to me is that you don't have faith in your own material. Be outrageous if you will, but be dignified.

Once we have begun to work together and I have sold your book, then—like one of my charming authors who has sent me an orchid for each of her books I've sold, or another who brings me freshly laid eggs from her hens whenever she comes to New York—you can send me chocolates, flowers, potpourri, or artisanal cheeses.

4. Be confident, not boastful. Be personable.

I am drawn to authors who, in their introductory letters, demonstrate that they are confident but not boastful. It's not a good idea to praise your own work, telling me how wonderful your book is.

It always amazes me how the flavor comes across in a query letter—not only of the work but also of the personality of the author. Whenever prospective clients start their letter with: "I am looking for a New York literary agent who will aggressively market my book," I read no further. I have learned from experience that this is not the kind of client I am interested in working with.

Being a literary agent is not just my work. For me, the line between work, books, writers, ideas, and my life is blurred. Many of the authors I represent have become personal friends of mine and my family, friends

> I AM DRAWN TO AUTHORS WHO, IN THEIR INTRODUCTORY LETTERS, DEMONSTRATE THAT THEY ARE CONFIDENT BUT NOT BOASTFUL.

with whom we have the good fortune to share something of the world about which they write.

One such sharing was the journey my husband and I took with an author to experience firsthand the magic of the Pacific gray whales off the coast of Baja California. I have spent time meditating with one author in a Zen Buddhist monastery. I've stayed with one of my cookbook authors on the rugged Greek island where she and her husband now live. I've traveled and given a writing workshop with another client while she gave a photography workshop. And with one of my more intrepid authors, I climbed New Hampshire's Mt. Monadnock on the hottest day of the year.

5. Seek the wonderful one-liner.

It is rare and hard to come by. If you're able to sum up your entire book with a title or a one-line description, that's gold. Take for instance the title of a book I represented by Nina Wise. This was the title suggested in her pitch letter: *A big new free happy unusual life: self-expression and spiritual practice for those who have time for neither.* What more need one say?

Author Rolf Potts described his book *Vagabonding* as "an uncommon guide to the art of long-term travel." Or another described a book on a writing practice as a way to "write the mind alive."

Recently I received a pitch letter for a book by two authors living in Paris. They described *Made in France* as "a cross between *A Year in Provence* and *Born to Shop Paris.*" I couldn't resist that delightful combination from the sublime to the ridiculous, and now we are working together.

These one-liners can be especially evocative for a work of fiction. So, before you send off that final draft of your pitch letter, let your intuitive imagination run wild. Get together with clever friends. And see if you can come up with a delicious one-liner that says it all.

6. Be authentic.

In addition to terrific writing, there is another quality I really value and always seek. This quality often shines through, even in a letter. It's authenticity. By this, I mean the assurance and dignity that comes from being genuinely knowledgeable and truly intimate with the subject you are writing about. You've immersed yourself in it, and gained a certain intimacy. You've walked the walk, so you can talk the talk (or write the write).

This authenticity makes me feel as if a book *had* to be written. Not just because the author would love to be published, but also because the author has something of importance to say, something to add to the world. From a practical point of view, this authenticity helps with a key aspect of a good pitch: clear focus and good organization.

7. Be honest.

How much should you tell me about your project's checkered past? If, with your pitch letter, you enclose all the kind rejection letters you have received from other agents, you've told me too much. I am surprised at how often would-be authors do that. Maybe they feel the letters are an indication of how close they've come to being accepted. But mostly it just tells me how thoughtful many agents are.

On the other hand, if you don't tell me that, under another title, your book was sent out by another agent and rejected by twenty publishers . . . then you haven't told me enough.

I would love to share some of the pitch letters I have received, but it is telling that I haven't kept any. There is no cookie-cutter approach to writing a good query letter. Provided you write well and are coming from an authentic place, everything else is up for grabs. You can be as provocative, outrageous, sentimental, cynical, vulnerable, or humorous as you choose—whatever reflects who you are and what you have to say.

I will go out on a limb and say with absolute conviction that, as with everything else in life, so much of what transpires between an author, an agent, and a book is timing . . . and chemistry. Your eyes meet someone else's on the street as you're waiting for a bus, on the subway, in an art gallery, across the proverbial crowded room, on a ledge hanging off a mountain cliff, and something clicks. In other words, one either falls in love . . . or doesn't.

This, in my opinion, holds as true for people as it does for books on parenting, religion, travel adventure, science, business strategies, sports, cooking, and fiction. And when that "click" happens and a spark is ignited, one tends to rationalize: it was that charming query letter, his blue eyes, the subject is timely, the author has such a fabulous voice, it's such a great title, and so on.

But for me, the truth—alas and thank goodness—is both more simple and more mysterious.

We cannot end here, however. After all, what can any of us do about chemistry, something over which neither you nor I have any control? While I believe in the mysterious, I refuse to accept a "que sera, sera" approach.

When it comes to writing, as one of my clients always says, "Trust in God, but tether your camel." So take responsibility for all the details listed herein, and the mysterious will take care of itself.

SARAH JANE FREYMANN has been a literary agent since the 1970s. Born in London, she moved to America with her family when she was six and attended the Lycee Francais in New York. There, she learned it was okay to smoke, flirt, drink endless cups of coffee, and be madly in love with Existentialism, so long as one also stood up whenever a teacher came into the room.

The Sarah Jane Freymann Literary Agency has placed authors with many publishers, including Random House, Ballantine, Bantam, Broadway, Chronicle, Clarkson Potter, Dutton, HarperCollins, Morrow, Penguin USA, Riverhead, Rizzoli, Simon & Schuster, and Viking. The eclectic list reflects her diverse interests. The agency has a strong commitment to serious self-help and spiritual books; selected titles have sold over 100,00 copies and been published in many foreign editions. Several cookbook authors have won the prestigious Julia Child Award and one, Cookbook of the Year. The agency also has an affinity for narrative nonfiction, representing renowned naturalists and journalists; also memoir; travel, with lavishly photographed coffee table books; health; and books on lifestyle, illustration, and design.

Sarah Jane brings to her work a conviction that *story* (in fiction or nonfiction, conveyed via words or image, for entertainment or insight) is still our most powerful magic.

CHAPTER 5

Practicing Pitchcraft®

by Katharine Sands

It's the pitch and nothing but the pitch that gets a writer selected from the leaning tower of queries in a literary agent's office. Are you writing a novel that will keep readers turning pages, instead of turning in for a good night's sleep? Will your book show readers how to talk to the dead, trim their thighs, manage their money, make better love—or all at the same time? Then get ready to distill the most dynamic, exciting, and energized points about your work: your pitch.

Your pitch is the passport that you carry into the literary marketplace. Why is pitching your work so important? Because whether for fiction, faction, nonfiction, thriller, chiller, cozy, category romance, or chick lit, it's the pitch and nothing but the pitch that gets an agent's attention.

The writing you do about your writing is as important as the writing itself. To effectively introduce a novel or book idea to a literary agent, you must persuade him/her that there is a readership for your book. The writing about your writing is part "hello," part cover letter, part interview for the coveted job of book author. It's the best of the best of the best of your writing. If you were an Olympic figure skater, it would be your triple axel on the ice.

Yes, agents do deeply care about the craft of writing. But understand that now you are taking your work into the literary marketplace. Like any other industry, the book business—the actual business of books—has certain quirks and processes and challenges. For you, the writer, these are separate from the creative act itself.

"Publishing must tread the tightrope between art and commerce," says agent Michael Larsen of San Francisco. "Publishers want books that they can publish with pride and with passion, but to survive, they must publish books that sell."

An agent needs to know from the get-go why you will appeal to readers. You must put aside your deep connection to your work and even the amount of work you have put into it. Your work is literary wares that you are now selling in the literary marketplace.

While many agents became agents because they love literature, venerate books, and wrote papers on the novels of Jane Austen in school, this alone does not spell success for an agent in the business. One succeeds by having what P. T. Barnum described as "the ability to see what is all around you just waiting to be seen." We see raw material, raw ideas, and the gleam in authors' eyes. Then, we envision how these could be grown into a book. We ask ourselves how your writing will be considered inside a publishing house, how your writing—as a literary property—would succeed in its bid for publication. This is paramount in our minds from first write to last rights.

The way you query an agent—the way you introduce your work—must be influenced by these things. They are more than trends. If you want to understand and speak the language of bookselling, answer the question posed by editor Max Perkins (who discovered Hemingway and Fitzgerald), still being used by editors today: "Why does the world need this book?"

Make sure the reasons readers would like it are clear. The way publishing professionals look at your work is the difference between how a loved one looks at you and how your doctor looks at you. To your loved one, you are a sight for sore eyes, loved, chosen. But to your doctor, you're a bunch of symptoms and a gaggle of body parts. You're still you; but you are regarded differently. Literary agents read writers' works to diagnose the page, to make a prognosis—a professional assessment of how that work will fare.

Your Query Letter

Imagine you are Atticus Finch arguing for the life of an innocent. Because you are. Your query letter is a plea for life.

START BY WRITING LONG DESCRIPTIONS OF YOUR BOOK, YOUR MARKET, YOURSELF. THEN SHRINK THEM DOWN TO QUERY SIZE.

> A good query answers the three questions I will have: why [nonfiction writers] are uniquely qualified, who the audience is for the book, and what the competing books are. . . . For fiction I'm just really looking for good writing, I think the letter should really pique my interest in some way. If the letter isn't well-written, it is unlikely that I'll believe that the novel will hold my interest. The letter is the first indication for me of their ability to communicate.
> —Anna Ghosh

Go ahead, give these a try: Start writing long descriptions of your book, your market, yourself. Then shrink them down to query size. What is your strongest area? Your credentials? Your book idea? The potential market?

> One page, that's how brief your query letter should be. Never, ever go longer than one page. You need to distill your brilliance, your wisdom, and your expertise into one potent page-long brew that will leave a reader reeling from its power. Here is a quick exercise . . . : Sit down with one blank page of paper. Write out a two-paragraph description of the book. Write out a two-paragraph description of the market for your book. Write out a two-paragraph description of yourself, the author of the book. Okay, now pretend you are Ernest Hemingway. No, you don't have to run in front of a herd of bulls: all we want you to do is simplify your writing. Turn wordy paragraphs into punchy paragraphs.
> —Sheree Bykofsky

PRACTICING PITCHCRAFT   43

But how to reduce your novel to one paragraph? Don't try. Tell the beginning of your story, which requires only three elements: the setting, your protagonist and the problem that he or she faces. Convey these elements succinctly and colorfully, and your prospective agent may well wonder, 'Gee, what happens next?' To find out, they may well ask for your manuscript. Bingo. Your fiction query has done its job.

—Donald Maass

Here is a sample fiction query (excerpt) that does its job:

Blue Honor is told through the eyes of Emily Conrad, daughter of a wealthy farming family in Vermont, who falls in love with Joseph Maynard, a young lieutenant with a commission under General McClelland in the Army of the Potomac. *Blue Honor* interweaves the lives of three families—and the deeply felt injustices of Henrietta Benson, an escaped slave who takes refuge in the Conrad home—with the important political events from the succession of the South to the surrender of Lee to Grant. Set against a vividly created landscape of Federals and Confederates, *Blue Honor* examines the conflict between duties and desires.

My debut novel is a story of love and its struggle to survive amidst a country's struggle to hold together. My name is Kelly Williams and I hope my story will appeal to readers who loved the way documentarian Ken Burns brought this era's period and portraiture to life, by writing a satisfying book for readers who loved *The Killer Angels* and *Cold Mountain*.

Here's another example of how to practice pitchcraft, for a book titled: *Elvis and You: Your Guide to the Pleasures of Being an Elvis Fan.*

Elvis and You is a guide to the universe inhabited by Elvis Presley and his fans presented in a way that's entertaining, enlightening and undeniably unique.

Elvis and You is about the many joys of Elvis—things to do, places to go, activities, projects, adventures, guilty pleasures—hundreds of ways to interact with and get closer to Elvis. No other book succeeds in offering such a comprehensive guide to experiencing Elvis.

Quite simply, *Elvis and You* is a book that celebrates every aspect of being an Elvis fan with a big emphasis on the fun. Because in addition to his monumental talent and staggering appeal one of the few things on which all of his biographers agree is that Elvis Presley was known for his rollicking sense of humor and relentless pursuit of a good time.

Elvis often asked the people around him, "Y'all havin' fun?"

Elvis and You answers that question with an enthusiastic, "Yeah, baby!"

YOU MUST CLEARLY CONVEY: I CAN BE A SUCCESSFUL CLIENT FOR YOU.

Notice how authors Laura Levin and John O'Hara tell you that you're going to have fun—and you do. See how this shines with authority and humor and delight. Note how they follow the agent's golden rule: "Show, don't tell." The same principles apply to serious and practical nonfiction as well. See how they clearly address the famous question posed by iconic editor Maxwell Perkins: Why does the world need this book? The authors have the answer: "No other book succeeds in offering such a comprehensive guide to experiencing Elvis."

Building a Platform

You must clearly convey: I can be a successful client for you. When reviewing writers' query letters and proposals, an agent is thinking: who would I call about this project? Which editor would be right for this? Less frequently are writers today seen as artists who need monies to live on while they create. More and more, publishers are looking for hooks, media sound-bites, and platforms that have been identified by the writers themselves.

You might cry out, "But I'm a writer not a woodworker. What do I need to know about platforms?"

This crucial publishing term, the author's "platform," is too new to be found under "P" in the indexes of classic books on the craft of writing and the writing life. Once, writers could focus solely on prose, and publicity was the province of a publisher.

Today's publishers use "platform" to mean the groundwork that is being laid by a writer. For writers, a platform sets the stage for reaching readers through marketing and publicity. Simply put, your platform is a list of all of your book's selling points.

"In the context of publishing, a platform refers to the author's ability to manifest meaningful sales through her own efforts, whatever they may be, outside of anything a publisher might do," says Jeff Herman, author of *Jeff Herman's Guide to Book Publishers, Editors, and Literary Agents*.

To describe your platform, detail all of the ways you are promoting your proposed book to readers—media attention, academic and literary journals, online promotions, lecture tie-ins, official author websites, cross-promotions, targeted advertising, e-mail newsletters, holiday and specialty retail catalogs, national and regional periodicals, ongoing author appearances, features and interviews.

Fiction writers build their platforms with blurbs from published writers, literary awards, and reviews, and through participation in readings, events and book festivals.

If you are wondering: did Ernest Hemingway have to think about building a platform? . . . no, he did not. Before the era of the superstore and the conglomeration of book publishers, Hemingway could devote himself to lion-hunting and running with the bulls.

How to Get Started

To build your platform, here are questions to consider: Do you have access to mailing lists? What might work for publicity purposes? Where might your book be promoted—conferences, professional organizations, public events? What are your current public speaking venues (seminars, workshops, professional meetings, readings) where book promotion would be possible? Develop your answers to build your platform.

Writers often assume their selling points are obvious, but they may not be. An acquiring editor needs have to confidence not just in the writing, but in the platform. Editors refer to a writer's salability when discussing projects with sales reps, who in turn must pitch to booksellers.

"When a publisher buys an author these days they are buying the whole package, which includes the platform. And the platform is the prospective author's ability to reach a large segment of their reading audience (via radio, television, websites and newsletters)—the author's visibility to the market and ability to reach the market," notes literary agent Sheree Bykofsky.

Publishers want to launch books to the widest possible audience. And your platform will lay the foundation for a successful book. Remember, you are doing your publisher a favor by pointing out your book's potential, and you are doing your reader a favor by getting your book published.

Practicing Pitchcraft®, a checklist

1. Interview yourself.

Pretend you are about to be interviewed on your favorite talk show. What would you say if you were on *Oprah*? What would you want your listeners, your readers to know about your work?

Think of and write out five questions. Answer them. Your answers can now be crafted into your pitch in 25-50 words. Practice your pitch in front of the mirror or the cat. Think of your pitch as a show—produced, written, and directed by you. Your query is a kind of performance; think of it as theatre of the page.

2. Practice your pitchcraft in the form of a sound-bite.

What are the best words and phrases to use? Remember to pick a set of complementary descriptive words that work well together.

3. Have you identified your hooks?

Hooks are the most exciting elements to compel your reader and propel your story. Think of a way of building in a cliffhanger, a question in the reader's mind to be answered by more reading.

"The best query letters have a strong hook in the first two lines. What is a strong hook? Something that grabs the reader's attention and keeps them reading," says Sheree Bykofsky.

4. Think of your pitch as a movie trailer.

Imagine your setting, your world, your universe for someone who has not lived in it before. You, the writer, are a camera. Put the camera on one character, the setting, the aliens. . . .

Have you set up the reader and communicated quickly your concept and the overview, the impact? Have you identified what is provocative and compelling in your overview, your argument for the book's life, your insights, what's fresh and unique, your ability and authority.

Have you told a story arc? "It starts here, ends there, boy meets girl, boy loses girl, boy gets girl." It is the old Hollywood chestnut, but it works.

"Study ads, movie trailers, junk mail," says Jeff Herman. "Junk mail is a free mail-order course in how to write excellent copy. Junk mail is a billion-dollar industry that test markets how to write copy that will have an impact."

Are you leading with the most important points?

Do you have evidence, statistics, articles, Zeitgeist? Point out why readers want this book. Argue your case. Pretend your book is on trial. Indeed, an acquisitions editorial meeting is a trial for life for your work.

Do the descriptive words, tone, and intention match? If you are writing a dark and disturbing thriller, the pitch should reflect that. For chick lit, on the other hand, you want a cute, punchy title and voice.

5. Communicate the excitement!

Writing is solitary; publishing is collaborative. The key point to understand: you want to get others excited about what is exciting to you. If you don't get them to read your work, you are not going to get anything else. An assistant or editorial reader's job is to review and pass the promising queries to the agent. Each query gets a cursory glance from the reader (invariably named Jennifer).

She looks for a minute and makes the decision to read more or to reject it. This is why it's so important to give a reader a reason to read more, and why you have to do it fast.

Agents know the most interesting books on bestseller lists are the ones nobody could have predicted. "There is no formula for getting on *The New York Times Bestseller List*," says Charles McGrath, Book Review Editor for that prestigious paper. "We don't want the list manipulated. Its complex methodologies are kept deliberately confidential to keep people from manipulating it."

To everyone's surprise, a New York City high-school teacher named Frank McCourt spent twenty years telling his students stories of his impoverished childhood in Limerick, then published his memoir, *Angela's Ashes*, which quickly rose to the top of that bestseller list. The author went on to become a much-loved literary figure, winning the Pulitzer Prize and every kind of accolade.

And who could have imagined a single mother on the dole would spend ten years conjuring up a wizarding universe that would set the publishing world on its ear, as J. K. Rowling did, with her phenomenally successful Harry Potter series. It was so successful, in fact, that *The New York Times* decided to create a new bestseller list for children's literature. "We had been thinking about it for years. *Harry Potter* pushed us over the edge," said McGrath.

"Now is the most exciting time ever to be alive, and it's the best time ever to be a writer," says Michael Larsen of the Larsen-Pomada agency. "Information is doubling every eighteen months, and the age of information is also the age of the writer. There are more subjects to write about; more media and more formats for your books to be published in; more agents; more options for getting your books published; more ways to learn about writing and publishing; and more ways to promote your books and profit from them than ever before," says Larsen.

It is indeed an exciting time to be writing. Machines cannot produce content. We need hearts and minds for that.

We need writers!

KATHARINE SANDS is a literary agent with the Sarah Jane Freymann Literary Agency. She represents a range of authors in diverse categories: category and literary fiction, chick lit, and dysfiction to faction to nonfiction (popular culture, entertainment, personal growth, leisure activities) to home arts (lifestyle, cookbooks, home design) to more eclectic subjects (travel, humor, and spirituality).

Titles represented include *XTC: SongStories*; *Under the Hula Moon* by Jocelyn Fuji (as co-agent); *The Tao of Beauty* by model Helen Lee; *Make Up, Don't Break Up* by Dr. Bonnie Eaker Weil; *Elvis and You: Your Guide to the Pleasures of Being an Elvis Fan*; *Asian Bistro: Sumptuous Recipes from Honolulu's Indigo Restaurant*, among many others. Katharine has been a guest speaker on writing and publishing topics for Poets and Writers, the American Society of Journalists and Authors, New York University, and the New York State Council on the Arts. Her book reviews have appeared in *Publishers Weekly* and *The New York Times Book Review*.

CHAPTER 6

Setting, Protagonist, Problem

An Interview with Donald Maass

by Katharine Sands

Sands: What catches your eye in a query letter?

Maass: The first job of the query letter is to provoke me to ask for the manuscript. A mistake that a lot of query letter writers make is this feeling that they somehow have to sell me on the whole novel, convince me that they're going to be the best client I've ever had, that their novel's going to be a bestseller, and all of that hype.

As an agent for fiction, everything that I have to sell is in the manuscript itself. Very rarely does the author have much of anything to do with whether a book sells or not. It's all in the writing. Is this a dynamite novel that I can't put down? Is it a great read that I feel that I could sell readily?

So the query letter really only needs to address the manuscript—not the author, not the author's ambitions, not the author's long-term plans, not how many years they've been writing, not how excited they may be, not how dedicated they are. I know all of that stuff. If somebody's finished a novel, they're obviously a serious writer. The question for me is: Is this a novel I can sell?

The first thing I need to know from the query letter is: What's the category?

A lot of people get hung up on that point. They don't know what kind of book to call their novel. We get all kinds of crazy designations. "Mine is a romantic-thriller science-fiction chick-lit book." What the heck is that? It's not helpful to have a category designation that tries to cover too many bases. The simplest way to think about the question is this: What section of the bookstore is your novel going to live in? Go to a bookstore and look around. Science fiction/fantasy, mysteries and thrillers, fiction, young adult, romance and women's fiction—choose whatever is the simplest way to categorize your book and the most useful way.

And if you can't figure that out, then simply call it a novel. I can figure out its category for myself as I read it. If really you can't narrow it down, it's better just to say "my novel."

The next thing I want to know: Is this a story I want to read?

What convinces anybody that they want to hear a story? Think about how we tell stories to one another. How do they start? How do I start telling a story? First, I locate it in time and space—Yesterday, I was walking down the street here in New York—so you can envision the place.

Second, who are we talking about? In your query letter, identify the protagonist by name.

Third, tell what they are doing. In particular, what is the problem that they're up against?

If you can convey those three things, you've begun to tell the story. Setting, protagonist, and problem. Once the problem is indicated, we want to find out what's going to happen next. That leads us to the next step in the story.

If I'm leaning forward as I'm reading a query letter and thinking, how or where does this go next? the query letter has already done its job. And it can stop there. Most authors feel that they've got to go on and tell me everything else that happened in the plot and try to cram it into one page as well.

And they do that because they're afraid. They're afraid that they're going to leave something out, something that might catch my interest, something that might make the difference, something that would really get me excited. The truth is, I'll listen to any story if you set it up right.

Setting, protagonist, problem, that's really all you need. Although it's helpful to add, somehow, one colorful detail that makes this story a little different than any other story like it.

WHAT CONVINCES ANYBODY THAT THEY WANT TO HEAR A STORY? HOW DO THEY START?

Sands: Can you make up an example?

Maass: My romance novel *When Bill Met Judy* is the story of two ordinary suburban people, both divorced, who find each other in a support group. Now there's nothing unusual about that situation. It's a story we've heard or feel we've heard a number of times before.

Except that this is a support group for little people. Now that's that one detail that turns a fairly familiar idea around and gives it that extra bit of originality that makes me go, oh, now I haven't read that story before! If you're pitching any kind of romance novel, for instance, we've all read that story before. The romance formula is the same thing over and over and over again. Man, woman, fall in love but something keeps them apart.

But when it's pitched well, there's one little thing at least that makes this version of the story just a little different than any other. In a query letter, put in that one little twist or difference that makes the story stand out.

After that, you don't need much of anything else. Because at that point I'm thinking, ooh, that's interesting, what happens next? And I will probably ask for at least a portion of the manuscript to read.

Now, about 95% of the query letters that we read do not give me just that much. They oversell, over-pitch, over-summarize, leave out or drown the essence of the story in a wealth of detail that just becomes a numbing blur to read. Most people put way too much information in query letters.

All we really need are setting, protagonist, problem, a colorful detail. That's enough to tell me this is a story I would like to go further with.

Having done that, you can offer a little bit about the author. This helps to personalize the author, particularly if there's something about their career or the life that qualifies them to write this particular story. If you're writing a police thriller and you happen to have been a Chicago detective, that's relevant, that's interesting. If you're writing a Chicago police thriller and you're a hairdresser in Miami, that's not particularly relevant.

More relevant are prior fiction publication credits, courses that you have taken, writers that you have studied with or even just how long you've been working. I'd rather hear that this is a fourth manuscript than this is a first manuscript, because that shows me that there is an author who's been working on their technique for a period of time.

There are exceptions, but most of the time a first manuscript is not really salable. It's a couple of manuscripts down the line that people really get the hang of the fiction form. So my overall advice is keep it short, keep it businesslike, keep it simple. And remember that the only thing the query letter really needs to do is make me wonder what happens next.

Sands: Tell me about a recent sale.

Maass: A surprising number of our clients actually just write to us cold. They just send in a really good query letter and things proceed from there. A book that I sold last week is a thriller by a journalist in Oregon—a World War II thriller. He sent in a letter; we thought that the premise was very good.

The guy had published short stories in a couple of science fiction magazines, but those sales were more than ten years ago. Now he was offering a thriller, a completely different kind of fiction. But the premise was really excellent. So I asked for 50 pages. And the 50 pages were well written. So I asked for the complete manuscript after that.

It was all about an unlikely hero, a New York hit man in the 1940s who works for the New York gangster Meyer Lansky. But he winds up being sent out of town with a suitcase full of money that's going to help finance an operation in Holland in 1942 to rescue a train full of 1,000 Dutch Jews on their way to be killed in Eastern Europe.

And I thought the idea of rescuing a train on its way to the Holocaust camps is itself pretty good. But put in the middle of that story a hit man from New York who is completely out of his element—and I just had to see what happened with that.

It turned out to be a wonderful story of this amoral hit man's transformation—first into a Jew, and then into a hero, as in the end, he almost single-handedly brings off this entire operation.

It's just a phenomenally good story. Great cast of characters, beautifully researched, wonderfully written. And we worked a lot on the plot to make it very tight and suspenseful, and raising the stakes, keeping pressure on, keeping the opposition one step ahead of the protagonists all the way.

He did wonderful work on the book and it came off beautifully. We spent about four or five months working on it and then I began to market it. I just got him a very nice six-figure deal last week from G.P. Putnam Sons for his absolute first novel. It's called *The Longest Night*, by Gregg Keizer.

When I pitch a story to an editor, I try to find those things that make the story just a little different, a little special. In this thriller, one thing I focused on as I pitched it were some of the great, emotional moments in the story. Such as a moment when this American Jew from the New York streets arrives in Amsterdam in 1942, he first comes upon a scene in the streets where Jews are being herded into a building, rounded up with their suitcases and yellow stars. And something stirs inside of him and he realizes for the first time that he is a Jew—and he can't believe that they're not fighting back.

That perspective on this proud American Jew who wants to fight back really sets a rousing tone for the story. So I would mention something like that just to bring the story a little bit alive.

You see, it doesn't take much more than just a little scene, or a moment, or a detail or two, to make a story seem interesting. And once you've got somebody's interest that's all you need to do, you can back off. You don't have to tell the whole plot. You don't have to do any more than

THE ONLY THING THE QUERY LETTER REALLY NEEDS TO DO IS MAKE ME WONDER WHAT HAPPENS NEXT.

that because at that point the editor wants to read the manuscript for themselves, just like I do when I read a good pitch in a letter.

It's very hard to trust that four short paragraphs will get your novel across to an agent. But the fact is that they do.

The number of short, businesslike query letters we get is maybe one in a hundred. The reason people overdo it in query letters is that they're afraid. They're anxious. They spent years working on this manuscript. They're highly keyed-up. They've got so much emotion, time, and sacrifice invested in the manuscript that they just go nuts and feel that they've got to tell me everything. All their anxiety comes pouring out on the page. And that's not helpful.

You've got to trust the basics of your story. If your story is good, it will only take a paragraph to put it over. If you have to write five, six, seven, eight paragraphs to summarize your story—then I wonder whether you really believe in that story. Do you really have confidence in it?

There's a lot going on in any 450-page manuscript. But at the core of the story, there's one thing that drives the narrative from beginning to end. One central problem. You can elaborate it for 400 pages but it's one simple problem. That's enough to drive a story. And that's enough to put in a query letter.

For instance, I've just been reading a novel, *The Dive from Clausen's Pier* by Ann Packer. It's about a woman who wants to leave her hometown and she is getting ready to except that at the very beginning of the story her boyfriend who she's getting ready to break up with, takes a dive off a pier at a lake and winds up paralyzed in a coma.

It's that situation that keeps her stuck in place. The novel's all about whether, in the face of this guilt and responsibility, she can shake loose from that and leave this comatose boyfriend behind.

It's a very tough dilemma and makes for a wonderful novel. So as you can see, it doesn't take a lot. Boil it down and keep it short.

Sands: Other tips?

Maass: A lot of books and people advise you to launch right into the story in the first paragraph of your query letter. I don't respond very well to that. Instead, I prefer something like, "I'm looking for an agent for my new mystery series." That's interesting to me, since I'm an agent who handles mystery series.

Paragraph two: "My novel is about so and so, a detective who has a routine case go terribly wrong when . . ." It's a simple and businesslike way to approach it. And yet so few people do that.

Sands: What lights you up about agenting?

Maass: One part of the job I like best is developing fiction with writers. I've written a book on taking your writing to new levels, called *Writing the Breakout Novel.* The other thing I like is negotiating deals. It's like playing poker with real money. Real big money. It's still fun when you find that great idea and you can help a writer to deepen the story. And then you turn it around and sell it.

That's just the best feeling in the world. All right, the second best feeling in the world.

Sands: The first being food, of course.

Maass: Right.

Sands: What general advice do you give writers who are starting out?

Maass: Learn from contemporary novelists. Not just the classics, but novels that are being written and published today. The fiction section of the bookstore is a university for fiction writers.

When you find a novel that you love, if you have a favorite author, don't just read their work, read it again. And then read it again and read it again—until you're not reading the story anymore, you're breaking the scenes down to see how they work. How did he do that? How much dialogue is there? How much action? How much exposition?

Take it apart. How are characters constructed? What are they doing in the first scene? Why do you like a character? What is the one thing that this character does or knows that no one else can do or know?

Everything I've learned about fiction I've learned from reading fiction. All the technique you'll ever need is on the bookshelves right now.

Sands: How does someone really grab you? Do you have the word hook in your mind when you're reading?

Maass: I don't really believe in hooks. I don't think there's any such thing as a bad premise for a novel. That is, in 23 years I've never heard a bad idea for a novel. But I have thousands of times seen perfectly good ideas poorly developed.

Hooks emerge from the story itself. It isn't something that's pasted on to the beginning of a story. Or if it is, it probably can't be sustained for 300 pages.

You asked what keeps me turning the pages of a manuscript. I can tell you what *stops* me turning the pages. Two things. The first is insufficient conflict. I'm talking about tension on every page of the book—from page one to page two to page three and so on.

The second thing is poorly developed characters. Characters that are not really distinctive or larger than life. And that's true even in literary fiction. In a literary novel, we may be reading about realistic people in realistic places. But the circumstances of the story need to be different—heightened, larger, special. A special time in somebody's life.

And how do characters respond to that? If they respond in the usual way, why would I want to read about it? I go through my ordinary everyday life in my ordinary everyday way, every single day. I don't need to read a novel about that.

What I do need to read is a novel about somebody doing something different. Acting different, acting outside of themselves in ways they don't ordinarily. There are ways to develop extraordinary qualities in characters, writing exercises to bring out the larger-than-life qualities in a character.

One exercise I take people through in workshops that I teach based on *Writing the Breakout Novel* is this: write down one thing that your protagonist would never say. Write down one thing that your protagonist would never do. Write down one thing that your protagonist would never, ever think.

And then find places in the story where that character must do that thing, say that thing, and think that thing.

If you can find a way to do that in your story, you're going to have that character break out of their boundaries. When people do this exercise in the workshops, I ask, okay, how many of you actually want to use these things that you came up with? And almost every hand in the room goes up.

Because they've pushed the envelope on their characters. Their characters are suddenly becoming bigger than themselves—and much more interesting to read about.

I also do an exercise where we craft a pitch in five minutes. I give people a framework in which to create their pitch which involves the very things I talked about before.

Tell me the category, the title, and the setting, the name of the protagonist, and the problem. And then find one colorful detail that makes this story a little different than others like it. And in five minutes, people write one paragraph, no more than five sentences that pitches their story.

IN THE LAST LINE OF YOUR SUMMARY, USE ONE OF SIX WORDS: LOVE, HEART, DREAM, JOURNEY, FORTUNE, AND DESTINY.

I also say, in the last line of your summary, use one of six words. Here are the six words: love, heart, dream, journey, fortune, and destiny.

And if you can work in one of those six words to the last line of your summary paragraph, it helps close off the presentation of the plot with a word that's poetic and evocative. It sends the story outward without you having to say much about it.

DONALD MAASS is president of the Donald Maass Literary Agency in New York, which he founded in 1980, and a past president of the Association of Authors' Representatives (AAR). He represents more than 100 fiction writers, including mystery writer Anne Perry, thriller writer Gregg Keizer, historical novelist Jack Whyte, and science-fiction writers Diane Duane and Todd McCaffrey. He sells more than 100 novels per year to top publishers in America and overseas, such as Warner, Ballantine, G.P. Putnam's Sons, Harcourt Brace, Penguin Canada, and others, often for six- and seven-figure advances.

He is himself the author of fourteen pseudonymous novels, plus a number of books for writers, including *The Career Novelist* (Heinemann) and *Writing the Breakout Novel* and *Writing the Breakout Novel Workbook*, both by Writer's Digest Books.

CHAPTER 7

Talent Always Jumps off the Page

by Ethan Ellenberg

Before I started writing this piece, I reviewed my client list and found that of the forty active clients I currently represent, I had sold the first book for eighteen of them. Nearly all of them came out of the "slush" pile.

They include Eric Rohmann, the 2003 Caldecott Gold Medalist for *My Friend Rabbit*; bestselling novelist Laurie Breton for *Final Exit*, her first novel with a trade house (after two earlier novels by a small press); and Tom Philpott, whose nonfiction masterpiece *Glory Denied* was excerpted by *The New Yorker* and garnered a paperback sale of a half million dollars.

I'm very proud of this record. For an agent, there is nothing more exciting than discovering new talent. On a recent panel at The Romance Writers of America national conference, I was asked what I look for in a writer. The answer was easy: a story that excites me.

Talent always jumps off the page and always demands a hearing. There is always room on most agents' lists for a book that absolutely seizes their attention.

That said, the first contact between a writer and an agent is the most important one. The vehicle of that contact is the pitch letter, so it's worth taking the time and making the effort to make sure the pitch letter is as good as possible.

Before this makes you too nervous, let me pass this along: I have found a strong consistency between the pitch letter and the completed manuscript. You don't have to re-invent yourself to write a great pitch letter. The same personality that fills your book—a product of your talent and imagination—should naturally fill your pitch letter.

There is, however, a form to the pitch letter, so let me share with you what I think works. There's a big difference between fiction and nonfiction, so I'll describe the perfect fiction pitch first.

THE SAME PERSONALITY THAT FILLS YOUR BOOK SHOULD NATURALLY FILL YOUR PITCH LETTER.

Fiction pitches

It's good to start with a single, attention-grabbing sentence that articulates the core story element of the book. For *The Andromeda Strain* by Michael Crichton, I would write something like this:

> An entire town wiped out without a visible cause, the bodies filling the streets, forces a government disease investigation team into the most dangerous mission of their lives.

It sounds like back-of-the-book copy. And it should, because back-cover copy tries to grab the reader and get them instantly "hooked" by the story itself. Here are two examples from actual letters I've received. This is from Whitney Kelly Gaskell:

> In reading about your agency, I learned that you represent mainstream women's fiction. My completed novel, *Pushing Thirty*, is a modern romantic comedy that would appeal to the readers of *Bridget Jones's Diary* and *The Nanny Diaries*.

I subsequently sold *Pushing Thirty* to Bantam, where it was published in 2003.

This pitch is from an author I mentioned earlier, Laurie Breton:

> I am seeking representation for my 100,000-word romantic suspense novel, *Midnight Confessions*. Ten years ago, murder tore them apart. Now it's brought FBI Special Agent Carolyn Monahan and Boston Homicide Lieutenant Conor Rafferty back together to find the serial killer who's terrorizing Boston.

Laurie's book was published by Mira in 2003 as *Final Exit* and became a *USA Today* bestseller.

The second paragraph continues to develop the story; it should introduce the main character and provide the ending (or crescendo if you want to keep the ending secret). By the time I finish reading this paragraph, I should know what your story is—beginning, middle and end. I should also know what genre it fits. And if you don't get too extravagant ("more spiritual than the Bible!"), you can compare it to other books.

Here's an example from Whitney Kelly Gaskell's *Pushing Thirty*:

> *Pushing Thirty* is the story of Elie Winters, a consummate Good Girl who's spent her life playing by the rules. On the surface, it looks like Elie has it all—a successful career as a litigation associate with a Washington, DC law firm, wonderful friends, and a kind boyfriend. But as her 30th birthday looms ever closer, Elie starts to feel like she's lost an instruction manual to her life. She despises her job, her boyfriend bores her silly, and she's the last of her friends to remain single. Worse, her dysfunctional family is driving her nuts, and she's somehow become enslaved to her demanding pet pug, whom she suspects is the reincarnation of Pol Pot.

This should follow with a single, short paragraph on your credentials for writing the book. This can include credits, like short stories published. It can be as simple as:

I've been a big fan of fantasy for years and carefully read and study the market on an ongoing basis.

It's a mistake to include your employment, your marital status, the number of your children or pets. If you don't have prior writing credits, that's fine; it's not unusual in commercial fiction. Whatever you do, don't add irrelevant credits (my cat loves this book) or information that has no bearing on my decision.

It's also a mistake to include too much information on your other work. I have never taken a client who told me they had ten novels just like this one, ready to go. If I'm interested, I always ask in the first conversation we have about pre-existing work and future plans, but don't put it in the pitch letter unless it's something simple like, "I'm working on my next fantasy novel." Here are examples of two good credential paragraphs:

> I graduated magna cum laude from Syracuse University in 1994 with a B.A. in History and as a member of Phi Beta Kappa. I continued my studies at the Tulane School of Law, where I served as a member of the *Tulane Law Review*. In 1997, I published an article on a United States Supreme Court gender discrimination case in the *Review*. After graduating from law school in 1997, I clerked first for the Texas Court of Criminal Appeals, and then in the United States District Court before opening my own law practice focusing on criminal appellate law. *Pushing Thirty* is my first novel.
>
> —from Whitney Kelly Gaskell

> *Midnight Confessions* is the fourth novel I've written, and I have plans for a sequel. I have published two books (*Black Widow* and *Coming Home*) with Neighborhood Press, a small Florida publisher. Response from readers and interviewers has been gratifyingly positive, but distribution and availability of both books has been limited. Although my current publisher has expressed an interest in seeing more books from me, I am hoping to move on to

the next level and find a bigger publisher for my next book.

I believe an agent can help me in my quest.

—from Laurie Breton's *Final Exit*

Because I'm so passionate about good writing and I'm anxious to quickly size up the talent I'm considering, I do ask that your first submission to my agency include the pitch letter, an outline or synopsis (3-5 pages), and the first 3 chapters. This way I can immediately plunge in and see what's there. I am aware that some agents only want the pitch letter. In all instances, follow the agents' individual guidelines.

Work on your pitch letter. Make sure it's focused, intelligent, and clearly shows you know your genre and audience. It's a simple letter, but like a poem, all the more powerful for being simple. I don't believe long pitch letters work, and if they do, they do despite the excess of information they inevitably contain.

Nonfiction pitches

Nonfiction is different, and nonfiction pitch letters must contain information that fiction letters do not.

For the first two paragraphs (my one-sentence "grabber" and my second-paragraph story summary), the nonfiction pitch letter can utilize this approach. If I was going to pitch a book on auto repair, my first sentence would be something like this:

Everyone owns a car; but did you know that more than half of the most common repairs can be performed by the average person with just a few tools at a fraction of garage prices?

My second sentence would continue with that theme: how much money could be saved, how easy the repairs are, etc.

The third and fourth paragraph is where things change. You can choose your own order, but for nonfiction books credentials are much more important. You should prove that you are qualified to write the book you intend to write. Also, take a paragraph to demonstrate some knowledge of the audience, often including competing books.

Your conclusion should sum up why your book is needed by your audience.

Nonfiction is very diverse. Although certain books don't need much in the way of credentials, for most cookbooks, craft, history, journalism, health, and so on, you must have some solid credentials.

For nonfiction, besides the pitch letter, I suggest you include a complete book proposal. This should include an introduction describing the book, your credentials, and market analysis and competitive works. A complete table of contents and sample chapter is also very helpful. Great writing convinces, so sample material is always welcome.

Pitch letters need to reflect the talent and professionalism of the writer. They should be straight forward, intelligent, and reflect a good understanding of the genre and marketplace. There's no magic formula, however, and a lot of different styles work. Don't beat yourself trying to make it perfect or copying it from some guide that claims to have all the secrets.

I, for one, always look forward to that next discovery and the pitch letter that brings it to my door.

Ethan Ellenberg heads his own literary agency based in New York City. He has been a full-time agent for 18 years. Prior to opening his agency, he was contracts manager of Berkley/Jove and associate contracts manager of Bantam. He handles a wide variety of commercial fiction, including romance and books for women, science fiction, fantasy, thrillers, and mysteries. He has a strong interest in children's books. Nonfiction interests include biography, history, current affairs, health, cookbooks, and spirituality.

For more information, visit his agency's website, www.EthanEllenberg.com, which includes submission guidelines and forthcoming books.

YOUR PITCH LETTER IS A SIMPLE LETTER, BUT LIKE A POEM, ALL THE MORE POWERFUL FOR BEING SIMPLE.

CHAPTER 8

The Providential Diamond

by Joseph Regal

At the first agency in which I worked, I got a quick and useful education in just how difficult it is to sell new fiction. I was looking through the files of a talented, somewhat shy writer the agency had taken on, reading through the correspondence as her work was sent back again and again, watching as her lack of confidence in her own work was only magnified by the many rejection letters she was receiving.

Even the polite ones didn't help. Many finished with, "This is a particularly difficult time for fiction," or "The market is very tough on first timers at the moment." Knowing that even those readers who liked her work felt that it wouldn't sell to a large enough audience made her wonder whether there was ever a chance she'd be read outside a few regional literary reviews.

Fortunately, her agent, Diarmuid Russell, persisted. Eventually he sold Eudora Welty's work, after more than thirty rejections, during that "dark time for fiction": 1942.

As anyone who has tried to find an agent (or as any agent who has tried to find a publisher) knows, times have always been tough for new fiction writers. The market is extremely competitive; everyone has a novel "in them"; and the years during which publishers thrive are few enough that they are more the exception than the norm. Every once in a while the door opens and a slightly larger than usual group of neophytes gets an invitation to the dance, but in most eras the refrain is as it was in Eudora Welty's day: fiction is hard.

Therefore, the best bit of advice is also the most obvious: make sure your work is as good as it can possibly be before you send a query letter. What does that have to do with making the perfect pitch? It doesn't matter how good your pitch is, how pithy and well-crafted, if the work simply isn't ready for the world. Agents are not here to steer you or to offer editorial advice; we are here to sell your book. While rare is the agent who handles fiction who does not do editorial work with an author after having taken him or her on, it's work typically done after the author feels the book is perfect—just as there's often further editorial work done once the book sells to a publisher.

So if your novel is not polished, if you haven't really thought about each line, if you don't feel completely comfortable with every page and part of it—the characters, the plot, its length, its depth—then put this book down (after you buy it and bring it home, of course) and go back to work. No agent is waiting for something that's "almost" there; none of us are hoping a talented newcomer will send ragged, unfocused writing, no matter how promising. If your instinct is that another pass would make it better, make that pass. And do it again, until you are certain that you have reached a point where there isn't a single thing more you could think of that would make the book better.

But if you have already dedicated those hard, rewarding hours, if you do feel you've done everything that needs to be done, then relax: the easiest thing in the world to write is a query letter for a novel. Unlikely though it sounds, it is true. There are two simple reasons for this, twin poles of secret truth for every literary agent: we all want to say no, and the best, happiest moment in a fiction agent's career is when s/he discovers the unexpected jewel in the forest of words.

The idea that every agent who gets your query wants to reject it is probably less than encouraging—depressing or enraging may be more like it. But think of this: thousands of query letters come in each year, and we can't possibly ask to see all the work people offer to submit. On top of that, you're competing with people from M.F.A. programs who have an "in" through one of our writers, with friends of friends who get special attention, and of course with the writers we already represent, who tend to feel we are more obligated to their new manuscripts than to someone from the "slush pile." So the object of every agent going through the day's query letters is to say no as quickly and painlessly as possible so that we can get to the work that supports our business.

If agents want to reject you as quickly as possible, then why is a query letter easy to write?

Because as much as we all want to say no as quickly as possible, none of us wants to miss that providential diamond, that unknown, unexpected manuscript that makes our hearts pound and our pulses race.

Your goal, then, is *not* to sell the book with your letter. Your goal is only to write a letter an agent cannot say no to, for fear of missing something that just might be special. After all, unlike nonfiction, fiction is judged almost entirely by the writing. You can sell a work of nonfiction by an average writer if the topic is fascinating and underexplored; you cannot sell even the best idea for a novel if the writing isn't very good. So when it comes down to it, your perfect pitch is to give the agent no reason not to ask to see actual pages of the work. Later, if the agent rejects the actual book, well, at least you got a real audition.

Here are the rules of writing a letter we can't say No to:

Keep it short—preferably one page. The agent will not want to read a four-page outline of your novel; s/he will not want to know every twist of the plot. The agent doesn't want a page-long bio, nor an essay on how important your novel will be to readers, or even an explanation of why it will sell more copies than John Grisham's best.

Just write a brief introduction of your work, one paragraph long (if that seems challenging, think of it like writing a description of the book for the back cover). Then write one paragraph about yourself: Have you published anything before, or is this the first thing you've written? Have you had success in other areas of life? Do you have any experience that might be useful in selling the novel? Think of it as the "personal" part of a resume: a few well-chosen details (summa cum laude at college, worked as a rodeo clown, and lived in India for a decade) give the agent a sense that you're distinctive, and encourage him that you yourself, quite apart from the book, might be of interest to publicists.

As I said, writing this letter should be easy: in fiction, all that matters are the sentences and what they add up to. If no one has heard of you, if it's your first novel, if you're 17, if you're 70, if it isn't "high-concept" or "Hollywood"—none of this makes any real difference if your writing is compelling and you know how to tell a story. So resist the urge to persuade and simply attempt to inform.

YOUR GOAL IS ONLY TO WRITE A LETTER AN AGENT CANNOT SAY NO TO, FOR FEAR OF MISSING SOMETHING THAT JUST MIGHT BE SPECIAL.

Send letters only to agents who handle the kind of book you've written. Obvious though it sounds, I get letters every day from people hoping to interest me in their romance novel, or in their commercial novel in the mode of Jackie Collins. I have nothing against romance (or Jackie Collins), but I have never read it and don't have any desire to. So sending me a query for it is a waste of postage.

There are plenty of reference books that explain which agents or agencies handle what kinds of books. Not every agent is listed, but with at least four guides to choose from, many are, and while researching a perfect match may take some time, it's not as time-consuming (or expensive) as sending letters to every agent you can get an address for.

Beyond the library of reference books, you can also check with the Association of Author Representatives to get a list of members. (Not to say that good agents don't exist who aren't members of the AAR, but every member subscribes to its Canon of Ethics, so there is a set of rules in place that governs their behavior.)

Lastly, there are a number of websites that track, though incompletely, the various weekly sales of agents, the most well-known being Publisher's Lunch (www.caderbooks.com) and the various sites and newsletters attached to the industry's trade magazine, *Publishers Weekly*.

If all else fails, read the acknowledgments in the novels you most admire to see if you can spot the name of the agent. While it never used to be the practice for novelists to acknowledge anyone, that has changed over the last ten years (in part because of M.F.A. programs and the debt students often feel to their teachers). You should be able to find the agent mentioned about half the time—particularly in first novels, which is where you should look first. Any agents handling first novels are likely looking to add to their client lists.

I should add that while many agents will request an exclusive submission, I do not recommend you do so. It is in your best interest to send pages to whichever agents request them; if one asks for an exclusive, don't acknowledge the request explicitly, just send pages. If the agent loves the work and wants to take you on, s/he won't ask whether you sent the pages to anyone else first.

The caveat: while it is in your interest to submit to several agents at once, do not play one off against another. I have had writers call me to say that another agent wants to sign them up and they need an answer from me by tomorrow. Well, good for them: I don't need to read their material, knowing they've found another home. I won't audition, or be played off against another agent. If that troubles you, then avoid the problem of having to stall a less desirable agent who has asked to take you on before you've heard from anyone else by submitting only to small groups in which anyone who says yes would make you happy.

If you get past No with your query, but then the agent rejects your pages, don't fret: many, many talented writers have been rejected not once or twice but dozens of times. It's just as difficult for us to find a publisher as it is for you to find an agent; we face more rejection every week than you could imagine. I've had novels that took four years and five revisions to sell, that needed a change of the narration from third to first person or vice-versa, that had to be edited down from 600 pages to 400. We get rejected constantly, and often sell writers whose names ring throughout the ages only because of bull-headed persistence. Not everyone can recognize that providential diamond when it appears—including us paid professionals—so don't let a mere thirty rejections discourage you. (Of course, if each of those thirty rejections is substantive and voices a similar complaint, it might not be the worst idea to pay attention and revise, either.)

Fiction is *always* hard. But making the perfect pitch for fiction means getting the paid professional to read the novel and judge your prose and your characters, not your query letter. Do your research, submit to appropriate agents, and write a brief, simple letter, and you'll likely get a chance.

JOSEPH REGAL, after a career as lead singer in a rock and roll band, got his first job in publishing at the Russell & Volkening literary agency in 1991. There he worked with Pulitzer Prize-winning, bestselling authors Anne Tyler, Eudora Welty, and Annie Dillard, as well as Nobel Prize-winner Nadine Gordimer, television anchorman Jim Lehrer, and the president of the Children's Defense Fund and bestselling author Marian Wright Edelman.

Within three years he became the managing agent, building his own list of writers, which he took with him when he founded Regal Literary Inc. in 2002. He has been quoted in *The New Yorker*, the *Washington Post*, the *Los Angeles Times*, the *Chicago Tribune*, and *Rosebud*.

CHAPTER 9

Getting Ahead of the Curve

An Interview with Robert Gottlieb

by Katharine Sands

Sands: What jumps out at you first when you consider a new writer's work?

Gottlieb: Well, in today's book market, for commercial fiction and nonfiction, the idea for the book is fifty percent of the equation. And the other fifty percent is the author's track record. If the author doesn't have a track record, then it's the author's background for promotability and marketing purposes.

Sands: Tell me a great discovery story.

Gottlieb: Well, a great discovery story is Tom Clancy, who I discovered at the American Booksellers Association convention, in Washington, D.C., some 20 years ago. He was being published by a small press called the Naval Institute Press. They were located in the back of the exhibition hall. At the time, I was very young and not very knowledgeable about the business. I didn't have a lot of contacts.

So instead of hanging around the big booths where all the big agents and editors were, I started looking at the smaller publishers to see what they had to offer. And I discovered Tom Clancy's galleys at the Naval Institute Press booth.

I was working at William Morris, which had a policy of not sending agents to conferences unless they had author-clients being featured. So I had to pay my own way down there. I had to find my own lodging and take time off from work, which they allowed me to do. And that was how I began searching for clients.

Sands: Do you still keep an eye out for new writers?

Gottlieb: My philosophy is that you can discover an *established* writer. What do I mean? There are writers whose careers may be stalling—writers whose careers may not have a sharp enough upward arc. So you can discover ways to reinvent them, to get them publishing in more challenging directions.

When Fern Michaels came to me, Kensington Publishing was shipping 400,000 copies of her books. I moved her to Pocket Books when I took her over for representation, and now she's up over 900,000 copies a book.

For new authors: yes, I do like to discover new authors. At this point in my career I'm not doing that as often as I used to do, but when I see something is interesting, I can always match a good project with another agent here.

Sands: What goes through your mind when you consider taking on a client?

Gottlieb: My instincts have to kick in to say that I can do something for that author. If those instincts *don't* kick in, that's a clear signal that I'm the wrong person to be working with that writer, whether it's the material, the track record, or the promotable and marketable qualities that we need in today's business and economic atmosphere.

Sands: What advice do you like to give writers?

Gottlieb: That being a writer is an evolving process. Very few people hit it the first time out. Most authors who are successful, like Janet Evanovich, have been at it for over 25 years. It's like any art form. You have to practice it; you've got to continue doing it. If a book doesn't sell, if a manuscript doesn't attract the attention of an editor or a publisher, put it in a closet and start your next book. But keep on writing.

In these endeavors, only a handful of people really succeed out of the enormous numbers that try. But if you believe in yourself, then you have to keep at it.

Sands: How can a writer get you excited about their story?

Gottlieb: Since I'm in the commercial fiction business, the rules of engagement for me are different than for an agent who is representing upmarket material. You can be a very successful novelist in the upmarket area by writing dynamic characters but mediocre stories, because it's a literary adventure.

That's a different business than the one I'm in. In my business, if you write great characters but a mediocre story, I can't sell it. But a great story with mediocre characters may be a bestseller.

Sands: What do you see writers do wrong when they set out to pitch, query, or propose a new book?

Gottlieb: The right thing to do is to keep your pitch or your query letter short. Think about what's interesting about you as an author that a publisher and an agent will feel is appealing. Take a look at what's out in the marketplace, because you do want to be ahead of the curve, not behind it.

If historical fiction in hardcover is not succeeding in the commercial book business, then you shouldn't be pursuing that. You should be doing what is succeeding, which right now is contemporary fiction.

If a story is going to work in a novel, you can usually tell in the first 50 pages. If you as a writer can accomplish *that*, then you should be able to accomplish, in a few paragraphs, a sharp and smart description of your book that will catch someone's eye.

Sands: How do you think a writer can hone their pitch to best catch someone's eye?

Gottlieb: In the age that we live in, people have a shorter attention span than ever before. So introduce yourself in the letter—and then get right into the pitch. Make it a couple of paragraphs, no more. Extrapolate from your material what makes it exciting. Run it by some of your friends. Get opinions on your writing, because what may be interesting to a writer about their book may be one of the *least* interesting things about the book to the public. So it's always a good idea to have friends and family look at your query letter before you send it.

Sands: Do quirks ever work? Or outrageousness? Or creative submission packages?

Gottlieb: Generally not. If you're talking about a book that's over the top like *The Nanny Diaries*, maybe. But on average, no. It makes an agent may think the person's a clown, and you don't want that.

Sands: What can a writer do to stay ahead of the market trends?

Gottlieb: Take a good look at what's working. If the cruise industry is building bigger and bigger ships, you're not going to easily succeed by going to a cruise company and suggesting that they build smaller ones. Instead, think about how you're going to increase business for that company. It's the same thing for publishing. Look at what's succeeding. And then consider what space in publishing you want to enter into. Make that decision, then enter into the space. Not the space that you may have emotional connection to—but perhaps the publisher is less interested in—because then the odds are even worse. And the odds are already tough as it is.

Sands: Care to make any predictions about the Zeitgeist, what the new trends will be?

Gottlieb: I think there are two trends that parallel each other. One is fiction that is sexy and fun, because people want relief from everyday life. And the other is fiction that has high adventure, that takes people somewhere else, like the TV show *The Amazing Race*. The reason people

THINK ABOUT HOW YOU'RE GOING TO INCREASE BUSINESS FOR THAT PUBLISHER. LOOK AT WHAT'S SUCCEEDING.

GETTING AHEAD OF THE CURVE   75

watch it is because they love the idea of being taken somewhere else that's exotic and different.

Sands: When you speak to writers' groups, when they ask you what to do next, what advice do you have for them?

Gottlieb: There are certain things you can do. Look at the market-place and ask, where do I fit in? *before* you start a book. Not *after* you start a book. A lot of writers make this mistake. They start a book and write it, and then they ask, where do I fit in? That's a mistake. They should start with the idea and take it and ask, where does that idea fit in? Is it with the trend? Or is it going against the trend?

Sands: Do you like it if a writer uses blurbs?

Gottlieb: If Clive Cussler has read your manuscript and loves it, that's a great blurb. If a writer that no one has ever heard of has read it—or if your writing teacher who was published 35 years ago reads it and gives you a blurb—no, that's not useful.

Sands: How many new clients do you take on these days?

Gottlieb: Not many. I would say maybe two or three, maybe as many as five a year. Depends on if there's a slot that's open. Am I expanding my list? Now that I'm running a company, I have people working with me to whom I can refer good prospects. So I can bring the benefit of more than one brain to the table on the agenting side for the client. I may not be present at every conversation, but I'm behind the scenes on every conversation.

Sands: How did you come to found Trident and what is its mission?

Gottlieb: Its mission is to represent authors and intellectual property in an innovative and intelligent way in the twenty-first century. To get away from what I consider classical agenting, which is to sell the book, then it's up to the publisher to do the rest. So I formed Trident to test the vision that I had.

For instance, I represent Frank Herbert's estate, the Dune books. The estate was making money from the backlist sales, but I was able take that concept and create prequels to *Dune*. Those prequels changed the whole economic model for the estate. All of us together envisioned creating a whole new future for *Dune*, when normally these great properties over time just simply decrease in sales as the generations move on. But we revitalized the intellectual property, creating millions of dollars in profits. So those are some of the unique things we do.

Sands: So, if you're known as a star-maker, should the new writer ever think about coming to you?

Gottlieb: The best time for me to step in is when the writer is hitting a certain degree of traction that requires someone like me to be involved in their lives. Janet Evanovich came to me when she needed a higher level of representation to take her to a whole new level. Now, if Janet had come to me after she had written just one novel, and it was her first, I wouldn't have been able to do that for her. But Janet was well established and on her way. And I felt that I could help her get to where she wanted to be.

Sands: How did you become an agent?

Gottlieb: I started in the mailroom with the William Morris Agency.

Sands: So that's not a myth? People really do start in the mailroom?

Gottlieb: When I graduated from college, my father suggested to me that I think about starting at the bottom of a company like William Morris. So I went into the mailroom there. I took the job because I felt that they had a predictable and serious program for training agents. And I worked in the mailroom for eight months, and then as a secretary for another four-and-a-half years. And then was made an agent. And within twelve years of starting in the mailroom at the William Morris Agency, I was on their board of directors.

Sands: What lights you up about being an agent?

Gottlieb: Being around creative people. I like that. Creative people create worlds and opportunities that expand your horizons and your intellectual interests.

LOOK AT THE MARKETPLACE AND ASK, WHERE DO I FIT IN? BEFORE YOU START.

Sands: What should a writer be honing or crafting or developing?

Gottlieb: An author should be writing and thinking creatively. And an author should also find good business representation.

An author should stay involved with the business side.

If an agent ever says to an author—if the author is asking questions—"Don't bother me" . . . or, "I know more than you, don't worry" . . . that's the time to start worrying.

ROBERT GOTTLIEB was born and raised in New York City. After graduating from Elmira College in upstate New York, he began in the mailroom of the William Morris Agency as part of the company's Agent in Training Program. In 1977, he moved into the company's Literary Department as an assistant, and in 1982, became an agent. Just seven years later, he was promoted to Senior Vice President and became one of the youngest agents to ever head the Literary Department. In 1992, he became an Executive Vice President.

In September 2000, Mr. Gottlieb started Trident Media Group, where he now serves as Chairman. Trident Media Group is a new media business that represents clients and their intellectual property in all areas of entertainment: motion picture, television, theatre, and emerging media. Its impressive roster includes Deepak Chopra, Stephen Coonts, Catherine Coulter, Janet Evanovich, Allan Folsom, Elizabeth George, Dean Koontz, and Jerry Oppenheimer. The agency has also represented prestigious book deals for celebrities, including Jerry Seinfeld, Sir Anthony Hopkins, Mel Brooks, Aretha Franklin, Drew Barrymore, Paul Reiser, Brian Wilson, Tony Curtis, Carl Reiner, Muriel Hemingway, and Tony Bennett.

The company recently merged with the Ellen Levine literary agency, which brings award-winning literary clients to Trident such as Russell Banks, Michael Ondaatje, Garrison Keillor, Louis Sachar, and Todd Gitlin.

CHAPTER 10

Niche Your Pitch

From First Proposal to Profitable Career

by Michael Larsen

Fully 90 percent of all nonfiction books sold to trade publishers are acquired on the basis of a proposal.
—John Boswell, *The Insider's Guide to Getting Published*

From Pitchcraft to Nichecraft

Your pitch can be a one-line hook for a book that must seduce an agent, an editor, a publisher, booksellers, the media, and everyone else that you talk to. But it's a short pitch. Your proposal is the long pitch for your book and your career.

A proposal gives you the opportunity to make a pitch for a series of books and for a working marriage with your publisher that may last your whole writing career. To practice nichecraft, find an idea for a series of books that you will enjoy writing and promoting. The right idea will enable you to build a career book by book, reader by reader, talk by talk, and city by city. So align your pitch with your niche.

If you have an idea for a book that will interest enough people, and you can prove to a publisher that you can research, organize and write a book about it, you can get paid to write your book. But it requires a fundamental shift in your thinking from being an artist to being a merchant, from being a writer with something to say to being an author with something to sell.

An "In the Bleachers" cartoon by Steve Moore shows a jockey sitting at the starting gate saying to himself: "Why am I dressed like this? Who are all these people? What am I doing on a horse? Where am I?" The caption says: "Seconds before the start of the race, Felipe suffers a mental lapse commonly known among jockeys as 'rider's block.'"

Jockeys may have a problem, but writers shouldn't. Now is the best time to be alive and the best time ever to be a writer. One reason is that at this amazing moment in history, the world is awash with ideas. Another reason is that there are more models for you to follow than ever. You can emulate the books and authors you admire but do what they do differently and better than they do it.

There's a *New Yorker* cartoon by Mick Stevens that shows Adam and Eve sitting together under a tree in Eden, and Adam is saying "I can't help thinking that there's a book in this." There's a book in any idea that you can dream up. There will always be more ideas for books than writers to write them. The challenge is to balance the long view and the short view, to find the one idea that is the best idea for you to write about now yet will also enable you to create a career.

In 1976, a guy named Jay Conrad Levinson wrote a self-published book called *Earning Money Without a Job: The Economics of Freedom*. I saw a story about him in the *San Francisco Chronicle* and called him. Then I sold the book to Henry Holt, and it's still in print.

He wanted to write a book based on classes he was teaching at the University of California Extension on marketing for small businesses. In his proposal, he titled the book *Secrets for Making Big Profits from Your Small Business*. However, in the same proposal, he also used the phrase "guerrilla marketing," and as soon as I saw it, I knew that the book had the title it needed. (Jay's title became the subtitle.)

Since *Guerrilla Marketing* was published in 1984, Jay has written or coauthored more than 20 guerrilla books in what has become a virtually endless series. The books all sell each other (as well as the audio and videotapes based on them).

Jay has a website, www.jayconradlevinson.com, writes articles and columns, and is well-compensated as a keynote speaker. That's nichecraft. People don't always recognize Jay's name, but they always recognize *Guerrilla Marketing*. That's the power of branding, of creating synergy so that everything you do sells everything else that you do.

How can you tell if you have the idea for your breakthrough book? Here are five telltale signs for spotting the idea of a lifetime:

- You are passionate about writing, promoting, and giving talks about the concept.

- You know that you have the ability to write about it.

- You can do what it takes to promote it.

- You can see its potential as a series.

- You can see the books' potential for subsidiary rights such as foreign rights and book clubs.

Four Steps to Take ASAP When You Have an Idea

Someone once said that "Getting an idea should be like sitting on a pin; it should make you jump up and do something." The moment you have an exciting idea for a book, take these four steps as quickly as you can:

- Test the idea on your networks of publishing people, professionals in your field, and if you're a speaker, your speaking network.

- Check the competition online and off.

- Read all about it. The more you learn, the more you earn. Make yourself an expert on your subject by reading the most important competitive books and browsing through the others. For any kind of book you want to write, models (both bombs and bestsellers) abound.

- Write your long pitch ASAP. Unless it's a book that only you can write, don't assume that you're the only writer who has your idea. Ideas are in the air because the raw material for them is in the media. So write your proposal quickly without sacrificing quality. Then sell it before another writer beats you to it or interest in the subject wanes.

> Nothing is particularly hard if you divide it into small jobs.
>
> —Henry Ford

The Parts of an Irresistible Proposal

Writing a proposal can be the most creative part of doing a book. Why? Because an idea is an endlessly malleable abstraction limited only by the form you give it. A nonfiction book can be a how-to book, a biography, a memoir, a humor book, a history, a reference book, a gift book, or an illustrated book.

So there is no one way to write a proposal any more than there is one way to write a book. The following approach has evolved over the three decades my partner Elizabeth Pomada and I have been agents, and it continues to evolve as what editors need to see to say "yes" evolves.

But it's the fastest, easiest way we know to make your pitch rejection-proof and obtain the best editor, publisher, and deal for your book. Every line you write must motivate agents and editors to reach the next line, and each part of your proposal must convince them to go on to the next part.

Here's an overview of the three parts of a proposal:

Part I: The Introduction

Your Introduction has to prove that you have a solid, marketable, practical idea and that you are the right person to write and promote it. The Introduction section includes an Overview, Resources Needed to

Complete the Book, and About the Author. They give you the opportunity to provide as much ammunition about you and your book as you can muster.

Depending on the kind of book you're writing, you may not need all of them.

EACH PART OF YOUR PROPOSAL MUST CONVINCE THEM TO GO ON TO THE NEXT PART.

1. Overview

An Overview includes:

- Your subject hook (the most exciting, compelling thing you can say in as few words as possible that justifies the existence your book—a quote, event, fact, trend, anecdote, statistic, idea, joke). Your subject hook may be an anecdote about someone using your advice to solve a problem that leads to a statistic about the number of people with the problem.

- Your book hook (your title, your selling handle, and the length of your book):

    Your Title. This is the two-second pitch that must convince browsers who read it to pick your book up and look at it. The titles for most books have to tell and sell—say what your book is and give book buyers an irresistible reason to buy it.

    Your selling handle. This is a sentence that ideally begins, "(Your title) will be the first book to . . . " As other contributors to this book explain, you can also use a Hollywood pitch by comparing your book to one or two successful books, as in: "(Your title) is *Dr. Atkins' New Diet Revolution* for cats," or "(Your title) is *Seabiscuit* meets *What to Expect When You're Expecting.*" Your pitch or selling handle will get a workout: You will use it to interest agents, editors and everyone else you ever talk to about your book. Editors will use it to interest their colleagues in who will decide whether the house makes a bid for it. Your publisher will use your pitch to help sell subsidiary rights and interest the media and booksellers in it.

    The length of your book. A page- or word-count.

- Your book's special features (such as humor, structure, anecdotes, checklists, exercises, sidebars, the tone and style of your book, and anything you will do to give the text visual appeal). Use competitive books as models.

- A foreword by a well-known authority. Find someone who will give your book credibility and salability in fifty states two years from now to write a foreword.

- Answers to technical or legal questions. If your book's on a specialized subject, name the expert who has reviewed it. If your book may present legal problems, name the intellectual property attorney who has reviewed it.

- Your back matter. Does your book need a glossary, resource directory, bibliography, or footnotes?

- Markets for your book (both the groups of people who will buy your book and the channels through which it can be sold). Start with the largest ones.

- Your book's subsidiary-rights possibilities (such as movie, foreign or book-club rights).

- Spinoffs. If your book can be a series or lends itself to sequels, mention up to five of them in descending order of their commercial appeal.

- A mission statement that pitches your passion. If you feel a sense of mission about writing and promoting your book, describe it in one first-person paragraph.

- Your platform (what you have already done and are doing to give your ideas and yourself continuing national visibility). Editors at big houses will need this info to pitch your book to the house's editorial board, which usually decides the fate of your book.

- Your promotion plan (a list in descending order of impressiveness of what you will do to promote your book when and after it's published). At the beginning of your career, if your idea or your ability to promote your book isn't as strong as it needs to be to excite Big-Apple publishers, you may find small publishers more receptive.

Small and medium-sized houses outside New York don't need the promotional ammunition big publishers do.

- Lists of books that will compete with and complement yours.

2. Resources Needed to Complete the Book

This is a pitch to prove that your idea is realistic. Starting with the largest expense, list your out-of-pocket costs of $500 or more (in round figures). This is not for office expenses, but for a foreword, permissions, travel or illustrations. Include the total cost.

Even if you and your agent decide not to include these costs when submitting your book, you need to know them because they affect the time and money you need to write your book—and the negotiation of your contract.

3. About the Author

Include everything not in your platform that you want editors to know about you, in descending order of relevance and importance.

Part II: The Outline

Your Outline is a pitch for the content and the structure of your book. Write chapter outlines that, for each chapter, start with the strongest anecdote or slice of copy for that chapter, followed by about a page of prose.

Aim for one line of outline for every page of manuscript you guesstimate; for example, 19 lines of outline to describe a 19-page chapter.

Part III: Sample Chapter

Follow your outline with the sample chapter that best shows agents and editors how well you will make your book as enjoyable to read as it is informative.

Your proposal is now pitch perfect!

Getting Warmed Up

Author and speaker Sam Horn coined the word authorpreneur® to capture the calling of successful authors. "Authorpreneurs" are writers who make a living by coming up with ideas, writing books, and selling the rights to their work in as many media, countries, and forms as possible.

These authors know that their books are too important and valuable to just let their publishers promote them and hope for the best. So they do everything they do to ensure their books' continuing success, and they practice nichecraft so they can create synergy between everything they do.

It all starts with the right pitch. With the right pitch to the right agent, editor, and publisher at the right time, you'll hit a home run. Now's the time to start getting warmed up. Good luck!

MICHAEL LARSEN is a partner in Larsen-Pomada Literary Agents, a San Francisco agency that represents adult fiction and nonfiction. Since it was founded in 1972, the agency has sold books to more than 100 publishers.

He is the author of *Literary Agents: What They Do, How They Do It, and How to Find and Work with the Right One for You*. With Jay Conrad Levinson and Rick Frishman, he also coauthored *Guerrilla Marketing for Writers: 100 Weapons for Selling Your Work*. This article was adapted from his book *How to Write a Book Proposal* (3rd ed.), published January 2004.

Michael and his partner Elizabeth Pomanda are also co-founders of the San Francisco Writers Conference that takes place on President's Day Weekend in February; for more information, see the website at www.sfwc.biz. For other questions, you can reach Michael at www.larsen-pomada.com.

CHAPTER 11

It's the Quirks That Make It Interesting

An Interview with Barbara Lowenstein

by Katharine Sands

Sands: Did you always have an eye for talent?

Lowenstein: I know what's commercial. I think I have a good eye for what the reader is looking for and what sells.

Sands: What are you looking for in a commercial novel?

Lowenstein: The character has to really stand out—have a great voice with interesting quirks. To get fiction published today, you really have to be very good. Because there's no mid-list anymore. It's either top of the line or mass-market. And even for mass-market, a writer really needs to have something special.

In nonfiction, they need to look at their competition, know who their audience is, who has similar material.

Then, break out and be different.

Sands: How would a writer do that?

Lowenstein: By studying the markets; by reading *Publishers Weekly.* Writers can read what is being reviewed—and how it is being reviewed. They can go to conferences or workshops; they can network with other writers.

Sands: You do a lot of discovering.

Lowenstein: A first novel is more exciting than a second novel, because it's a fresh voice. Nobody's heard of them, and there's no baggage. You don't have to worry about sales figures from a previous novel. You have nothing to overcome except the work itself. The second novel, on the other hand, can make or break a writer. If the first novel just does okay and the second novel fails, you're finished.

Unfortunately, for many talented writers, it's not always their fault; there are many reasons why a book sinks. The editor left, nobody took the work seriously, the book didn't get good reviews. Or there could be some good reviews, but they didn't get the right review in the right place.

For fiction, the work has to stand on its own. For nonfiction, the author has to be an expert. They need a platform—which means name recognition. Years ago, authors were expected to do the seminars and lectures *after* the book was published. Now you have to have had a string of seminars, lectures, and workshops around the country *before* trying to sell a book to a publisher.

For example, we represent doctors Kathy Fields and Katie Rodan, creators of an acne product called Proactive. It's the number one acne product in the country, so everyone has heard of it. They have their own line, sold through infomercials, and they also have a second line sold in high-end department stores.

So we went after them, and finally they agreed to do a book. When we pitched to the publishers, we were able to say that four million people use this product. We put these clients together with a wonderful beauty writer, and the book will be a huge success.

Sands: What secrets or strategies can you impart for that all-important query letter?

Lowenstein: You know, agents have an ego. So one of the things I like to see is an original letter or e-mail. I don't want it to have been mass-mailed it to 600 agents. The letter should be concise and professional. The other thing that helps is if they have a connection with the agency. Otherwise, it's likely to go into the slush pile. And, yes, we've gotten some fantastic clients from the slush pile. We do take the slush pile very seriously. Nancy Yost is a partner in the agency, and she discovered Mary and Pam [Perri] O'Shaughnessy in the slush pile.

Sands: Are there things you're looking to pick out?

Lowenstein: No, the work just has to grab me. There has to be a real market for it. Publishers aren't getting excited anymore unless they can print at least 25,000 copies on a first print run.

Narrative nonfiction could be a little less than that. Obviously, the best thing for an author is to have a track record in some of the literary magazines.

With fiction, an author should have had short fiction or essays published before they come to us. For example, if they've been published in literary magazines or if their short stories have been anthologized, then that will help us get a deal.

Authors have to prepare themselves so that there's some name recognition. God knows, with 40,000 books being published a year, there has to be a reason why a publisher is going to sink money into their work.

But once in a while, something is different. Then all these rules go out the window. I met a young 22-year-old woman when I was in California. She has a great voice, and I think she's going to be a wonderful commercial novelist. She doesn't have much published yet, but then she's only twenty-two. She was in a class with one of my clients, Gina Nahai.

Gina is a wonderful literary novelist who teaches at USC–Irvine in California, and the author of three novels, including *Sunday's Silence*. She's from Iran and writes sort of in the genre of magic realism. She is a beautiful stylist, and I love that. You read a sentence and it flows so marvelously and magically that you wonder, how in the world did she put all these words together like this? That's what we look for. Somebody with extraordinary talent that's literary or commercial and has

> A FIRST NOVEL IS MORE EXCITING THAN A SECOND NOVEL, BECAUSE IT'S A FRESH VOICE.

unusual characters and plot. So when she sends us clients—students that she thinks are ready to be published—naturally we consider them very seriously.

Sands: You seem to have such an openness to the new, young writer.

Lowenstein: We are definitely open. But we're also very specific about what we want and need to sell. It's not me making the rules—it's the market. So yes, we're looking, through scouts and through contacts at writing programs at the universities. Yes, we're very interested in young, talented writers. And it certainly helps if they've had any well-known writers read their work—if they really spent some time at their craft and they know some important writer that could give them a quote, that would certainly help.

For example, Stephen Byler studied in the Writing Program at Columbia with some very well-known writers. When he came to us, he had about five quotes ready to go with the submission. That, of course, got our attention! And we sent the quote list to the publishers when we submitted the book. That really made a difference. The best way to get an agent is to know somebody that's represented by the agency.

Sands: You also seem to have a strong multicultural bent.

Lowenstein: For nonfiction, we saw a great need in the marketplace for African American books. I honestly think it happened after the Clarence Thomas hearings, when the American public saw that there were many educated African Americans from the greatest Ivy League schools in the country. I think that was when the publishers realized that they were missing a huge, huge market.

So we started a new agency called Lowenstein Morel—partnered with Madeline Morel—and started creating projects for African American markets. We represented the first black women's health book, *Body and Soul* by Linda Villarosa, at that time the editor of *Essence* Magazine. We also represented Hugh Price, the former head of the National Urban League, who wrote *Achievement Matters*; Gwendolyn Goldsby Grant, an advice columnist from *Essence*; and many other African American experts who authored books on health, relationships, parenting, etc.

We recognized that there was this huge market that no one was paying attention to, and that is exactly when the publishers started wanting these books.

Sands: How can a writer know his/her work is ready to send?

Lowenstein: If they're in a writers' group, they will have worked through all of the drafts with their group. And if they are in a writers' program, the instructor will have looked at it. That's why you can't write in a vacuum. It just doesn't work—you need some perspective.

Sands: Tell me how you began and what your first discovery was.

Lowenstein: I started at the Sterling Lord Agency in the late sixties as an Assistant to the Dramatic Agent. Every morning I couldn't wait to get up and go to work. They had the most fantastic authors—Jack Kerouac, Ken Kesey, Gloria Steinem, Terry Southern—it was just unbelievable. And I was always a really great reader, so it was a dream come true.

I left there after two years to take a year off to travel and when I came back I got a job as an associate editor at Lancer Books. My job was to create a line of digest-size, trade paperbacks on crafts, cooking, psychology, self-help. I did two books per month, finding writers and hiring illustrators. It was my baby and I just loved it. I worked at Walker for a little while, selling rights. And then I started the agency in 1976.

Sands: What are some questions a writer should ask a prospective agent?

Lowenstein: How long have they been in business? Who do they represent? Do they have an office? We have a full staff here: a contracts person, a bookkeeper, four agents, and two assistants—a full set-up for the services we offer. We have co-agents around the world and work with a number of Hollywood agents as well.

Sands: Do you like gimmicks when writers approach you?

Lowenstein: No, they don't work. One guy sent us postcards every other day telling us how he was going to be sending us chapters of his novel. We were bombarded with postcards—it just got annoying.

IF SOME IMPORTANT WRITER COULD GIVE A QUOTE, THAT WOULD CERTAINLY HELP.

Ultimately, with fiction, the writing has to speak for itself. And with nonfiction, they have to have something to say, but mainly they need a way of selling the book, they need a platform.

I think it's very hard for writers now. When I started out, there were 14 paperback houses and 50 hardcover houses. Now there are four paperback groups and five hardcover groups and the publishers have cut their lists. So the market has really shrunk.

Sands: What advice do you give to writers to attract an agent's eye? Do you go to conferences?

Lowenstein: We have a good connection at the University of Iowa. One of our agents, Dorian Karchmar, graduated from the Nonfiction Program at Iowa, so she goes there and to other top M.F.A. programs every year and talks to the fiction and nonfiction students. One of our big books this year was *Mrs. Kimble* by Jennifer Haigh, a graduate of the workshop. She got a two-book, huge six-figure deal. The writing programs are fabulous. We also have people in Southern California and Northern California scouting for us, going to workshops to find talent.

I personally don't attend anymore. But Julie Culver goes to the romance writers conferences, Nancy Yost goes to the mystery conferences, and Dorian Karchmar and Eileen Cope go to literary fiction conferences and graduate programs.

Sands: Any more tips for how writers should talk to an agent?

Lowenstein: They have to take this very seriously. This is my livelihood, and I don't really want to waste my time with anybody that thinks they can knock out a book. It takes a tremendous amount of effort, for the writer and for us. We work at everything. We want to know the sales figures. We want to see the art copy for the cover. Nine times out of ten it has to be changed. We want to give input. There's so much work involved nowadays to get an author launched, I need authors that are very dedicated. We take our writers very seriously and everybody works really hard. I'm sort of an old-fashioned person, I run it like a real organization, not some creative endeavor. We are business people and we want to get the best possible deal for our clients.

Sands: What do you tell your authors to get ready for this job?

Lowenstein: Experience life. The more life experience, the more you'll have to write about. It's something that has to come from inside the writer. Is this a fresh idea? Have I done the research?

For nonfiction, they have to have done the legwork. Somebody just called me today—recommended by two of our clients. She's a relationship expert. So I asked her where she has been published or what radio or TV shows she's been on. She said, well, she writes for a city newspaper in the South. That's not going to get the attention of the reader. The book wasn't really different from any other relationship book on the market, and we had to turn her down. I told her to spend the next two years building up her reputation and then come back to me.

Sands: How does a writer communicate that they're going to be a successful client for you?

Lowenstein: They start by going to writers' conferences. These conferences really give them an inside look into the publishing industry. They get to network with editors, a few agents, and other writers. And the fact that they have invested their time and money in these workshops tells me that they're serious.

BARBARA LOWENSTEIN started her publishing career at the Sterling Lord Agency as an assistant to the dramatic agent. She then moved on to Lancer Books, where she started the first line of trade paperbacks in the industry. There she published self-help, psychology, how-to, crafts, and cooking titles. A brief stint as Director of Subsidiary Rights made her realize that starting her own literary agency would allow her to combine her editorial skills with her gift for selling: thus was born Lowenstein Associates in 1976.

Twenty-eight years later, the agency, now known as Lowenstein-Yost Associates, represents a varied roster of over 150 authors of fiction and nonfiction from *New York Times* bestsellers to Pulitzer Prize nominees. Barbara looks for leading experts in their fields, including women's issues, business, psychology, health, science and social issues, and is interested in strong new voices in fiction and narrative nonfiction.

She is also known throughout the industry as an intrepid world traveler, whose far-flung journeys to such remote spots as Nepal, Tajikistan and Irian Jaya allow her to combine her love of adventure with human interaction.

CHAPTER 12

Making Your Book Into a Movie

by Laurie Horowitz

Welcome to my office. Sit down in my big stripy guest chair. It's huge and has the advantage of fitting the most colossal behind. All are welcome. From your vantage point, you are looking out the window toward one of the ubiquitous Starbucks. You feel yourself at the hub of something, sitting at the corner of possibility. Scoot up in that enormous chair, and I'll tell you some of the things I've learned about how books get made into movies.

As you can see, my desk, my credenza, and even the floor are covered with books in all stages of production. There are manuscripts, galleys, finished hardcovers, old paperbacks. There are even some scripts, book proposals, and treatments. I have a phone sheet as long as my arm, and when I turn on the computer I have hundreds of e-mails (and not all of them are offering to help me lose weight in my sleep).

Where to begin? I check the calendar for meetings. Yes, there are meetings, many of which result in some connection being made between a book and a buyer. There are lunches and appointments and calls to make. And all of this is important, but what I really want when I come into the office in the morning is to find a gem, a story that needs to be made into a movie, a voice that sings. I'm not looking for the karaoke singer, screeching someone else's song, but the distinctive voice that has something new and interesting to say. Every time, I come upon this, it excites me as if it's the very first time.

Where do these submissions come from? The majority of the books I receive come from agents who represent books to publishers (we have a policy of not accepting unsolicited submissions). Since 99.9% of my submissions come from literary agents, my pile of manuscripts has been vetted by people I respect.

That still does not guarantee that a given book should be made into a movie. Some of the most beautiful books do not translate well to film. That certainly doesn't make them bad books. Some books are highly internal and poetic. Film and literature are different media. Beautiful writing does not always transfer smoothly to screen—a medium which is highly visual and is, perhaps, based more in action than in language.

Some books on the other hand are just itching to be made into movies. They are plot-driven, full of colorful—maybe villainous—characters who scream to jump onto the screen.

The process

Let me, briefly, take you through the process, so that you will have a better idea of how to see your story on screen.

You write a book. It's the absolute best book you can come up with. If you are a humorist, it's hilarious. If you are of a more serious bent, it moves the reader to feel something he or she has rarely felt before. Write the best book that is in you and, especially if you want your book to be a movie, think a little about your audience. If you think you'd be the only one sitting in the theater to watch *My Hideous Life With My Ex-Wife Lorraine*, maybe you should broaden your horizons.

Your book captures the interest of a fine literary agent who represents books to publishers and, in the best-case scenario, sells your manuscript to a publisher. At this point, you think your dream has come true.

But, maybe, in the back of your mind, you remember another dream, the celluloid dream (I don't think film is made of celluloid anymore, but you get the idea).

At some point, your literary agent will contact someone like me and ask me to read the book. I will be very grateful to be considered and will read the book with care and with a view toward making it into a movie.

Let's take the best case. I love it without reservation, and I come up with a list for you and your literary agent of potential buyers. We will determine together whether that list includes everyone you ever envisioned. I will then send the book to the people on the list, making sure to call first and "pitch" the book.

Let's stop here to discuss some useful things to think about when pitching your material. For simplicity's sake, let's call them "the three Cs":

Be Courteous. Be Concise. Be Creative.

- *Be Courteous.* Presentation is important. There are many people vying for attention in the film world. I favor a professional approach. Make sure you are remembered for the good things, rather than for a funny hat, heavy cologne, or questionable hygiene.

- *Be Concise.* Be aware of your audience. I've seen more people lose an audience by continuing to pitch after their point has been made. Once you have sold them, stop!

- *Be Creative.* This may seem at odds with being courteous and concise, but it is not. Use colorful words. Create fascinating characters. Structure your story with a beginning, middle, and end. Make sure your main character has moved emotionally from one point to another by the time the story ends. You must convince your audience that your idea is so dramatic, moving, funny, interesting, etc. that it is imperative that they buy it. You are an artist, a craftsman, and also a salesperson. Sell your idea and your ability to execute it.

Remember, whoever buys your story will be working on it for a long time. They will invest money, time, and energy. Respect your potential buyers. They are busy people. Their interests are the same as yours. They want to create something entertaining, meaningful, lasting, and profitable. Make sure that what you have to offer them is worth their time.

So, I have called the buyers, pitched the book, and sent them the manuscript. We wait with restless anticipation while they read it and then the calls start coming in.

"It's too small."

"It's too soft."

"It's just right." Ah, that's what we wish for. Opinions are manifold in a business that traffics in opinion. Just because someone doesn't want to make your book into a movie, doesn't mean you don't have a good book. Sometimes the subject matter, the tone, or the scope of the piece is not a match.

You only have to find one person whose vision matches yours to get an offer. But your best-case scenario is if more than one producer or studio wants your book, because you are likely to make a better deal.

A typical book-to-film deal

A typical book-to-film deal is structured as follows:

There is an option price. For this option price, the producer will have the right to develop your book into a movie for a specified period, say, 12 or 18 months, with an option to renew for another similar period of time.

There will also be a purchase price structured into the deal. It is difficult to predict what your purchase price might be. It is not unlike determining the price of a vase in a Third World market stall. Slow day at the market, and the price will go down. But if two or more people are grabbing for the same vase, well, that vase could end up being expensive. Though this is a simplification and doesn't always apply, there is a rule of thumb you can use: If you are getting around 2.5% of the budget of the picture as a purchase price, you are probably getting a fair deal.

There are many aspects that go into making a deal, and you need a good agent or lawyer to help you. If you try to navigate the waters yourself, you may end up worse off than the character in *Castaway*. And he only had a volleyball for company.

That brings us to you, sitting at home with your book. You are reading this piece presumably because you like the idea of seeing your book on the big screen. My first advice to you is . . . forget about it. Write your book. Don't think about Hollywood. Decide whether you want to be a novelist, a nonfiction writer, a screenwriter, or something else entirely. The happiest authors I know treat anything that comes out of Hollywood as pure gravy.

That being said, there are a few questions I can answer that might inspire you in your own pursuit of the dream.

Do people sometimes sell their book to film based only on a partial manuscript?

Sometimes. A good example is *The Horse Whisperer*, a book that sold to Hollywood on approximately ninety pages and a synopsis. I read those ninety pages, and I read them again and again because, in my heart, as a salesperson, I wanted to know what grabbed the attention of so many for so much.

This is the answer I came up with. They were a knock-out ninety pages. They were highly visual, and established a conflicted family and characters you were interested in after only a few pages. In a very cinematic way, the first pages cut between a tired truck-driver in the snow and two innocent little girls out for a ride on their precious horses, early in the morning. Truck driver. Little girls. Truck driver. Little girls. And an inevitable collision looms that is going to change their lives forever.

That collision is a horrible moment.

And it made you want to know what happens next. How would it all resolve? It was, in a word: riveting.

Can you succeed by writing short stories and literary novels?

Yes. I recommend David Schickler's book, *Kissing in Manhattan*, as a good example. Several, if not most, of the stories have been optioned for film. Mr. Schickler has been commissioned to write several of the screenplays. I attribute his success to the world he creates and to his unique and appealing voice.

Can you be a great success in both the worlds of literature and film?
Pulitzer Prize-winner Michael Chabon is known for his fine literary work. He is a successful novelist who repeatedly sells books to film. He is so trusted as a writer that he is even able to sell treatments (several pages that show what he intends to write). He is also a respected screenwriter. He has a voice, literary longevity, and has proven repeatedly that he can deliver. Also, he has prosperous relationships with producers specifically known for choosing excellent literature and making successful movies from good books.

Now, what about you?

It's all very well to see how others have become successful, but how do *you* do it? Here is a list of some of the things to do if you want to pitch a book to Hollywood:

- Write a good book.

- Find a reputable agent to represent that book to publishers.

- Have that agent send the book to a Hollywood agent who represents the film rights to literary properties. (Someone like me.)

- Don't be afraid to ask for a chance to talk to that agent and give your input.

- As long as you feel comfortable with your representation, continue writing and keep your fingers crossed.

And be aware: It is not common for the film industry to buy an idea from an untested writer. A person must prove an ability to write a good script before anyone will be willing to buy a "pitch" from them. The best demonstration of the ability to write is a sample of your work. It helps even more if you have sold something. Also, while the person who wrote the book is sometimes offered an opportunity to write the script, that is not the norm.

So, we have traversed the landscape. Let me give you some final unsolicited words of advice.

We all have our wild dreams of villas in the South of France or the equivalent, but unless those dreams inspire you, focus on the writing and the villas will take care of themselves.

What are you really here for, as a writer? Isn't it to give of yourself? To offer your unique way of seeing the world? To entertain?

Your writing is your gift to the world. And if you wrap it up beautifully, in the way that only you can, I believe the world will graciously accept it. And, it may even write you a thank-you note.

LAURIE HOROWITZ is an agent with Creative Artists Agency where she specializes in selling the film rights of books and other literary properties to the film and television community. A graduate of Boston University Law School and a member of the Massachusetts Bar, she has been a presenter at the Maui Writers Conference, the San Diego Writers Conference, and The Learning Annex. She also serves on the board of the James A. Michener Center for Writers at the University of Texas at Austin.

CHAPTER 13

Pitches That Worked

by Rita Rosenkranz

As with its musical and sports counterparts, an author's perfect pitch is defined by utmost clarity and precision. And it can trigger an agent's almost visceral response and instant embrace. Yes, you must research an agent's areas of interest and track record; otherwise, the perfect pitch can be lost on an inappropriate agent. A project that catches my attention presents with confidence and commitment either a familiar subject approached freshly or a less well-known subject approached commercially. Offered in person at a writer's conference, via query letter, or generated by my entry in an agents' directory, the perfect pitch is a powerful summary of the book. It offers enough particulars to help anchor my understanding of the work, but not so many details to bog down the description.

An author should realize, too, that a perfect pitch might not register for reasons beyond the author's immediate knowledge or control—anything from personal likes and dislikes to imperfect timing (the agent has just signed up a similar work or has a book in the same category that is performing poorly).

Of course, I hope the perfect pitch will be followed by a perfect proposal. I mostly handle adult nonfiction titles, and the majority are sold on the basis of a proposal. The proposal is the single most important element in getting a publisher to buy a book project. It is the base from which I can convince an editor that the work is interesting, worthwhile, and likely to make them some money.

A great proposal is a faithful distillation of the full work. It makes clear the project's parameters (photographs? line drawings? original if not exclusive sources?), and leaves no important questions unanswered. It outlines the book's contribution to the marketplace and potential audience. For example, a proposal for a self-help book will outline groups affected by the problem or condition addressed, organizations linked to the problem, and the numbers of people involved.

I like to know that the author is closely aligned with the subject, either personally or professionally, to make the marriage of author and subject make sense and supportable in the marketplace. Publishers expect authors in most nonfiction categories to have a built-in "platform." This is the author's established audience, thanks to prior publications, media connections, professional or university affiliations, lecture circuits allowing for back-of-the-room sales—whatever helps achieve a competitive edge. Publishers big and small will be influenced by this information.

A perfect pitch generally avoids mentioning the author's 38 unpublished works. While an author might assume a lengthy resumé of unpublished projects suggests prolific talent, it raises more doubt than interest. Why has the author waited so long to find a home for his work? It's much harder to map a strategy from such a trunkload. And since an agent's own passion invariably is infused by the author's, such a constellation of choices confuses the agenda, unless the titles are limited to a planned sequel or series.

Do not spend valuable time—whether pitching on the page or in person—apologizing for taking up the agent's time. Authors are an agent's lifeline, and most of us depend on a continuing stream of new clients. I like to think we are mutually reliant. We need you, too! Do not create an awful, and possibly irreversible first impression, with a typed cover letter with the agent's name (misspelled and) filled in by hand. However superficial these blemishes might be, they make saying "no" easy.

Pitches that have not engendered my excitement include cover letters stating that the author is past his prime and has little time left to publish. This is one reliable way to make an agent more anxious than eager. (In my own defense, my oldest author, the distinguished diarist Edward Robb Ellis, published well into his 80s, and my youngest author was 13 at the time of publication, so I hope to not be accused of ageism.)

Pitches that have fallen flat for me include, "I like the authors you represent, so I am making you the guinea pig for my first query for my new book." Too often a pitch will refer to a "nonfiction novel." Does the author mean a work of fiction inspired by a real story? All novels are works of fiction and sold under that category. In any case, with a bit of research, this author would have known I don't solicit fiction, sparing himself the cost of postage and a needless rejection.

Other baffling pitches include: "Don't read this query letter unless you are willing to look at yet another project about a former mental patient." Or "I am not actually the author, but rather, channeled the writings, in a meditative state, from 1960 to the present."

AUTHORS ARE AN AGENT'S LIFELINE, AND MOST OF US DEPEND ON A CONTINUING STREAM OF NEW CLIENTS.

Pitches that worked

Pitches, excerpted from the original queries, that have worked for me and have lead to successful publications include:

> As someone who started her own business after working in the corporate world, you must have experienced some of the frustrations many knowledge workers still face. It is your current success as a literary agent that makes me eager to talk with you about representation for my book, *Work Naked: Eight Essential Principles for Peak Performance in the Virtual Workplace.* . . . The title grew out of public response to my revealing commentary on telework that Sue Shellenbarger published in her *Wall Street Journal* "Work & Family" column. I teach workshops, present at major national

conferences, and publish articles on telework and change management in the course of promoting my consulting practice; I will use these same channels to promote my book.

Cynthia Froggatt's letter showed the research she had done (noting my career change) and made clear her ability to promote her work. And I just happened to have read Sue Shellenbarger's column when it first appeared. Cindy's book was published by Jossey-Bass.

> *Precious Cargo* tells the story of a daring submarine rescue mission in the Pacific during World War II, when forty Americans and top secret Japanese battle plans were snatched off the beaches of Negros in the central Philippines. It is the story of how these refugees—missionary families, sugar men, coconut men, escaped POWs—survived 2½ years in the mountains, living in primitive hideouts, always one spare step ahead of the enemy. . . . Though this is my first book, I am an Emmy Award-winning freelance television photojournalist. Over a career spanning three decades, I've traveled to sixty countries on assignments as diverse as following popes and presidents to covering revolutions in Iran, Nicaragua and the Philippines. Current clients include *60 Minutes, 20/20*, the BBC, and Discovery Channel."

Steven T. Smith's dramatic description of his project, coupled with his credits, excited my interest. Steven's book, retitled *The Rescue: A True Story of Courage and Survival in WW II*, was published by John Wiley & Sons.

Betty DeRamus' *Forbidden Fruit: True Love Stories from the Underground Railroad*, under contract with Atria Books (Simon & Schuster) instantly captured my heart with the author's brief but evocative description, which was circulated through a manuscript marketplace at a writers' conference:

> My book tells true stories about runaway slaves in love.
> It describes what six couples endured to spend their lives together.

. . . Betty DeRamus is a columnist for the *Detroit News* and a Pulitzer Prize finalist. Her essays on black issues have appeared in *Thinking Black* (Crown), *The Darden Dilemma* (HarperCollins) and *Essence* magazine.

This original, commercial approach to a subject of growing interest, coupled with the author's impeccable credentials, made me believe in this work.

In these times of great mobility and inconstancy in the publishing industry, it is especially important for the new as well as experienced author to be vigilant about the details of the publishing process. May your perfect pitch lead to a successful publication!

RITA ROSENKRANZ, a former editor with major New York houses, founded Rita Rosenkranz Literary Agency in 1990. She specializes in adult non-fiction, featuring a list that goes from the decorative—such as *Flowers, White House Style* by Dottie Temple and Stan Finegold (Simon & Schuster)—to the dark—*Saving Beauty from the Beast: How to Protect Your Daughter from an Unhealthy Relationship* by Vicki Crompton and Ellen Kessner (Little, Brown).

She represents health, history, parenting, music, how-to, popular science, business, biography, popular reference, cooking, spirituality, and general interest titles. She works with major publishing houses as well as regional and with regional publishers that handle niche markets.

CHAPTER 14

In the Singles Bar of the Literary Persuasion

by Esmond Harmsworth

Since I am based in the resolutely low-key city of Boston, I pride myself on my restraint. I simply will not, ever, fall for hype. Boston is known for its red-brick houses, its tranquil parks, and its extreme aversion to hoopla. Razzmatazz, gaudy marketing, and outrageous bells and whistles may well work for you in Peoria, Palo Alto, or Poughkeepsie. They won't get you in the door in Beantown.

This is a city where the classic local recipe is baked beans. You don't get much more restrained than that. And where, as the famous saying goes, "Ladies do not buy their hats; they inherit them." A visit to one of Boston's many charity functions will quickly convince even the greenest neophyte that this is the truth. Many think it applicable not just to bonnets but to the rest of the wardrobe as well.

So I don't look for books that come too easy. Come-hither pitches without any substance behind them. Gaudy flirts in peek-a-boo blouses with nothing but a perm and a smile. Goofy studs crushed into supertight jeans and muscle T-shirts. Don't take me for a literary celibate or an intellectual snob; to interest me, new books don't have to be written by a Cabot, a Lodge, or even a Franzen. They simply need to have been written by a writer.

And, the good news for writers is that 90% of the mail I receive is clearly, indisputably, undeniably not written by a writer.

But, while I may project a hardened shell, an alligator's skin impervious to even the mildest seduction—despite appearances, I am indeed looking. Looking hard. If there were the equivalent of a singles bar where agents go to meet authors, I would attend nightly, nursing my venti dark-roast as I surveyed the crowd for my perfect pitch. I might look coy, might gaze into a writer's eyes for a moment, and then not return the affection. Don't we all, sometimes?

But, underneath it all, I'm anything but a professional flirt. I'm looking for the real thing. And while I might look tough, while I'm certainly hard to please, I never show disdain. And sometimes on a magic evening I find exactly what I'm looking for.

So, what does it take, seriously, to get me on the phone? It is usually the phone. Whenever a pitch comes in by mail, and grabs me in some immaterial way, I call the author. Most of my replies by mail are the simple "no," unfortunately rendered in one of our ghastly form letters. This is the simple result, dear author, of volume. As one becomes known, the demands of politeness become crushing, and rudeness and anonymity are, displeasingly, inevitable results.

Yet to say that form letters are not "personal" in any way isn't true. My taste and my occasionally impulsive rejections are unerringly personal—to me, to my reading and taste, not to you and yours. I've certainly sent my share of forms to authors whose books later appeared in the stores—the good slapping-down we need and occasionally get. No one's taste is infallible. May you quickly find a better match. But I know passion when I see it.

Working as a partner in a firm, I look at each pitch and ask two immediate questions. Can I sell this? Followed quickly by: Do I want to? To want to, I simply have to like it and to "get" it. Nonfiction can be judged on the market. How big is the readership for histories of Zanzibar? How many people really care about the science of earwax? Is it really true that 99% of the population suffers from a deficit of Vitamin Z?

NO ONE'S TASTE IS INFALLIBLE. BUT I KNOW PASSION WHEN I SEE IT.

But fiction is always, always a matter of taste. With nonfiction I look for books that contain valuable information and ideas that aren't already out there. With fiction, I look for work that, quickly or slowly, I will come to love.

My job is to advise authors on their work, to shape their work to make it true to their vision and at the same time interesting to the largest possible number of publishers (a project that requires Astaire-like editorial agility), and to do this I have to understand the work. I have to want to read the book, to know why others would want to buy it and what they might enjoy or detest about it. I have to help to make the book satisfying to a large audience without weakening its spirit. I have to guide Dante through the inferno, avoiding such hellish pitfalls as selling out, blandness, falsity, cliché, or avoiding challenges that must be met. I must critically judge the book, and assess its strengths and weaknesses in plot, character, prose, and atmosphere. And to do that sort of work, to be a guide of sufficient confidence, strength, and wisdom, I sure as heck better like Dante's writing. Because if I don't I won't have enough stamina to be the best guide I can be.

With fiction, the surest way to fix my bleary eyes on the page is to describe a good concept.

This is the hardest thing to define but perhaps the most important. The best novel ideas are based on concepts that are new but not strange, that fit that esoteric niche on a publisher's list for something that's not like everything else but is in its own way immediately recognizable. Reading a perfect pitch is like a fabulous, intriguing introduction: I know you, you're a book!

This why it helps prospective authors to compare their work to other, more established wielders of the pen. It's not to copy or to steal; it is to emulate in the best sense of the word. Such comparisons also point us to the work's audience—a necessary guide to the overtaxed brains of busy agents.

It's especially helpful if the pitch conjures up something that fills some sort of a void. The book should be like other books only so far, and the difference should seem advantageous and smart. A recent author sent me an incredible novel she described as like the work of Anita

Shreve, only more literary. The novel is a serious, challenging historical novel set in 19th-century New England. I took it on after reading the first draft.

Another author sent me a completely unsolicited e-mail regarding a book set in Manhattan, the story of four mothers with two-year-old children living in the East Village, coping with life, babies, and partners in between yoga classes and visits to the art center. High concept, indeed. I asked for the novel to be sent to me overnight and loved it.

Another author met me at a conference and beguiled me with the story of a young woman, abandoned by her mother as an infant and brought up by an aunt, who suddenly discovers her mother is the maternal superstar of a *Home Improvement* or *Cosby Show* style sitcom. I leapt at the chance.

Or another author, again a conference attendee: she told me that she wrote mysteries about a forensic scientist equal to the work of Patricia Cornwell. Within ten pages I agreed and signed her up.

This does, however, bring up a potential pitfall. For a Bostonian agent, understatement is often the key. I find this to be true with editors as well, even those in Gotham. Sometimes the coy call, "Are you sure you'd like to see it?" bears greater weight than "You'll love it, you've gotta grab it!" It may be because we are all contrarian deep down inside and dislike spoon feeding. Or, because we love the thrill of discovery and our greatest high is in finding El Dorado on the page. If the hand guiding us there is too forceful, we know credit for the discovery will elude us. And that discoverer's credit is one of our most elusive and satisfying pleasures.

Remember that, as you craft your pitch, I must also be crafting mine. I am the intermediary, not the destination, not the date but the matchmaker, and I must take your carefully drafted personal and turn it into a work of art guaranteed to magnetically attract those of the right sex and persuasion. Sometimes too much detail derails my own process and fixes the novel in my mind, in an unalterable way. For me to be the salesman, I must have an ownership stake in the novel's pitch as well. This is why I recommend authors send pitches that are brief, succinct, and to the point.

SOMETIMES THE COY CALL, "ARE YOU SURE YOU'D LIKE TO SEE IT?" BEARS GREATER WEIGHT THAN "YOU'LL LOVE IT, YOU'VE GOTTA GRAB IT!"

I greet long synopses with dread memories of CliffsNotes. Two kids from bitter, feuding families meet accidentally, fall deeply in doomed love, and leave a world chastened by chaos is better than a dreary, moment-by-moment summary of *Romeo and Juliet*. Do we need to know Mercutio's brand of tights? So, tell us your heroine jumps under a train and leave it at that. We don't need to know whether your modern-day Karenina or Bovary chose Amtrak or a New Jersey metroliner. And we certainly don't need to know the names, ages, and professions of all those standing on the station platform, witnesses to her martyrdom to love.

Do not think, though, that my Boston residence implies a love of modesty. Shun this "virtue" as you shun dull prose. It's not just because my roots are in flashier locales like New York and London. It's because your work will arrive on my desk, a white page unaccompanied by any trumpets or garlands—except for your brief recitation of your experience and accomplishments. Be modest up to a point and serious when you describe your work; but never be shy about describing your experience and accomplishments.

Alright, you say, that's all very well for those with books under their belt, *New Yorker* publications, the happenstance that "Dad" is known to most of us as Updike or Naipaul or "Mother" as Quindlen or Steele. But what about the little guy? Well, a secret: those with such overwhelming advantages already have agents. You're not racing against them.

A huge number of the competition are crazy, loony, or just plain strange. They scribble bizarre notes on scratch paper and mail them to me. They include (and all these queries were actually received): a grandma advocating families spend every night together smoking marijuana; a person who insisted he is in a secret marriage with an ex-President; "authors" with a strange obsession with ant extermination, gummi bears, or nudist colonies.

Others are writing works that contain grammatical errors, misspellings, or things that just don't make sense. This covers about one third to one half of the daily harvest. To write, you must make your work sing, choose each word with care and measure, even on your cover letter! If you don't, what sort of impression will you make? Precise word choice is more than anything the key to a writer's talent. If you are in doubt about one single verb or noun of your book, wait until certainty comes before submitting.

The majority of the rest simply don't feel new or exciting. They rely more than is acceptable on the most tired clichés. Their work seems like that of other writers but without any freshness, any twist, like a clone that only has 75% of the genetic material of the original. These can be outshone by good writers—with ease.

Some of the rest are, as I have said, just not what I like to read and they go, often, to other agents. Others seem like possibles whilst to others they are immediate actuals, and those agents get them first, as they should.

So show us your experience. If you've written anything for publication it is a plus. You have that jaded knowledge of deadlines, pressures, or the demands of an editor of some sort. This is of incalculable value.

And, show us your fire. We need to know you are serious, that you understand this is an intensely demanding profession that gives its favors to few, and even then rewards most with money that is, frankly, embarrassing. You must have passion to back up your talent, be prepared for the third or fourth book to be the "big one" if the first is a sleeper, be willing to market your work with uninhibited pride. What have you done to prepare? Do you know the works of authors you like forwards, backwards, and any-which-way? Have you studied with your idols in a class or conference? Have you sent out written work for publication and pressed on past the "no's"?

So let's imagine your pitch and I meeting. Sometimes the pitch immediately catches my eye, the coffee cup falls and I rush over, business card in hand. At other times, to interest me in your work requires more flirting. Say you really are reinventing the wheel, writing something quite unlike everything that's been published and you don't have any credits. Don't tart up your work with pizzazz. Be clear about its nature and ambition, but get a supporting opinion. Have at least one other author, from a class, a conference, or your rolodex, read it and give a "blurb" in advance. That helps us know that your unusual, unique creation will indeed satisfy an audience. This is always the big question with new books that are so original one has to invent an audience to greet them.

Remember that this singles bar has rules, and one of them is that you have only moments to make a good first impression. There's a lot of competition for my hand. One reason it's best to avoid cosmetic marketing devices—the Wonderbras of pitch letters—is that I really need to quickly see the substance of the work. Too much disguise and I'll move on. I must be able to know what I'm getting and be excited about getting it, all in five minutes or less.

But, like the Supreme Court said of pornography, you know it when you see it. That spark of excitement, that rush to the head. And despite my overwrought prose and pretenses, I am not jaded in the least—no more than 10%. I may not be the innocent high schooler ready to fall head over heels into a crush. But I'm open to new romance.

The perfect pitch doesn't have to be perfect. If it has the mark of character about it, if it intrigues me, if it sticks to plain form but still embodies passion and ambition, I'm game.

I'm free Tuesday night. Are you?

ESMOND HARMSWORTH is a founding partner of the Zachary Shuster Harmsworth Literary Agency. Born in London, he was educated in England and graduated with honors from Brown University and Harvard Law School.

He represents both fiction and nonfiction. In fiction, he focuses on literary fiction, mystery, and crime. His nonfiction list is varied and includes biography, true crime, popular science, business, media, politics, history, memoir, international affairs, and psychology. He is also in charge of the agency's foreign rights department and deals directly with London publishers.

Books recently represented include the novel *The Spinning Man* by George Harrar (Putnam); the narrative nonfiction adventure story *The Darkest Jungle* by Todd Balf (Crown); the *New York Times*-bestselling and Edgar Award-winning *Black Mass: The Irish Mob; The FBI and a Devil's Deal* by Dick Lehr and Gerard O'Neill (PublicAffairs); *Investor Therapy*, a book on investing and psychology by Dr. Richard Geist (Crown Business); *Madalyn Aslan's Jupiter Signs* by Madalyn Aslan (Viking Studio); and the mystery *Lover's Crossing* by James C. Mitchell (St. Martin's).

CHAPTER 15

The Secret Is Reduction

by Andrew Stuart

There is no paint-by-the-numbers formula for constructing the perfect pitch. Like so many things, the perfect pitch is the product of a number of elements coming together in the right way at the right time. The idea may have hit at just the right moment and there's no competition; the author may be ideally suited to write the particular book, so his or her credentials trump the quality of the pitch itself; or the writing is so fine that the pitch, whatever its structural weaknesses, is still persuasive.

Publishing is not necessarily a meritocracy. Certain people, namely celebrities or infamous figures, can get their books published based not on any intrinsic quality of the writing, but because of their high profile. But let's be honest; this article is meant for the rest of us, writers who have to convince an agent that we are a risk worth taking. I'll assume that you, dear reader, are not a celebrity, nor have you shamed yourself in front of the world. You are a decent, hard-working person trying to get an agent to help you get your book published.

While there are no magic bullets, that doesn't mean there aren't basic rules to follow to ensure that you'll receive serious consideration, rather than the all-too-frequent form rejection.

The secret to a great pitch letter is reduction. Reduction of the storyline to one or two sentences; reduction of the plot elements to a handful of sentences; reduction of the themes and ideas to a one- to two-sentence description; reduction of your target audience to a paragraph; reduction of your ten-page single-spaced précis to one page (maybe two, if you can't figure out the formatting and you really have a long bio).

Here, then, are a few staples that form the polished, professional pitch letter:

1. Always be able to summarize your book in one sentence.

While this sounds terribly crude and insulting to the majesty and integrity of the work, it is a fact of life. All agents and editors want a simple tag line that they can use to wrap their minds around your book and sell it. They don't want to have to figure it out for themselves. That annoys them. And when they get annoyed, they pass on you.

The tag line is a trickle-down phenomenon: Agents use a persuasive tag line to sell your book to the editor; the editor uses it to sell to the publishing folks shelling out the money for your book. Once the editor buys the book, he'll use the tag line to sell the book in-house to sales and marketing people; finally, the sales reps usually have no more than a few seconds to sell individual books in their publisher's catalog to book buyers in the big chains. It is imperative that that one-line description be as sparkling and effective as possible right from the outset.

No matter how elaborate your plotline, no matter how profound and paradigm-shattering the ideas and narrative techniques, you need to be able to say in one—if you must, two—sentences what the book actually is. *Ulysses* is a reworking of the Odysseus myth that recounts a day in the life of Leopold Bloom through an experimental stream-of-consciousness technique. *Moby Dick* is the story of one man's pursuit of a whale. *King Lear* is the tragic story of a king's test of his daughters' love.

Are such tag lines misrepresentative of the full breadth of the book and do injustice to it? The answer is an unequivocal yes. But they're a starting point; they give you the pivot around which you can then fill in the details.

The perfect pitch letter should give the agent the impression that the author can write and has a good story to tell, but also has a sense either of the market for the work or simply an inner confidence and maturity that increases the possibility that the work will be impressive.

Provide a one- or two-line description of what the book is. This description can also give an idea of who the target audience is, as well as the general context in which you'd like your work considered. "A compelling techno-thriller in the spirit of Tom Clancy, [untitled] follows secret agent Jake Steed in his pursuit of a maniacal former Soviet general who is threatening to launch a nuclear weapon." Or, "a cross between *Bridget Jones' Diary* and *The Exorcist*."

Perhaps, "an action-adventure thriller that will speak to readers of *Into Thin Air* and *The Perfect Storm*." Or, "narrative nonfiction that will speak to readers who made bestsellers of *The Professor and the Madman* and *Longitude*."

YOU NEED TO BE ABLE TO SAY IN ONE—IF YOU MUST, TWO— SENTENCES WHAT THE BOOK ACTUALLY IS.

2. Provide a one- or two-paragraph breakdown of the plotline.

Americans are renowned for their short attention spans. Agents are no different. An agent who receives many query letters each day does not want to slog through a blow-by-blow account of a Byzantine plotline. Just focus on the major plot points, and you'll be fine. All the ins and outs of the plot can be appreciated later—once the agent has agreed to review the manuscript. (Keep in mind, you can always include a more detailed synopsis page that is separate from the pitch letter.)

In addition to laying out your concise description of the salient features of the plot, this part of the letter is also the space where you can indicate any other features that make your book unique. For example, if your work relies heavily on a particular myth or is an updating/adaptation of a famous work of literature; if there are particular stylistic innovations that are crucial to the work; if your work is marked by extensive historical or scientific research.

3. It helps to let the agents know that you are aware of the market in which you are writing.

Mentioning competitive titles, current trends, or popular issues at least lets them know that you are thinking commercially. "Books such as *X* and *Y* were huge bestsellers, and my book deals with a similar topic." Or, "The market for accounts of eccentric personalities or unusual historical figures has grown in recent years." Or, "there have been no thrillers that dealt with this topic." And so on.

That said, be cautious that you do not overstate the reach of your target audience. Don't say that since your novel has a female heroine and women make up 52% of America, you know your book will be of interest to approximately 140 million people. Or that because a third of last year's bestsellers dealt with political issues, your novel with a politician as the hero will have a huge audience. Be focused and specific. And above all, be realistic.

4. Provide one paragraph detailing your own credentials, particularly as they relate to the project.

Don't worry if your bio is low on stellar credentials vis-à-vis the publishing world. Ultimately, a successful novel or work of nonfiction should be able to speak for itself. Certainly, awards, fellowships, and academic accolades should be listed. If you are writing a historical novel set in ancient Rome, of course mention that you majored in ancient history in college. However, for that same novel, it's not necessary to mention that you were voted most likely to succeed in your high school senior class, or that you won the talent contest at your company's Christmas party. Be relevant.

Don't provide every detail of your life. There's no shame in saying that this is your first novel. Actually, it can often work to your advantage, as publishers and agents are also intrigued by the prospect of finding a fresh new voice, one unblemished by a weak sales record or a bunch of unsold manuscripts.

5. Do as much research as you can on the agents to whom you are sending pitch letters.

You can find out who the agents are by reading the "Acknowledgments" sections of books, through writers' services on the Internet, or often just with a vigorous Google search. It's not a matter of flattering the agent; it's to show that your query is not just another cold call, a stab in the dark. You've selected this agent to consider your book because you're familiar with the kinds of books they do and the topics that interest them. This is a touch that can make the unsolicited query seem less random.

6. Be aware that tone is a sensitive issue.

Do I try to be funny and soften them up with a humorous conceit before they get to my work's description? Do I phrase things in the second person, and try to set up a mode of camaraderie with the agent, whom I've never met in my life? Or do I just describe the virtues of my book and myself, and let the agent make up his mind if he wants to read it?

THERE'S NO SHAME IN SAYING THAT THIS IS YOUR FIRST NOVEL.

While some people don't mind attempts at humor or quirkiness, my personal preference is for the straightforward description. One writer's sense of humor or imaginative conceit is another agent's writhing agony—followed by a moment of exercise as they toss the crumpled letter into the dustbin.

Cuteness and idiosyncrasy are okay if that's the nature of the project you're submitting: a humor book or a book on cat astrology, for example. But if you're going to opt for the quirky humor approach, be sure that it works. Otherwise, you'll kill your project straight out of the gate. Ultimately, you can never go wrong with an honest description of what it is you're doing. To quote Jack Webb's signature exhortation in *Dragnet*: Just the facts, please.

There is no guarantee that even the best of pitches will get the consideration that is its due. The aforementioned tips, however, will at least increase the odds that you are able to distinguish yourself from the rest of the pack, and aid you in that all-important category: getting noticed and taken seriously.

ANDREW STUART, prior to starting the Stuart Agency, was an agent at The Literary Group International for five years. Before that, he was an editor at Random House and Simon & Schuster.

He represents a wide range of award-winning and bestselling authors, from Pulitzer Prize winners and entertainment figures to journalists, academics, policy makers, and novelists. Clients include Wendy Northcutt, author of *The Darwin Awards: Evolution in Action* and *The Darwin Awards II: Unnatural Selection*; Pulitzer Prize-winning journalist William Dietrich; bestselling novelist Mary Monroe, Mike Medavoy, David Wolper, Nasdijj, Mark Dery, and David Callahan.

CHAPTER 16

The Serendipity of Slush

An Interview with Jane Dystel

by Katharine Sands

Sands: What do you look for in a query letter?

Dystel: The query letter has to be written in English. And too often it isn't. For instance, if somebody says they have a "fiction novel" for me, I stop reading. Obviously if it's a novel, it's fiction. So I know that they haven't been careful.

And the query has to be written in a thoughtful, intelligent way. I like people who write to us to have done some research in terms of how to present ideas to agents.

As far as nonfiction is concerned, I am looking for fresh ideas. Now there are no new ideas; it's just the way they're presented. So I'm really looking for a fresh way of presenting ideas.

And the author needs some kind of credentials to be writing what they're writing. Sometimes they don't have them when they come to me, but can develop them along the way. You can't get credentials overnight, but, depending upon the idea, you can build them. And if I'm interested enough in the idea, then I'm going to help the author do that. For instance, if they have a lot of teaching experience, maybe we can get them out on the lecture circuit.

I think credentials are more important than the platform. If you have both, it's wonderful. But many people are not on a speaking tour, or don't have a television show.

Sands: What's going through your mind when you first look at a query or hear an author's pitch?

Dystel: What's the idea? And then, who can I sell it to? As I'm listening, in my own head I have to come up with a half a dozen editors' names—so-and-so would love this. I spend a great deal of time with editors trying to figure out what they're interested in. It's part of what we agents do. If I can't come up with half a dozen editors right off the bat, forget about the credentials and the platform. I can't help.

I may become very emotional about an idea and want to say, I love this, it's the best thing since sliced bread. But then I'll step back, as a businesswoman, and consider, what if I can think of maybe only one editor who will be as passionate as me? Is it worth the time it will take to help create the book proposal the right way—to just go to one editor? Maybe not. And some other agent might have some other ideas that I don't have. So I might pass.

That's the way I work with nonfiction.

Fiction is different. Fiction is much more emotional, more subjective, for everybody. I'll give you an example. I have an author that we represent, and tried to sell his first novel. It was very strange. Beautifully written. And I couldn't sell it.

But I loved his writing. So he put that work aside and now we are developing another novel of his. I read it on Friday, and the more I read, the more I loved it. It's very odd and very quirky and outrageous and so clever.

Cleverness I think is what grabs me most about a novel. I do a lot of traditional suspense thrillers—but even those have to have a certain cleverness about them. It's the uniqueness of the voice and the idea that really attracts me in fiction.

I THINK CREDENTIALS ARE MORE IMPORTANT THAN THE PLATFORM. IF YOU HAVE BOTH, IT'S WONDERFUL.

Sands: If you were to teach a course in how to write a query letter, what would be in it?

Dystel: First, they've got to really grab me in the first paragraph with the idea of their book. And I want to hear why they think it has merit. But the writing of the query letter is everything. It's got to be written very, very well. It's got to get me in one page. I don't want it to be any longer. Incidentally, I read every query letter that comes into my office.

Sands: Personally?

Dystel: Yes. I read every single letter. Authors like Thomas Moran, who wrote *The Man in the Box* that won the Discovery Book, his was a first novel that came over the transom. And I've now sold seven novels of his, two under a different name.

I pick up a lot of people over the transom. It's a very important source. Obviously most clients come through referrals, but the slush pile is an important resource. I learned that years ago as an editor.

Sands: How did you become an agent?

Dystel: First I was an editor, then I was a publisher. I was on the other side for 18 years. And I had gone as far as I could go. And I was really sick of inventory. Being in a returnable business, as a publisher that's all you're worried about. Inventory. One of the main books I published was *The World Almanac*, an annual, and I printed two million copies a year, and took back a million. You know, after eight-and-a-half years it was enough. I wanted to become an agent.

And I was taken in by a brilliant agent named Jay Acton. I was with him for eight-and-a-half years before I went out on my own and built this agency. And that was a long time ago.

We're now doing 80% nonfiction. I would love more than anything in the world to build the fiction side. And that's what my goal is now. But it's hard to find. You know from that first query letter if you're getting that novel.

Sands: What other mistakes do writers make when they query?

Dystel: One of the biggest mistakes that novelists make is that they tell me that they have five novels that they've written. And that makes me think, oh my God, they're not focused. What are they doing?

That's a big no-no. Usually I don't read any further. Because I know that they're not really focused on that one book that they're really keen to have published.

THE WRITING OF THE QUERY LETTER IS EVERYTHING. IT'S GOT TO GET ME IN ONE PAGE.

Sands: What lights you up about being an agent?

Dystel: The serendipity. Not having any idea of what's going to happen in the next minute. I have no idea. I love it. I just had a phone call, a wonderful call. I have a client who's published a bunch of novels, but I couldn't sell this particular novel for the longest time. Then, it was picked up by the last publisher. And it has been nominated for every possible fiction award except for the National Book Award, and it may be nominated for that. That really is so fabulous.

So many times, it has happened to me that the last publisher buys it, after I've gone to 40 and 50 publishers. And the book does sensationally well. And the author goes on to have a wonderful future. That really excites me. Because all you need is one to start them off, if you can start them off well.

And I explain to my authors if a particular one is not a good publisher for them. I'm going to tell them what the pitfalls are of being published by someone who's really not going to support you very well. Because if your first book doesn't make it, there is no second.

Of course, you can make it in different ways, not just in the unit sale. It's the reviews and all of the stuff that happens around the publication. A small publisher is not going to have a huge unit sale usually. But one of the things that really excites me about what I'm doing is building writers. That's what I'm in business to do.

Sands: For the talented newcomer out there, how should they approach you? What will catch your eye? What will make them stand out?

Dystel: That new idea. With nonfiction, the answers to three questions are absolutely essential. What is the idea? Why do you think it works? Why are you qualified to do it? And the quality of the writing itself is important, especially with narrative nonfiction.

For fiction, if I'm interested in the category and in what the novel's about—which they have to be able to digest into a paragraph—I'm going to ask for a sample. Sometimes I'm so interested I'll ask for the whole manuscript, but most of the time, just the first 50 pages.

Sands: What does the writer sitting at the keyboard need to understand about what has to be there?

Dystel: When they're writing a query letter, they have to think like they're talking to us personally. First of all, these query letters that go out over the Internet to four million people—those are automatic "no's." I read one paragraph and think: everybody in the world has just gotten this letter. I'm not going to spend any more time on it.

We have a very good website. So go there and learn about us, what we're interested in, and write to that. I ask to see more for almost all of those letters. The writer who does the research about the agent, and then writes the letter as if they're having a conversation with that agent, now that's interesting.

You can't go to ten agents with your submission unless you write 10 different letters. Personalizing a query letter in some way will get the agent's attention. It really will.

It might not make me want to take it on, of course, if I'm not interested in the subject or if I can't think of the six editors I can go to. And if you go to our website and find out, oh my God, this is not the right agent, then just go to the next. A lot of agents have websites. Or go to *Jeff Herman's Guide* to find out what we're interested in.

A writer should know who they are querying. One part of writing a book proposal is finding other books that have the same market. So look inside those books. See what the acknowledgments are, especially the agents' names. Do some research.

Sands: What is some other advice you like to give writers?

Dystel: Don't ever give up. And try to get as much feedback as you can. Rejection is a tough thing to take. But don't give up. Just try to learn.

It's hard with fiction, because we don't give feedback in terms of why it doesn't work for us. But if we don't like something, but we love the writing, we'll ask them for the next thing. And we'll mean it. We don't ask lightly, because we don't have the time to do the reading.

But one thing that people say about me is that I just keep persevering—if it can be sold. Of course, if I go to twenty people with a piece of nonfiction and don't sell it, and after hearing the editors' opinions, I believe that they're right and I'm wrong, I'm going to stop. Because I'm also a business person.

WE HAVE A VERY GOOD WEBSITE. SO GO THERE AND LEARN ABOUT US. A WRITER SHOULD KNOW WHO THEY ARE QUERYING.

Sands: Do quirks or outrageousness or whimsy ever work?

Dystel: That's a gigantic turnoff. They're thinking that they're getting more of my attention by sending these things, but it's really a turnoff.

Sands: What about after you do sell the book?

Dystel: Oh, I love getting flowers, if I've earned it. And I never forget those flowers. I never forget that lovely thank-you note. So after we've done the work that's nice, as long as it's not excessive. But if it's before we've done the work, I wonder why you think it's necessary to send me that stuff. It's not a good thing.

Sands: Tell me a good discovery story.

Dystel: Oh, I have a great discovery story. I have a client who I love dearly; her name is Mary Doria Russell. And she spent close to ten years trying to find an agent for her novel *The Sparrow*. I think she went to over thirty agents. Now, when the novel came into my office, it was over 800 manuscript pages. And, if loosely described, it fell into the science fiction category—which I didn't handle at the time.

So I was ready to pass. But my partner worked with Mary to get the novel down to a little over 500 manuscript pages and convinced me to read it. And I fell in love with it right away and sold it within two weeks. *The Sparrow* became a classic. It was followed by a sequel called *Children of God*. And now Mary is doing a third novel, quite different from those first two books.

Ten years and over thirty agents. And it's really weird; if you describe *The Sparrow* in that cover letter kind of way, it's about Jesuits going into outer space. So it sounds quirky, maybe too quirky. But when you read it, the writing is brilliant.

Sands: You have a separate client list for cookbooks. How is pitching a cookbook different from any other kind of book?

Dystel: Cookbooks depend on (1) idea, (2) credentials, (3) platform.

Mostly the credentials. This is a very difficult category to sell these days, even though and I've been doing it for almost 18 years. You have a very finite number of editors for cookbooks. It's not like with fiction, where you might have four editors at a house overlapping in their interests. In cookbooks you only have one.

So you really have to be spot-on. I sell 95% of every cookbook I take on. But I'm very particular.

I say no to most cookbooks these days. Because I know what's going to work and what isn't.

Sands: Back to fiction, how do you fall in love with a new character? What would speak to you?

Dystel: I cannot fall in love with a character I don't like. But this is subjective. Even within our agency we have novels where somebody will say I hated the characters and somebody will say, oh, I loved the characters.

So I have to like the characters. I think that's universal. Editors feel that way. If you read a novel and it's a really interesting story but you hate everybody in the novel, you're not going to buy it.

I've got to be able to relate to what motivates them. I've got to be able to believe in what they're doing, that what they're doing is real. Unfortunately, it's difficult to sell fiction, which is why I love it so much.

There are a lot of opportunities. Advances are down. But there are a lot of new publishers, small ones.

It's certainly not as easy as when I came into this business.

But I'm a person who enjoys challenge. And, I mean, you have to have a strong backbone.

JANE DYSTEL has been an agent since 1986. Her publishing career began at Bantam Books, after which she moved to Grosset & Dunlap where she became a managing editor and later an acquisitions editor. She went on to become Publisher of World Almanac Publications, where she created her own imprint.

As an agent, Jane quickly developed a reputation for honesty, forthrightness, hard work, and commitment to her authors and their writing careers. Her agency, Dystel & Goderich Literary Management, founded in 1991, has steadily grown to include a diverse and impressive client list.

Her roster includes such luminaries as television's Judge Judy, yoga instructor Gurmukh, actress Valerie Harper, gossip columnist Cindy Adams, actor Richard Dreyfuss, and Pulitzer Prize-winners Thomas French and Walt Bogdanich. She has also nurtured the careers of acclaimed novelists Mary Russell, Lorene Cary, Gus Lee, Thomas Moran, Reed Arvin, and Jewell Parker Rhodes and a number of young fiction authors, including Tayari Jones, Joe Konrath, and Michael Weinreb.

Her cookbook clientele includes superstars like Lynne Rossetto Kasper, Lidia Bastianich, Bobby Flay, Michel Nischan, Alice Medrich, Nina Simonds, Mary Risley, Gale Gand, Mary Goodbody, Julia Moskin, Jonathan Waxman, Flo Braker, Raghavan Iyer, and many others.

[Sample query letter for a nonfiction book:]

[date]

Jane Dystel Literary Management
One Union Square West
Suite 904
New York, NY 10003

Dear Ms. Dystel,

I am the author of several magazine articles and three business books (one published by AMACOM; two by Peterson's). I'm writing you because I am now turning to more general nonfiction, and I feel an agent could better represent my work—especially the book I'm now writing.

It's entitled *Falling: A Brief History of an Extraordinary Sensation*. Like Diane Ackerman's *A Natural History of the Senses*, or Witold Rybczynski's *Home*, my book will be an entertaining and educational essay on a topic that seems familiar, but that, when explored, yields a fascinating new perspective on who we are.

Why falling? Because falling, after the 60 million years our ancestors spent evolving in trees, is built into our bodies and brains; it's in the grip of our hands and the swing of our shoulders; it may have even formed our consciousness, according to one recent theory. Falling, or the risk of it, is at the heart of much of our recreation, sport, and entertainment; it also forms a universal, almost instinctual metaphor in our language, myths, even our spirituality. In short, falling is a primal force in our lives; a fundamental part of being human.

In my book, I broaden the definition of falling to include activities in which we fly through the air, momentarily free of gravity, and those in which we flaunt gravity's pull through balance or climbing. Falling is also not only something we do, it is something we watch others do.

The history of falling is filled with surprises. Parachutes, for example, at first weren't used to save lives—they were used to *risk* lives. For more than a century only daredevils used them, and only to scare the daylights out of a paying crowd. It was a daredevil, in fact, who came up with the idea of packing a parachute into a backpack. His aim was to hide it, the better to horrify his audience.

Mountaineering, which started out as a gentlemanly hike to have a good look at nature, quickly became a game of who could take the biggest risk, with climbers intentionally choosing the most dangerous routes possible. Today, some climbers, called free soloists, scale cliffs of a thousand feet or more with no safety equipment whatsoever. A single slip means death.

Roller coasters evolved from ice slides built by Russian peasants, and by the late 1800s coasters had not only very steep drops, but some had loops that turned riders completely upside-down. Victorians, it turns out, had something of a mania for falling. Aside from roller coasters, they flocked to see Jules Leotard, inventor of the trapeze (and yes, of the leotard), turn somersaults in mid-air. They also made the Great Blondin wealthy, gasping and even fainting at his antics on a tightrope stretched over Niagara Falls.

The mania for falling has only seemed to increase in recent years. Witness the phenomena of extreme sports, most of which are just normal sports with an extreme dosage of falling added. Snowboarders, extreme skiers, rock climbers, skydivers, and others, have pushed their sports further and further towards pure confrontations with gravity. Skateboarding, in-line skating, and BMX bicycling would never have become events in ESPN's X-Games if the athletes didn't use ramps to shoot themselves high into the air.

These subjects will give *Falling* a nice measure of sensationalism, but there will be more to my book than that. Readers will discover how the metaphor of falling fills our language and literature, from myths such as Icarus's melting wax wings, to expressions such as *to fall from grace*, right down to the formation of words themselves: falling is so equated with a sense of loss that its Old English root, *feallan*, is also the root for *fail*, *failure*, *fallacy*, *fallible*, *false*, and *fault*. This deep metaphor may account for why stories of individual falls can be so compelling, such as these, which will be told in full in the book:

• Lt. Col. Bill Rankin was flying ten miles above the earth over a violent thunderstorm when the engine in his jet fighter failed, and he had to bail out. Without a pressurized suit, he assumed that the blast of air at 500 miles an hour—air that was 70° below zero—would kill him. It didn't, and instead he fell into the storm. When his parachute opened automatically at 10,000 feet he was swept into updrafts, spun like a doll on a pendulum, pummeled with rain and hail, shaken by thunder, and surrounded by huge shards of lightning. Altogether he was aloft for more than half an hour before the storm released him, and he landed.

[Several other examples were included.]

And there will be more: how we sense falling, and how that sense evolved; why it can feel good (a recently discovered "thrill gene" may in part be responsible) and what people do when it feels bad (virtual reality is now being used to treat acrophobics); what it means when we dream about falling; and what we know about people who choose to die by falling.

As you requested in your submission guidelines (which I found on your website), I've enclosed an outline and a sample from the book—in this case, the first chapter and much of the second (about 10,000 words), which is all I have completed so far. I have only approached one other agency with this project, where it was declined. Please feel free to contact me by phone, or mail at the numbers above. Thanks very much for your consideration.

Best regards,
Garrett Soden

[Sample query letter for a spiritual/inspirational book:]

Jane Dystel
Action & Dystel, Inc.
928 Broadway
New York, NY 10128

Re: A Book Proposal for *The Wind is My Mother*

Dear Ms. Dystel:

In 1987, I was ready to die. In a twelve-month period, I filed
for personal bankruptcy, I lost my business to an unscrupulous
business partner, my lover committed suicide, and, after rebound-
ing into a relationship with an old boyfriend, I got dumped for a
19-year-old receptionist. My life was at its darkest point, and I
had gone so far as to make a plan for how to end it. Then I met
Bear Heart.

His words gave me hope, and my work with him since that
time has dramatically changed my life. I didn't have to be a rocket
scientist to see that a book on his life and teachings could help
and inspire countless others the way he helped and inspired me.
The Wind Is My Mother: The Two Worlds of a Native American, by
Marcellus "Bear Heart" Williams with Nancy Lynn O'Donohue,
will do just that.

Bear Heart is a paradox—a man deeply rooted in Native
American legend and healing, yet so accessible to white people
and so captivating a speaker that he has become a bridge-builder
between cultures. Having made headlines and been featured on *A
Current Affair*, Bear Heart is a media-experienced storyteller who
is both entertaining and newsworthy. His message will make for a
fascinating book relevant to mainstream audiences.

The stories and spiritual guidance in *The Wind Is My Mother*
come at a crucial time in American society. To truly understand
family values, we may need to listen to Bear Heart as he illustrates
the powerful connection between generations in Native American

culture. To truly understand "environmental politics," we definitely need the guidance of someone like Bear Heart, whose teachings give us a new appreciation of how to live sustainable lives on this planet.

My nine years of in-depth study with Native Americans, plus my work as a video producer and writer, make me uniquely qualified to help Bear Heart tell his story.

I expect this book will sell extremely well to mainstream audiences, hopefully surpassing the over 500,000 copies (each) sold for several other books of related themes (*The Education of Little Tree*, *Lame Deer: Seeker of Visions*, *Rolling Thunder*, and the books of Lynn Andrews and Carlos Castanedas).

I would be happy to send you a proposal which includes newspaper clippings and a 3-minute videotape of Bear Heart's television and video appearances. I look forward to your response.

Thank you very much.

Sincerely,
Nancy L. O'Donohue

[Sample query letter for a novel:]

[date]

Ms. Miriam Goderich
Jane Dystel Literary Management
One Union Square West, Suite 904
New York, NY 10003

Dear Ms. Goderich:

I hope you remember me, or more precisely, my work. A few years ago you read and liked my novel, *Hold Fast Your Dreams*, though you ultimately decided not to take on the representation.

I have just completed a commercial thriller, ***The Courier***, which I'm hoping you'll have an interest in representing. Because you've read my previous work, I've taken the liberty of including an abbreviated, one-page synopsis, and the second chapter, which introduces the courier, Simon Leonidovich.

FYI, this work took first place in the Novel category at the Focus on Writers annual competition. There were 900 entries, the majority of submissions by published authors. I offer this information simply to let you know the work has gone through a vigorous screening process and was found to be "very polished, with outstanding commercial potential," by a panel of industry professionals and bestselling authors.

Would you be interested in seeing the full manuscript (approximately 85,000 words)? I look forward to your reply.

Very truly yours,
Jay MacLarty

Enclosures: Sample Chapter
               Abbreviated Synopsis
               SASE

[Sample query letter for an anthology of essays:]

[date]

Todd Keithley
Jane Dystel Literary Management
One Union Square West, Suite 904
New York, NY 10003

Mr. Keithley,

I am seeking representation for a project I am working on, *The Secret Life of Cowboys*, a collection of essays. Enclosed is a proposal for this book, as well as "Everything But Rope," one of the essays in the collection. I am currently finishing up *The Secret Life of Cowboys* and I am actively seeking an agent to help me get it sold.

I have been published regularly in *Big Sky Journal*, one of the most well respected magazines in the West, which features a number of acclaimed contributors including William Kittredge, Mary Clearman Blew, Rick Bass, James Crumley, and Pete Fromm. I've also had an essay published in *Bugle Magazine*, short fiction in *Kinesis*, and my work is forthcoming in *Gray's Sporting Journal*, *Heartland USA*, and in the anthology *My Heart's First Steps: Writings that Celebrate the Gifts of Parenthood*. I've enclosed my most recent clips.

Thank you again for reading my work. If you would like to discuss this project further, please feel free to contact me at home or by e-mail. I look forward to hearing from you and I thank you for your time and consideration.

Sincerely,
Tom Groneberg

Enclosures
SASE

CHAPTER 17

I Want to Hear a Diva Do Opera

An Interview with Sheree Bykofsky

by Katharine Sands

Sands: What are some of the things you look for when you are pitched by authors?

Bykofsky: For a nonfiction project, I am interested in a timely, unique idea, a professional presentation, and an author who has the proper credentials—what publishers call a "platform." I want that author to be the very best person to write that book.

When considering fiction, I seek good writing. I want commercial fiction with a literary quality. I believe it requires a certain talent to be a novelist. I want to find writing that's awesome, but I like to represent novelists who won't actually use the word awesome.

I also want to work with likeable authors who respect what an agent needs to do to bring a project to life.

Sands: What advice do you have for writers who would like to be deemed awesome?

Bykofsky: Make the presentation to me as perfect as possible. First, make sure there are no mistakes. Show me that you don't write the kind of sentences that anyone could just slough off. Serious thought has to go into every sentence of a novel, the way every word does in a poem. Every word should be carefully chosen. I think authors need to take that kind of time to write. Write and then put it away. And then come back to look at it again.

Also, make sure you're not submitting to an agent just because you're sick of writing. Is your work ready—not just to be evaluated, but to be bought? If you have any doubt, there are professional editing services, writers' groups, classes, and conferences. Those are all great places to get good feedback.

Definitely ask others to give relentless criticism. Be open to listening to anyone who has any constructive criticism to offer. But don't make changes you don't 100% agree with. A writer should only make changes they believe will improve the material.

Sands: What common mistakes do people make in pitching you—written and verbal?

Bykofsky: Verbal is easy. Sometimes I'll sit down with an author and they'll give me a really great quick pitch or they'll find a compelling way to describe their book in one sentence—the same sentence they might use if they were on a radio show publicizing their book after it's published. At this point, they've definitely got me interested. And I want to request the book. But then they proceed to talk me out of it—they tell me too much. I want to see how it reads—I don't want to hear about it. I have to see how good the proposal is or how the novel reads. In the verbal pitch, I just want to hear enough to know whether I'm interested or not in seeing more.

In written pitches, the number one mistake is making mistakes. Number two is trying to go around a system that works, the protocol to send a query letter, synopsis, and a self-addressed stamped envelope.

Don't send flowers, candy, or scented stationery. One potential author sent me a follow-up to his initial query—to apologize for something he did wrong the first time. These kind of things do not make a good impression.

Sands: What does make a good impression?

Bykofsky: A well-constructed query letter, a self-addressed stamped envelope, and an author who's taken the time to learn about the publishing process. I must admit I'm impressed when an author tells me they've read my book, *The Complete Idiot's Guide to Getting Published* (now in its third edition), because they're telling me they've taken the time to learn not only about me and what I want in an author, but also about the business. An author who is well-informed about the business of publishing, before embarking upon it, increases his or her chances of getting published exponentially.

Sands: Tell me a discovery story from the slush pile.

Bykofsky: One day I was sitting there with my big bag of mail when a self-published book by Nicholas Boothman called *How to Make People Like You in 90 Seconds or Less* landed on my lap. The complete title appealed to me immensely. The book looked self-published and had a lot of neuro-linguistic programming jargon, but I was immediately impressed by the picture of the author, his letter to me, and the title.

So I dropped what I was doing and called him immediately. He was very engaging and made me like him in 90 seconds or less! I was very pleased to take on that book, and it's been a big success. I sold it to Workman Publishing, and Boothman is now working on his third book for them.

Sands: How about an e-mail discovery story?

Bykofsky: I generally prefer snail-mail queries with a self-addressed stamped envelope. If I receive an e-query, I tend to think that the author is not following my own personal guidelines. However, there are times when an e-query is so outstanding that I do make an exception and look at it.

It's also important to say that if I see something really good, a mistake or blunder can be easily overlooked. For example, I once got a query addressed to Maria Carvainis, another agent who is listed alphabetically after me in *Jeff Herman's Guide to Book Publishers, Editors, and Literary Agents*. It was a biography of Jimmy Carter.

I liked it. So I called the author and said, "I'm not Maria Carvainis, but I like your query." I said he was welcome to send his query to Maria, or I'd be happy to pass it on to her. But I asked if I could consider it, and he said yes. I ended up representing him and selling his work to the University of Georgia in an auction.

Sands: If someone were to take the Sheree Bykofsky course on pitching, what would they learn?

Bykofsky: That passion is everything. That no matter what you're selling, whether it's a book or a vacuum cleaner, you have to believe in your product.

You have to be the first person convinced that it is something important, worthwhile, fun, funny, entertaining, informative. You have to know every good thing about your product to be able to sell it.

In my own pitches to publishers, sometimes I extrapolate from the author's pitch because it was their language and wording that got me excited in the first place; they often properly convey the tone and content of the work I'm representing.

But personally, I'm very concise when I'm pitching. I recommend that authors do the same. Conciseness is a quality very much appreciated in this marketplace where everyone is vying for a small piece of everyone's time.

Sands: Do you have any exercises you might recommend to writers to improve their pitching skills?

Bykofsky: Sit down with a friend and practice making a pitch. If it's a written pitch, get someone to look at it before it becomes the real thing in the mail. Try to get some feedback from non-menacing sources.

Sands: What are your biggest turn-ons?

Bykofsky: I do like an author who, as I said before, shows me right off the bat that they've done some homework. They know who I am and are trying to find a good match. I also like someone who shows me they are a professional by approaching the query or pitch in a professional way. They remember to include an SASE, type the envelope, and have put thought into a good title that catches my eye and conveys the book's subject.

I like to know after reading the first paragraph what this book is about or what genre it fits into. Paragraph two should list the author's credentials and should tell me how they plan to promote the book. I also like them to include a phone number. And I like conciseness.

Send me a whole package that shouts professionalism, that includes a perfectly written query letter, a great, timely idea, good grammar, a good platform, an energetic author—someone who has taken time to learn the business and to learn about me. That gets me excited.

Sands: What hooks you when you're reading a fiction query? Character? Plot?

Bykofsky: The only thing that I need to hook me is good writing. I have a Master's Degree in English from Columbia and I like to use it. I know good writing. I want something that will appeal to a large audience, but I want the writing to be special. Some people can sing and some people can write.

When I'm at a concert, I don't want to hear an average, adequate singer; I don't want the song to be just good. I want to hear a diva do opera. I want the singing to have a great tone and quality. It's the same when I'm reading. I want not only a good plot but also good writing—the whole package. That requires talent.

I believe fiction requires an innate drive and talent. That can—and should—be nurtured and improved. But I don't think someone without an innate talent can learn how to do it well enough to appeal to me.

SIT DOWN WITH A FRIEND AND PRACTICE MAKING A PITCH. GET SOMEONE TO LOOK AT IT BEFORE IT BECOMES THE REAL THING IN THE MAIL.

Sands: What lights you up about being an agent?

Bykofsky: I love the pleasure of knowing that I help writers spread important messages that help the world. I love getting a bound book in my hand that would not exist if it were not for me.

I love books that are well-published and achieve success.

I like being a part of the excitement.

SHEREE BYKOFSKY is a New York literary agent, representing some 100 book authors in all areas of adult nonfiction, as well as select literary and commercial fiction. Her specialties include popular reference, business, health, psychology, inspiration, self help, humor, and cookbooks.

Clients include nonfiction authors Taro Gold, Nicholas Boothman, Jennifer Basye Sander, Gerald Meyers (former CEO of American Motors), supermodel Roshumba, and Richard Roeper (of Ebert and Roeper). Fiction clients include Donna Anders, Leslie Rule, John Richards, and Andy Straka.

Sheree teaches the basic publishing course at NYU's Center for Publishing certificate program and at the 92nd Street Y. She is author, co-author, or editor of more than a dozen books, including the bestselling *The Complete Idiot's Guide to Getting Published*; *The Complete Idiot's Guide to Publishing Magazine Articles*; and *The New York Public Library Desk Reference*.

She is also author of *The Best Places to Kiss In and Around New York City*; *The Big Book of Life's Instructions* (Harper); *Me: Five Years from Now* (Hyperion); *Popping the Question: Real Life Stories of Marriage Proposals from the Romantic to the Bizarre* (Walker); and *The 52 Most Romantic Dates In and Around New York City* (Adams).

Sheree speaks on all areas of publishing at colleges, writer's conferences, and seminars across the country, and has appeared on countless radio and television shows. She has a popular online column called *Ask the Agent*. Her website is www.shereebee.com.

CHAPTER 18

I Love to Tell a Publisher: "Have I Got a Virgin for You!"

An Interview with Harvey Klinger

by Katharine Sands

Sands: When writers pitch you, what do you look for?

Klinger: For fiction, it's the quality of the writing and the subject matter. Credentials don't come into play; it could be a housewife or an award-winning author who wants to switch agents. I might love the housewife's first novel, but find that the award-winning author doesn't interest me in the least. This is among the most subjective businesses around.

I don't like writers who try to pitch me with a sales pitch of their own. My attitude is, "That's my job." I just want a very short query. Don't do a big sales job on me. Let the material speak for itself.

Sands: How does a writer get you to read his/her material?

Klinger: If somebody goes to HarveyKlinger.com, they'll automatically have a strong sense of what our client list is like. I want to know that a writer has taken at least that much effort to check out who we are. You want me to know who you are—well, do you know who I am?

Sands: For fiction, if someone were to pitch after a panel or during a conference, what would jump out at you? What would work and what wouldn't work?

Klinger: Strong contemporary women's fiction; I feel like that's the core market right now. A great thriller. Women's suspense. Coming-of-age novels don't work; I've had them up to my eyeballs and they're a rough sell right now.

For whatever reason, I have always had—strange for a native New Yorker—a strong bent on Southern fiction. I have a lot of clients in the South.

Sands: Are there any stories that jump out at you? Pitches where you've just said, wow, I've got to talk to this person?

Klinger: Don't oversell yourself. Undersell yourself. I recently took on a first novelist from the middle of nowhere in Texas on the basis that she had written an incredibly good pitch letter.

First and foremost, it was very intelligent. It was very well-written. It combined her work and life experiences with the subject matter of the novel.

I always think that all fiction is autobiographical anyway, particularly first fiction. This novel was almost like a modern-day Romeo and Juliet, but with a happy ending. One of the main characters is a foster child, and she related that to the fact that she had worked with and taught a number of foster children.

So that jumped right out at me—how she combined her life experience with her writing. Because I have always believed that great writing comes from a place of passion in the writer. That passion can come from any place. It can come from within the realm of the imagination, but more likely than not it comes from life experience, whether personal or professional.

The letter was heartfelt. It was a great novel that was coming from a very personal place of passion and meaning. Knowing she had these experiences and being able to see how she combined them with a good contemporary plotline—the threads just came together.

Sands: How are you hooked in nonfiction?

Klinger: In nonfiction, I hate to say it, but we have to take our p's and q's from what the editors and publishers are hocking at us all the time. And that is the platform and professional credentials of the author.

The last thing I want to hear is everything you're going to be doing after the book gets published. That you can't wait to be on *Oprah* or can't wait to stand at the subway station and ply your book to everyone getting on at rush hour.

It's what you have done to date that matters. If you are a psychologist, where have you been speaking? Where are you giving seminars? Are you a regular with The Learning Annex or something similar?

If you're from a small town, do you have a center where you are constantly seeing people? Do you have an active website? I want to know how many hits you're getting on it.

Many, many years ago I shared office space with a publicist. Every day I saw her pitching and public-relations work in practice—what the shows and the columnists and everybody else was looking for. And it's what's the hook? What's the handle here?

Sands: Do you have any great pitch-from-hell stories?

Klinger: Well, I recall a pitch from a bodybuilder—he was a Mr. America this and a Mr. this and a Mr. that—and I sort of frankly took one look at him and thought, "This guy is scary."

It was a book on supplements. And, of course, he had interesting credentials, and he sort of had a platform. But I thought to myself, his English ain't very good for openers and he's just kind of spooky.

Sands: If you were going to teach a course in how to get you as an agent with a query letter or a pitch, what would be on that syllabus?

Klinger: Something about your background, a rationale for having written whatever it is. Where did this come from? There has to be a place within a writer where hope springs eternal and this is why I felt I had to write this book.

Tell me what it is about yourself that has driven you, because you must be driven to be a writer. And to be a good writer—it has to come from that place that is unimaginable to most people.

Be honest. Be honest. Don't be a salesman.

And be short. Be short. Give a thumbnail sketch of what this novel is about. I know really quickly whether or not it's something that's going to be of interest to me. And if it is, then what I like to do is just request the opening chapters and a synopsis. And if I like what I'm seeing, then we ask for the rest.

There's an impersonal nature that a lot of querying writers have. It's evident that they're just going through *Literary Market Place* or *Writer's Market*, and I'm in the K's, so I'm just sort of show up in the middle of their list of agents to contact. They are just playing 52-Pickup.

I respond to a pitch where I see you've taken the trouble to know something about me and my client list, and what this agency is all about. We are very hands-on. We do a lot of editorial work with our writers.

I don't respond to a pitch letter that makes it sound like this is the be-all and end-all. I respond to a writer who looks upon the agent/author experience as very much a collaborative experience. Because with the consolidation of the publishing industry, it's the relationship between the agent and writer that has more stability than anything else.

And writers want that element of stability in their lives because the writing experience is such a lonely one. When you are facing the outside world, you don't want to feel like you're totally alone out there. And also, your editor or your publisher can be out of work just like that.

But *I'm* not going anywhere.

And I like to know that a writer wants that cooperative, collaborative experience. That you do not look upon the agent as just your salesman. That here it is on a silver platter and now you're just going to take it out there and can get me a big, fat deal. And that will come through in a writer's pitch letter to me.

I will run so far in the opposite direction from sentences along the lines of "I am going to be the next Tom Clancy." Right away, I know this is somebody whose ego is ten yards long and five miles wide.

The way a writer can be most compelling is just by being themselves and letting the writing speak for itself. Capote used to say that when he would get in a manuscript he would read the first paragraph and the last paragraph, and if he liked those two then he would read everything in the middle.

Well, I don't like reading the last paragraph, because I always like to be surprised.

Sands: A writer has prepared a query to send to you—they're about to lick the envelope. What should they double-check before they seal that package?

Klinger: In this day and age, they should absolutely make sure they have checked my website. If you're sending me *Computers for Dummies*, then you haven't checked me out at all. And that's just going to go back lickety-split.

Then I know you have no idea of the kinds of books that we actually represent.

Do your homework. I don't think in this cyberspace era that that's a very difficult thing to do anymore. Show some initiative. Show that you're something of a mensch. And I will respond in kind. Don't waste my time; I won't waste yours.

Sands: I always tell writers to find the answer to Max Perkin's question: Why does the world need this book? Do you think that's good advice or not?

Klinger: It's good advice in theory, but on the other hand, I subscribe to the notion that it's already been all said anyway and it's just a writer coming in and saying it a little bit differently that just sort of appeals to us in a way that we haven't been moved yet.

I RESPOND TO A PITCH WHERE I SEE YOU'VE TAKEN THE TROUBLE TO KNOW SOMETHING ABOUT ME AND MY CLIENT LIST.

Sands: Then what advice do you give to newer writers, younger writers, or first-time writers?

Klinger: For first-timers—the luxury of a first-timer is that you haven't failed. I always like saying to a publisher, this one is the perfect virgin for you.

Sands: When you do your own pitch or submission letter to an editor, how do you approach it? Do you draw from the writer's pitch? Or do you have your own formula?

Klinger: I do not get into questions of marketability. I will get into a question of promotability, though, because I want to be able to tell them who the author is—especially in the case of a nonfiction author, where we know the talk shows, the newspapers, all of that is going to be very important.

I think that a press kit is a very good thing to have. I automatically say to my clients, I want a press kit. I also find these days that videos are very helpful.

For pitching fiction writers, I will say things like, when it's coming from me, "This is my next Bernard Malamud." I think editors like to have a frame of reference. They like having that handle. I think the worst thing that you can do is to just say, "This is a great novel."

I think the worst thing that a writer pitching me can say is, "I've written this great novel, and I know that you're going to want to see it."

Well, what's great about it? Tell me. If you think it's great, *why* is it great?

Sands: Do you have a great "I fished it out of the slush-pile" story?

Klinger: Well, let's see. I just fished a first novel out of e-mail. In fact, here's the postcard. Just got it yesterday. Her name is Julie Hilden. She wrote me a very intelligent e-mail in which, first of all, she told me that she was leaving her agent. And that she was the author of a nonfiction memoir called *The Bad Daughter*, which Algonquin had published.

Of course, I went to Amazon to see the reviews for that memoir. And the book had gotten very good reviews. So that piqued my interest.

And she had this erotic novel, which in fact her former agent had sent to some of my friends in the business, but would I read it? I thought, well sure, because she struck me as a writer to watch.

Sands: Do you find many authors via e-mail?

Klinger: Very few. But God knows we're getting a lot of e-mail queries, and I encourage it these days. It also indicates to me that that person has indeed gone to the website to check us out.

Julie Hilden was an e-mail success story. She wrote the facts, just telling me this is who I am, this is what I've done, this is what I've had published, and this is what my new novel is. Do you want to take a look?

And I just thought, well sure, I'd be a damn fool to say no.

But this query letter had all the bells and whistles going. So I called her after I read the novel, and she just sounded so great on the phone. Now Plume is publishing it, and it's called *3*.

She's also extremely young, which is always appealing. Because then I feel I can shape and mold them, and all they're going to do is listen to me. As well they should.

Sands: Are there any other elements you would identify for a successful query letter that haven't come up yet?

Klinger: My favorite word is always just *persevere*. Because I believe that if a writer believes in one's ability and one's talent, then it's no different than the actor who just says, "I'm going to make it."

Sands: How much does genre figure in? Do you want people to identify their genres?

Klinger: It's very helpful because we live in a very categorized world. And I know almost automatically which publishers are looking for which categories of material, particularly fiction and women's romance, mystery. I think a writer should absolutely identify genre.

I think the biggest problem for the writer is when it's really just a mainstream novel. If it is, then I look for the connection between one's personal or professional life experience and what you are writing about—that there is a connection you have been able to make personally. And your credentials: what you've been doing as a writer.

Sands: Do you like gimmicks with pitches? Has anyone sent you anything funky that worked? That got you to read them and/or represent them?

Klinger: Well, chocolate always works. At least then I'll read your letter. I won't say I'll represent your work. Dark chocolate.

Don't send photos unless you're gorgeous. Otherwise, don't send a photo. We have fun with them, but I don't recommend it.

HARVEY KLINGER received his M.A. in the Writing Seminars at Johns Hopkins University. He began his publishing career at Doubleday where he expected to become the next Max Perkins among editors. Instead, he left and worked for a literary agent for eighteen months and began forming his first client list. A two-year stint followed in association with an independent publicist.

Harvey created his own independent operation in October 1977 and has never looked back. He loves great fiction and nonfiction books that teach, enlighten, and help us cope in an ever-changing world.

A few of the diverse bestselling works he has represented include *What Women Want Men To Know* by Barbara De Angelis; *The Music of the Spheres* by Elizabeth Redfern; *Sophie and the Rising Sun* by Augusta Trobaugh; *Get Your Share* by Julie Stav; and *Sacred Ground* by Barbara Wood.

CHAPTER 19

15 Minutes to Fame

Pitching at a Conference

by Jason Cangialosi and Andrew Whelchel

As query letters and unsolicited manuscripts pile ominously around the walls of publishing's inner sanctum, writers must find new ways to beat the submission lottery. Writers' conferences across the nation offer a venue where the competition is stiff, but less abundant. It is a unique chance to truly convey the message of a manuscript and show an agent why the work will sell. For agents, conferences can yield great projects and lasting connections; for the writer, it's an opportunity to land representation.

Those who come prepared for their fifteen minutes deliver confident, smooth pitches about their work and enjoy a relaxed, positive appointment. Remember: agents wouldn't be there if they weren't looking for new projects. Developing, reworking, and practicing a pitch will make the meeting a comfortable and rewarding experience.

The idea is to make your book the natural topic of the conversation. Knowing how to answer questions and how to effectively convey the strong points of a manuscript will help ease any tension. Researching personal interests and a few of the agent's published clients can be useful in avoiding long, uncomfortable pauses in conversation.

What does an agent like to see?

Perhaps the most pondered question is what the agent might like to see at the meeting. In our personal experience, one writer in particular stands out. He sat down and gave a smooth pitch, offering insight about himself and his experience that would lend itself to a successful publishing venture.

He then produced from his briefcase a cover letter, three sample chapters, a synopsis, and two envelopes. He had seen the people before him try and fail to get their manuscript to be the one read on the plane ride home, so instead he provided one SASE for the return of the material and one envelope ready to be addressed.

"I brought this second envelope so if you are interested in the manuscript, it can be mailed to your office from the hotel," he explained. After some interest was established, he asked that the envelope be signed, first name only, after a space designated "Requested by:" to ensure it got into the appropriate hands.

It was truly a memorable introduction. While it didn't lead to representation, it did earn him several leads.

The introduction and presentation

Agents meet with dozens of writers over the weekend at a conference. A key factor in making a favorable impression on agents is the introduction. In roughly two minutes, an author can either completely enthrall an agent or lose their attention to the hundreds of other tasks on their mind.

Most of all, a writer must be natural in his or her approach so that the agents can also feel comfortable with being themselves.

In today's publishing marketplace, authors can no longer hide behind their words; it is the outstanding personalities that become successful. Agents want to visualize a writer talking about their book. How well you present yourself to an agent is an indication of how well you will be able to promote your published book.

Your introduction, then, is your "hook before the book." A solid handshake and thanking the agent is a safe place to start, but to stand out among the masses, it pays to be original.

Writers should prepare their material concisely. There is no need to give every detail. Treat the meeting as if it were the query letter; just be ready to give a short synopsis of the book. With guided ease on the writer's part, a natural, developed pitch should follow the introduction. The book's pitch will come across better if it is not recited off the page. Professional public speakers know how dry and impersonal most people sound when they read directly from the page.

You also makes a better impression by not relying on the page; it proves the book is a natural topic of conversation. Remember: short answers (similar to media "sound-bites") are not only effective when talking with agents, but also further down the road when utilizing the media to promote the book.

The question of body language is a topic too involved to cover here; just keep it in mind when you prepare to present yourself to an agent. Be affirmative in your intentions, personable in your approach, and ready for the full potential your book can achieve. These are paramount to secure an agent's positive perspective in a meeting.

Many authors let their nerves get the best of them before a meeting. This nervousness is a possible reflection that the writer is not fully prepared for the meeting or maybe their career as a writer. The pitch for the book should roll off your tongue with ease and confidence. More importantly, it should get the agent excited about hearing more. Keeping all these factors in mind, you can guide the conversation to your benefit, ultimately getting the agent to read your material.

Do not be over-confident or boastful in your introduction and pitch; no one likes an egomaniac. You should involve the agent in your pitch by asking where you should start in explaining more about the book. This is a good place to start once the pitch is out there. Foremost, it must be a pitch that packs a powerful punch.

IN ROUGHLY TWO MINUTES, AN AUTHOR CAN EITHER COMPLETELY ENTHRALL AN AGENT OR LOSE THEIR ATTENTION.

The face-to-face pitch

A good face-to-face pitch does not require reinventing the wheel. The best pitch is simple to remember, much like advertising. It should never be so long or so complex that the agent's eyes glass over. The few seconds spent delivering a pitch can be critical to the mood of the meeting. The gimmick of the stuttering Bible salesman asking if you would like to buy a Bible or have it read to you does not work.

A great pitch conveys tone, plot, and originality. Most pitches fit into one of two categories: the comparison pitch, where existing titles or similar story lines are used to draw ties to the manuscript and the "strength of the idea." One strong comparison pitch that did earn representation and then a multi-book deal from a conference was:

> If Carl Hiassan and Elmore Leonard conspired to write a
> novel about the contemporary west, it would be *Open Season*.

The second type of pitch is more complex to develop; it is the "strength of the idea" pitch. This is far more difficult to compose as it requires putting the best of the manuscript into a sentence or two that fully summarizes the project. It is a better pitch, however, for many writers who don't know what their work could be compared to. This approach still requires avoiding too many details that make a pitch cumbersome or confusing.

A writer who had won numerous awards delivered this "strength of the idea" pitch that started our meeting in motion:

> *Blood Spiral* is the chilling story of our human struggle to right
> our own wrongs—seen through the eyes of rampaging defense at-
> torney Bradley Hunt, as he tracks and destroys his past clients . . .
> in vivid detail and true thriller style.

Usually, a strong pitch will lead to questions by the agent and an opportunity to ask a few yourself.

If an agent asks a lot of questions after the pitch, it could mean one of two things. It is possible the pitch was not informative enough and the writer's introduction did not clarify the strongest points of the book—yet the agent is still interested. The more positive result is a sparked interest, and the agent is trying to fully visualize the book within the writer's career.

There are also a few questions a writer can ask an agent to better understand how they operate in their decision-making process. Help the agent to foresee them as an author on their client list by asking if their book is similar to any other titles currently represented by the agency. Another question worth asking is what you can do as a writer to best reach success. Asking this can give insight into what an agent's priorities are when they build the career of a client. Though the agent may not have specific answers, it shows that the writer is dedicated to their craft and their career.

Once all the cards are on the table and it is apparent that the agent still wants to play, the fifteen-minute meeting has served its purpose; it is a springboard for further contact. Most agents base their initial decision to represent someone not only on the material written, but also on what further material the writer has written or wants to write. The atmosphere a conference provides can offer ample ground to excite the agent with what they plan to write.

Agents also make their decision to represent someone based on a genuine chemistry that can exist in the working relationship. With an effective pitch, the first five minutes of the meeting is more than enough to obtain interest. This leaves the rest of the meeting to get to know each other.

By stimulating conversation about or beyond the book being pitched, a writer can plant the seed of interest with an agent. It is possible to tell how much an agent is really interested by when and how they intend to follow up the meeting. If the submission is requested and the agent plans to follow up with a phone call in a few weeks, the meeting was a success for the writer. What a writer should hope to hear is, "Let's talk later." An agent may make time to talk more during the conference, if they are excited about the project and the writer.

It's just as important to remember there are some things that should not be said—or at least certain ways in which they should not be said.

MOST AGENTS BASE THEIR DECISION NOT ONLY ON THE MATERIAL WRITTEN, BUT ALSO ON WHAT FURTHER MATERIAL THE WRITER WANTS TO WRITE.

A few of the common phrases that turn a conversation in a negative direction are:

- "I am an unpublished writer." Perhaps other agents have already passed on it. But if the manuscript is good enough, why make it an issue? Don't be dishonest, but don't start off on the wrong foot.

- "You probably won't like this, but . . ."

- "I've decided to give you a chance with my project."

- "I've tried several agents and publishers, and you are my last hope."

- "This may not be a subject that interests you."

Any situation can be turned to the writer's advantage. Stay positive, be confident, and be prepared.

ANDREW J. WHELCHEL, has been president of the National Writers Literary Agency (founded 1981) since 1997. The agency has since placed their clients' work with publishers such as Dell, Career Press, Random House/Waterbrook Press, McGraw Hill, Black Heron Press, and Putnam, as well as film production companies including Warner Brothers. Clients include bestselling mystery author C.J. Box (*Open Season*, *Savage Run*, and *Winter Kill*). Other titles include *Final Cut* by Reed Martin; *Rikers* by Paul Valponi; *The After Hours Trader* and *The Wizards of Wall Street* by Mike Sincere; and *Why is this Job Killing Me?* by John Kachuba.

With a background in film distribution, magazine publishing, and writers' organizations, Andrew speaks regularly at conferences such as the Writers Foundation Conference in Denver, the Kent State Summer Writing program, the Rocky Mountain Fiction Writers, the Southwest Writer's Conference, the Willamette Writers Conference, and others.

JASON CANGIALOSI, the Vice President of the National Writers Literary Agency,, operates out of New York City. With studies in media and film production, he covers a broad range of interests for the agency. He is a regular speaker at major writers' conferences across the country and has written feature pieces for *Authorship, BPM Culture*, and other periodicals.

CHAPTER 20

A Nation of Many Tribes

An Interview with Jim Fitzgerald

by Katharine Sands

Sands: How does somebody touch your heart, catch your eye, stand out from a stack?

Fitzgerald: The initial contact should be very short and should focus on the subject at hand. That's what attracts me. When I read a query letter, I look to see if they are on a fishing trip or whether they're really serious about writing a book.

The first thing I look for is to see that they're established and that they think of themselves seriously as a writer. Have they been published before?

The second thing I try to determine is whether they have a game plan. If, for example, for a nonfiction book, they've already done some interviewing or talked to people and done research, it certainly comes forth in the query letter or the initial pitch. Otherwise I regard it as a fishing trip.

Game Plan

Every piece of writing has its own little market—its own crowd, its own little feudal state of readers. Literary fiction is one of them. I like real young writers and coming-of-age books. It goes without saying that something has to be well written; otherwise you're not going to get to first base with anybody.

Then I think, who's the market? We're in a nation composed of many tribes. You've got motorcyclists, cheerleaders, literary types, business movers. How do you reach each of these groups? Who's the market?

Everyone's writing for somebody. No one is writing for the whole world.

When John Grisham first began, he was writing for lawyers. And that was in the pitch that went around. And it didn't sell. It wasn't until an editor at Doubleday (the 14th person, after the first 13 had passed on it) thought writing for lawyers maybe wasn't such a bad idea. It's a huge and dedicated market. You could do anything if you identify your market correctly.

Sands: What makes you say "eureka"?

Fitzgerald: If you know how you can get your book to that marketplace. That's the key. When I sold Sonny Barger's *Hell's Angel* book, I went over to HarperCollins and sat down and had a long marketing session with them on how to get that book to the marketplace. They were book people in New York. So they didn't know that there are Harley Davidson stores out there that are really lifestyle stores that aren't just selling motorcycle parts. These are stores where people who ride motorcycles on weekends go and hang around; this is a very upwardly mobile market. They're called H.O.G.s, which is short for Harley Owners Groups, and they spend a lot of money. And this book was by the man who is "a legend" to them.

It was an education for them. I showed them where the market was. And how to get to it.

As Willie Sutton said when he was asked why he robbed banks . . . the answer was simple: "That's where the money is."

The same goes with books. Get the book to the marketplace.

Sands: What makes you keep reading a new writer? And what makes you put it down for good?

Fitzgerald: When I get bored with it I put it down. When I already know where it's going. When I don't see any direction.

I have the Beau Brummel theory about writing. Beau Brummel said if someone noticed your clothes, you're overdressed. Well, if I notice your writing, it's overwritten.

It's true. When I read a book that's really good, it just floats away. I don't even see it anymore. I'm just immersed in the story, going and going and going.

But if I get hung up on clever writing, then I don't get anywhere.

Sands: Are there things that pop out as major negatives for you? Things that in a pitch or query would ring alarms? Or get an automatic turn-down?

Fitzgerald: If they start by listing the publishers that would be interested in their work; a red flag goes up. An author writes, an agent sells, an editor edits, an art director designs, and a publisher publishes and markets the book. Having worked on both sides of the fence, I know how it works.

Sands: What you can tell writers about how to craft the perfect pitch?

Fitzgerald: You don't have to embellish it with a bunch of history. State up front what your intention is. What are you doing? Be it a novel, be it nonfiction. State what it is, and then get into the rest of it. That's the main thing.

This is what my book is about. And this is who I am. And provide a good synopsis: What's the beginning, middle, and end?

And then just pick a chunk of writing out somewhere, and let me read it.

A good query letter is not much longer than three paragraphs. And at the end of the letter, I know what they're doing, what their intention is, and how to get hold of them.

WHO'S THE MARKET? EVERYONE'S WRITING FOR SOMEBODY. NO ONE IS WRITING FOR THE WHOLE WORLD.

Another thing writers do that really turns me off is to say that this will be the first book ever . . . on whatever. No, all the books on earth have all been written. They have. We're all just rearranging the alphabet right now. And putting new covers on and finding new slants, telling the same story in a modern context.

Rather than trying to make what you're writing about unique, make yourself unique. Make yourself as the writer unique. Find something to distinguish yourself, the writer, as aside from trying to distinguish the subject matter. Include your writing history, be it from the high school yearbook to the pet obits in your local paper.

Publishers are buying that particular book, but they're also buying writers. They love continuity and success.

And if you're going to write something—make a statement. Get out there and say it. Getting back to the original definition of publishing, it's very simple. It means to make public.

You're writing something and giving it to me, and I'm passing it on to the next person, who is saying, okay, let's print a hundred thousand copies of this, and share it with others.

Don't be shy.

JAMES FITZGERALD is a literary agent in New York. He sells and licenses books dealing with real culture. His clients include Sonny Barger of the Hell's Angels; David Toscana, a literary novelist from Mexico; Legs McNeil, author of *Please Kill Me*; Howard Safir, the former police commissioner of New York; the Harold Lloyd estate; and David Hilliard of the Black Panthers.

Prior to becoming an agent, James was an editor at St. Martin's Press, Doubleday, and the *New York Times*. His authors and books in that capacity included Douglas Coupland's *Generation X*, Leni Riefenstahl's memoirs and photography, Johnny "Rotten" Lydon, Arnold Palmer, Merle Haggard, photographers Amy Arbus and William Eggleston, Ice-T, Sarah Vowell, and a host of others that all have changed the world in their own unique way.

CHAPTER 21

How Much Is a Black Dress?

An Interview with Meredith Bernstein

by Katharine Sands

Sands: Tell me how you became an agent.

Bernstein: I was working for Henry Morrison, and went to a conference which turned out to be Hannalore Hahn's very first International Women's Writing Guild Retreat.

There was a woman there named Christina Baldwin who had written a book on journal keeping.

And I thought to myself, aha! she thinks she's Anne Frank too—as I had been a journal keeper myself from age 12 to 28. So, I introduced myself, we talked, and I asked to read her book—which I did on the train ride back from Long Island. I fell in love with it!

As it happened, I knew *one* publisher (he was a client of Henry's) and I called him immediately and pitched the book. I said, "This is a book about self-understanding through journal writing. And I think it could have a big market." He called me the next day and said, "Meredith, I want to buy the book!" And voila! That's how I became a literary agent. And that was 27 years ago.

That book is still in print. But the point was, that this author had connected with me on a visceral level—and her voice had resonated in my mind. When an author does this with any kind of subject matter—the reader *listens*. I try to look for material that other readers will also "hear."

That is the essence of a good query letter: can it pique the agent's interest? Does is express with a solid voice what it wants you to hear? If it's nonfiction, does it have the credentials or platform to make it stand out in the crowd. And most important: What are you doing that has not been done before? What is your spin?

Even if your spin isn't entirely unique, you've got to make it sound unique. Because that's what we're going to have to do when we present it to a publisher. So the more clever you can be, or the more creative you can be about the presentation of your material, the more likely I'll be able to sell it.

Selling is making the consumer believe that buying the product will somehow enhance his life. Whether the enhancement is a physical one, that allows them to do something better; whether it's the enhancement of the pleasure of reading for the pure joy of it; or whether it is just for knowledge, to learn something—whatever it is, it's about making a good trade.

You're buying that book because you believe that that book will give you something in return.

Sands: And in fiction?

Bernstein: In fiction it has to be a terrifically clever storyline, or a terrific voice telling me the story. The more you want to keep turning the pages, the more you want to be in the world that the author has created.

This is the success of *Harry Potter*. J. K. Rowling has created a world that you want to be in. It's an escape and a retreat, and almost a form of meditation in a way because you are transported. You are not in the real world. Your mind has been taken away. You are outside of yourself. So that suspension of disbelief gives you a freedom to be something that you aren't in your real life.

So when the author creates that for you it is a gift and you are just enlivened by it. And I think also for writers like Stephen King and others who are capable of creating a fear element, it's a very similar thing, on a different level.

And recently, a lot of people had recommended *Seabiscuit* to me. And I was avoiding it—why do I want to read about that horse?—but I absolutely flipped for that book. Because she pulls you in, the way that John Krakauer did in *Into Thin Air*.

That book is an even better example because, metaphorically speaking, that book was perfect. It was as if every chapter put you on the brink of a crevasse, looking into this deep hole, or took you to the edge of a cliff. And as he was ascending the mountain, you were ascending at the same time in terms of your interest and in the voice and the story he created. Every chapter left you teetering on the edge.

Laura Hillenbrand did the same thing in *Seabiscuit* in a different way. Was the horse going to make it? Would the horse win the next race? That is what the writer needs to do, whether it's in their book or their query letter. It's sort of a matter of seduction. Show me a little more. Show me a little more.

So what I'm looking for in a query letter is a sense of intrigue about what it is they're doing. If it's a well-written letter, they've said enough about the storyline.

But not too much. Enough to pique my interest.

Sands: How does a writer introduce a character in a way that might hook or compel you?

Bernstein: Possibly with some very clever piece of dialogue. If somebody says something funny or presents something in a humorous way that's clever, I will be very attracted to that.

Describe something in a way that I can envision it. Don't just tell me who the main character is. Give me some real description, something that embodies the character.

Sands: What do writers do wrong when they query you?

Bernstein: A, their letters are too long. B, they go into too much detail about their story. C, they bore me in the first paragraph.

If it doesn't grab me by the first paragraph or two, I scan. I look at the first two paragraphs, and then I look down to see if they have any credits.

Or if they tell me it's their first novel and it's 240,000 words—that's almost always a turnoff. I'm thinking, oh my God, they told me way too much.

And a lot of the nonfiction just feels like it's the same old thing.

But sometimes something wonderful just appears! Prior to becoming a literary agent, I had been a story editor for a film producer so I knew people in the film business. One day a woman I knew from that time called me and said that she knew a woman in California who was putting together shows for *This Is Your Life* and that woman was going to Europe to meet the couple that had hidden Anne Frank and her family. She said that if anything developed she wanted the film rights but I could have the book rights . . . was I interested?

You bet I was!

So I called this woman in California named Alison Gold and introduced myself. She said that somebody had turned her on to this couple in Amsterdam and she was flying there on her own dime with a translator, and she didn't know if they were for real, but she was going.

And I said, I'm going with you. So I flew to Amsterdam to meet four complete strangers, the couple and the translator and his wife. We met in the airport, checked into the hotel, and then an hour later we're sitting in the center of Amsterdam in Miep Gies' apartment.

We spent the next week, every day—Dutch English, Dutch English, Dutch English, interviewing Miep. It was a fascinating experience.

At the end of the week, Alison and I holed up in our hotel room and wrote out a working outline. Miep had given me access to her photo journal, which I photocopied to add to the proposal. And, of course, I had riveting stories to tell as a result of this intimate experience.

Because the "reality" of this project was unsure before I left, I had only mentioned it to a few publishers. But as soon as I came back, one of the editors (from Simon & Schuster) called me. And I quickly sold the book in a pre-empt. Needless to say, that book has been *very* successful and is still in print.

Sands: If a writer were to take the Meredith Bernstein course in pitching, what would you teach them?

Bernstein: You need a lure. It's like fishing. You need some kind of a lure, because we see so many. My father always used to say, "How much is a black dress?" You know, you walk by a window, and you can see twelve black dresses. Why does your eye go to one of them? What is it?

I'll tell you what it is: you think *one* of those dresses is going to make you look the best. So, the query letter has to make you as the writer look the best in your work. If the way that the writer presents the letter makes me feel attracted to that writer, then I'm going to want to see that piece of work.

Sands: What lights you up about being an agent?

Bernstein: I think there is absolutely nothing greater than when you get that manuscript and you start reading it and you fall in love with the voice of the story or whatever and you're thinking, I'm going to launch this career. I'm going to make this person's dreams come true. That is a large part of the joy for me.

And I have a slightly different attitude about agenting. My attitude is that money is the side benefit of what I do. Not every author starts with a big advance.

I'm very interested in the quirk of the author's eye. And that means their ability to tell me a story in a particular way that becomes memorable, captures my fancy, makes me want to be with the characters, reminds me of something. Whatever it is that captivates me, I want to be around them more.

That's why people keep going back to read book after book after book of a particular author. They have been captivated by the quirk of that author's eye. And that's what I look for.

THERE IS ABSOLUTELY NOTHING GREATER THAN WHEN YOU START READING AND YOU FALL IN LOVE WITH THE VOICE OF THE STORY.

Sands: Do you like quirks when a writer queries you?

Bernstein: Definitely. If somebody sends me something special, I may be prompted to call that person. On the other hand, if it begins "Dear Agent," I throw it away. And don't ask me about letters that are addressed to me but begin with another agent's name!

Sands: How much developing of a writer do you do?

Bernstein: I'm more like a coach. I'll say, perhaps, that the beginning didn't work for me. Or there's not enough tension, the story isn't getting off the ground. I think you've got one character too many. I don't like the female. I don't like the way the protagonist is being developed. I don't like a certain relationship.

I'm more likely to give broad brush strokes, rather than, on page 13, paragraph 4, you need to take out that dialogue and you need to put action in there. That's not my job. I think I'm really good at making my authors understand what their strengths are and making them feel confident. Even though I have been known to be "tough" on the phone, I feel that they really know I'm in their corner.

And I will go to the mat for them as long as I really like what they're doing. But if they've sent me four romances in a row and I can't sell any of them, I'm a little less enthusiastic. I might like them very much, but I'm in business, too.

Sands: If you were speaking to a group of writers, what would you want them to understand about you as an agent? And how they would get you to read their work, based on their query?

Bernstein: You have to animate what's inanimate in order for me to be drawn to it. You have to draw something in my mind's eye that I'm going to want to see more of. That's really the key.

It's about taking a chance on paper. Successful artists, in my opinion, no matter what their realm, have taken a chance on showing outside what's inside. And the closer they come to the authentic self in that expression, the more likely I am as the appreciator of that art form to be drawn to it.

For me, every day the way I dress is an opportunity to express myself in a visual way in the world. And I get tons of feedback every day. If somebody doesn't comment on what I'm wearing on a given day, I think to myself, I blew it. Something didn't work. And I often find that the more I take chances—the bolder I am—the more people love it.

That's what somebody needs to do in the query letter. Take the chance. Be bold. Say something.

Make your mark. I think everybody has a little bit of outrageousness in them, and people are just scared to death to let it out. And it's such a gift. Why not, that's what I say.

MEREDITH G. BERNSTEIN has been a literary agent for 26 years, and has had her own agency for almost 21 of those. She has also been a story editor for film producers on both the East and West coasts, and as a freelance reader. In addition, Ms. Bernstein has packaged two romance lines and co-authored the book *Sexual Chemistry* with Julius Fast (M.Evans/Pocket).

Her client list includes fiction (women's fiction, men's fiction, mystery, romance) and nonfiction (women's issues, personal memoirs, parenting, psychology, business, spirituality, science, travel, inspiration, humor). She represents many individuals who have accomplished memorable achievements. Among such clients are Miep Gies (the woman who hid Anne Frank's family and found her diary), NOW president Patricia Ireland, sailing champion Dennis Conner, and Chanrithy Him (a survivor of the killing fields of Cambodia).

"We love personal memoirs that bring out the heroic individualism." In nonfiction, she seeks authoritative works that shed new light on a given subject. Her agency is always interested in new ideas, new voices, and other original projects and creative endeavors that supersede genre.

CHAPTER 22

Adventures in Copywriting

by Debbie Babitt

Now you see him . . .

It begins at a prestigious music school in New York City. A killer flees the scene of a homicide and locks himself into a classroom. Within minutes, the police have him surrounded. When a scream rings out, followed by a gunshot, they break down the door. The room is completely empty . . .

Bet that got your attention, didn't it? That was the first paragraph of cover copy for a novel by a *New York Times*-bestselling thriller author. How about this one?

Sophie will never forget the day her best friend killed herself.

Or this?

> Nina Chickalini has a plan: Get out of Queens.

Here's an intro line of copy for a novel by a contemporary master of horror:

> [Hero} meets evil late one Monday morning when the doorbell rings.

And for a first sentence that winningly captures mood and tone and tells you exactly what you'll be getting in the book:

> After finally wising up to her drunken rodeo crooner lover ("Imagine Kevin Costner with an overbite"), [heroine] saddles up her dogs and takes her act on the road, leaving miles of heartache and highway behind her.

CAPTURE THE READER'S INTEREST RIGHT OUT OF THE GATE WITH A WHAM-BAM OPENING.

It's known as the fine art of copywriting. As a veteran copywriter and copy director at major New York publishing houses, I've always followed a simple rule of thumb for writing selling copy: Grab readers with a first sentence that builds to a powerhouse finish that gets them to buy the book. (No sweat, right?) So when you pitch your work—be it a query letter or a full-blown manuscript, the most vital requirement is catching your reader's interest . . . and keeping it.

So here are a few practical guidelines for writing that will sell you to your target audience, whether it's a reader, an agent, or that all-omniscient publisher:

Babitt's Copywriting Canon #1

Capture the reader's interest right out of the gate with a wham-bam opening. You don't necessarily have to say who or what the hero/heroine is; in fact, oftentimes it's more effective not to begin with the name of the hero and who he is and what he does, blah, blah, blah. Headlines are especially effective on the back covers of mass market books, and/or a front cover line (what we call a tag line) that's short, snappy, evocative, and tells the reader what he's getting into. It must also be brilliant and fascinating enough to make the reader turn the book over and start reading the cover copy. Here are one or two that spring to mind:

> A Novel about Sex, Love, Motherhood,
> and Happy Endings . . .

(This tells you exactly what you'll be getting: A sexy, romantic, family-oriented book that promises to be a light-hearted, upbeat read).

> Put a man and a woman together in a small town,
> and watch the temperature rise . . .

(Clearly a book about the chemistry between the sexes—lots of heat, sex scenes, and, of course, romance)

Here's one of my personal favorites for a book entitled *Shopaholic Takes Manhattan* . . .

> . . . But will she have to give it back?

Babitt's Copywriting Canon #2

Surprise the reader. Start going in one direction, then veer off into uncharted territory that keeps them intrigued enough to read the rest of the copy—in novel parlance, to turn the pages. But it shouldn't be so off-balance that it becomes off-putting. You need to strike the right balance by bringing the plot elements and characters of the story together in a way that signals the kind of book (read: genre) the reader's getting, but original enough to let him know this isn't your typical romance/mystery/horror, etc., novel.

What is it that distinguishes your book from the rest of the pack? A word to the wise: When it comes to writing copy for a specific genre, the reader usually wants to know that the author isn't straying too far from those familiar guidelines. It is, as playwright Edward Albee entitled it, *A Delicate Balance*.

Babitt's Copywriting Canon #3

Provide a few tantalizing hints about the story—just enough plot and character information/exposition to make them want to read the book.

To paraphrase Gypsy Rose Lee, "Make them beg for more. And then don't give it to them." (Not all at once, anyway.) This is guaranteed to keep the reader turning the pages. Whether you're writing a thriller, a romance or, yes, even a work of nonfiction—more on this later—you must release information gradually, like a time-released vitamin going into your bloodstream.

Babitt's Copywriting Canon #4

End on a high note. Give them a climax that teases, tantalizes, and marches them right to the checkout line. They won't be able to wait to get home and read the story.

THE THING ABOUT RULES? THEY'RE NEVER CUT AND DRIED. BUT THEY ARE GENERALLY EFFECTIVE.

The thing about rules? They're never cut and dried. But they are generally effective, as I've discovered from the copy that helps to sell the book (as opposed to copy that in a few rare cases might actually have misled the reader). This is based on authors and book buyers who have been surveyed about the blurbs that make them buy the book versus the ones that make them put it down again.

A quick word on author hype: Often, as copywriters, we're told to start the copy with a paragraph hyping the particular talents of an author, especially if they're consistent bestsellers like Danielle Steel or John Grisham. In their cases, we're usually armed with glowing reviews, which we obviously don't have with the first-time or fledgling author. That's when you really need to come up with great, selling copy to promote this unknown author.

You can apply these rules to everything from writing a query letter to creating a full-blown manuscript. I've had hundreds of query letters from writers pitching their work and ideas to me in the hope of getting a writing job, either as a freelance copywriter or a writer on my in-house staff. Like writing copy that gets someone interested enough to buy the book, your query letter is about getting your foot in the proverbial door. Most agents today will not even consider looking at your unsolicited manuscript, so you must write a query letter that will hook his or her interest.

I can tell a lot by writer queries. Great copywriters they might be, but if their queries are flat and dull and lack a sense of character and energy and narrative flow, I may never look at their copy samples.

Suppose you write me a great query letter, and I'm ready to tackle your samples. What do I look for in a sample piece of copy? The same high-voltage drama, energy, intriguing characters, active sentences (watch out for those passive verbs!—the feature that distinguishes the great writer from the mediocre is the former's brilliant use of active verbs); beginnings that draw me in; cliffhanger last sentences that leave me hanging and wanting to read more (i.e., to buy the book.) Writing a novel should be no different, which leads me to my next thought:

So you want to be an author?

Now let's say I'm writing copy for *your* book. You're in the exalted company of a published writer or a writer about to be published. Here's what I look for when I'm reading your manuscript: I'm looking for the hook into the story and characters that will help me write winning cover copy to help sell your book. (Speaking of hooks, a great book to read is Donald E. Westlake's *The Hook*.)

1. A story line or plot that's clear (though not necessarily linear) and gathers steam as it evolves, constantly building in narrative drive. Images help. Vibrant, compelling descriptions of places and settings that provide the necessary color and background. Then there's time period. Whether your book is historical, contemporary, or futuristic, there's always something you can tell me about a particular time and place that I never knew before.

2. Characters with qualities that are immediately accessible and who leap off the page because they're so wondrously alive and real and multi-dimensional, and therefore a gift to describe and talk about.

3. A clear beginning, middle, and end—nothing too muddled or obscure or simply esoteric showing-off.

4. Great moments of suspense—even if you're writing a romance or a saga or humor book or a work of nonfiction. In fact, the nonfiction books that usually make the bestseller list are described as being as dramatic and suspenseful as the best fiction. You don't want the reader to know how the story will turn out—whether the girl will get the guy or vice versa.

5. Chapters that end on cliffhangers. These keep me turning the pages and just might give me that slam-bang last line of copy. Think of soap operas or the novels once serialized in literary magazines. Pick up a book by Michael Crichton for chapters that accomplish this feat. Stephen King has been a master of the page-turner for years, with the bonus of creating flesh-and-blood characters you really care about.

6. Great writing style. Good copywriters should be like sponges: Capturing your unique authorial voice in their blurbs. (God, I've always hated that word; it actually diminishes what copywriters do. Let's change it to "copy.") If we can quote directly from your book, all the better. It means that you've written a book with what I call "selling prose."

Note: A series or continuing characters is always an interesting challenge; as your copywriter, I'm already familiar with your characters' histories, traits, etc. Now, along with you, I can reveal the arc of the character as he/she grows and develops.

To sum up

Write in such a way as to keep them turning the pages. If you're wondering how to get started—whether to begin with character, plot, or story, just remember the words of the great acting teacher and director Stanislavski: "Character *is* action."

Decide who your main character is—who's telling the story. If you don't know, your copywriter certainly won't. Keep your characters' secrets, exposing them at the most dramatic time. Create characters we'll care about, but don't give them away in the first sentence or first page or even the first chapter. Reveal them to us gradually; it makes for far more interesting and intriguing reading. And it's more the way it happens in real life: Do we ever learn the entire life story of someone we've just met?

Think of your query letter as a novel in miniature. Keep the conflicts strong and the tension high. Make each sentence build in drama and scope to the next one. Make us keep coming back for more.

That's the goal, of course: To write something that someone will want to read. Remember, you control the flow. Writing that gets the reader's attention is the first crucial step. But first it has to get *your* attention. You have to believe in it enough to be able to invest it with your passion and emotion.

Below are a few more sample pieces of copy that hopefully achieve all that has been discussed in the previous pages. (This time, I'm including names.)

And happy writing!

More samples

Lincoln Rhyme and Amelia Sachs are brought in to help the N.Y.P.D. handle the high-profile investigation. For the ambitious Sachs, solving the case could earn her an eagerly-sought promotion. For the quadriplegic Rhyme, it means relying on his protégée to ferret out a shadowy conjurer of death and destruction who baits them with gruesome murders that become more diabolically perfect with each fresh crime. As the fatalities rise and the minutes tick down, Rhyme and Sachs must move beyond the smoke and mirrors to prevent a terrifying act of vengeance that could become the greatest vanishing act of all . . .

—final paragraph of a thriller called *The Vanished Man*

He's the world's geekiest guy.
She's the woman of his dreams.
Only a major disaster could bring them together.
Now nothing on earth can keep them apart. . . .

Twenty-four hours ago, Genevieve Terrence was fantasizing about spending a hot weekend with her boss, major babe magnet Nick Brogan, on romantic Maui. Now she's stranded on a remote desert island after his nefarious scheme nearly got her killed. Lucky for her, brilliant computer programmer Jack Farley was on board. Now he's her sole companion in this unlikely paradise with nothing but driftwood, guava trees, and sharks for company. Who'd expect the shy genius—and the least alpha male she knows—to turn out to be the uninhibited stud of her wildest dreams?

—for a romance called *A Nerd in Shining Armor*

Poor Montana Moore—born during a flight from Seattle, with Idaho to the left and Utah to the right. Her parents compromised on Montana, who's still in flight mode as an airline attendant with one recurring fantasy: Walking down the aisle with that paragon of male perfection—wherever he may be. With her mother about to tie the knot for a fourth go-round, three-time maid of honor Montana knows she has to make big changes in her life. Becoming a nun is out of the question, so she's off on the adventure of her life: A cross-country quest for a man who can satisfy her emotionally, spiritually, sexually, and financially.

With its colorful cast of larger-than-life characters and winning blend of comedy, sensuality, and spirituality, *Baggage Claim* tells a heartwarming and hilarious tale of a woman who dumps the baggage of her past by claiming her future. And this time, she's traveling light.

—for a novel called *Baggage Claim*

The leaves of the calendar may be shedding faster than the sycamores on her family's decaying Mississippi plantation, but thirty-something southern belle Sarah Delaney isn't ready to sing the blues. Not when she's got a thriving detective agency and the outspoken, outrageously attired ghost of her great-great-grandmother's nanny to keep her on her toes. But the over-the-top, matchmaking phantom may have the last word on motherhood when Sarah takes on the controversial case of an accused baby killer . . .

—first paragraph of a mystery called *Hallowed Bones*

And last but far from least, copy taken directly from the pages of this adrenaline-pumped thriller:

If you contact the authorities, we disappear.
You will never know what happened to her.
We will be watching.
We want two million dollars.
Get the money ready.
Go home and wait.
There will be
No Second Chance

—from *No Second Chance*

DEBBIE BABITT was Copy Director at Penguin USA and Kensington Books in New York City. She has written copy for Random House, Simon & Schuster, Time Warner, and HarperCollins, among other prominent publishers. Ms. Babitt has worked with award-winning, bestselling authors ranging from John Grisham to Stephen King, Danielle Steel to Patricia Cornwell, Diane Johnson, Ken Follett, and Toni Morrison.

A former actress, playwright, and drama critic, she has recently completed a novel and is at work on her next book. She divides her time between Manhattan and Amagansett, New York.

CHAPTER 23

Don't Be Buffeted By Whims

An Interview with David Vigliano

by Katharine Sands

Sands: I don't think there are too many stand-up comics who went to Harvard Business School who became literary agents. How did that happen?

Vigliano: When I got out of Harvard, I got a job at Warner as the in-house packaging director. My job was to have ideas for books and approach people about doing books. Which was radically different at the time from what editors did—waiting for agents to come to them with ideas and projects.

My idea was, why be passive and wait for agents to come up with ideas? If we have an idea, why not go out and try to persuade people to do the books with us? It was very radical for publishing at the time; this was 1984. I was doing essentially what an agent was doing. And I tried to do four different books that Warner didn't want to do in-house that became *New York Times* bestsellers. So I said, well if I can't do it here, they're still great ideas, so why don't I just open up my own shop? Which is what I did.

Sands: How did *Generation X* by Doug Coupland come to you?

Vigliano: Through Jim Fitzgerald. But I think it was Peter Livingston, who had sold it to Jim as a nonfiction guide to Generation X. But then Peter died of AIDS. So the author was without an agent; he had delivered it but they weren't sure they were going to accept it, because what Doug had delivered was a novel. So Jim introduced me to Doug. And ultimately, they accepted it.

Then I got very involved in the marketing. I actually got a friend of mine at the *L.A. Times* to do a cover story in the View section on Doug and on *Generation X.* And that triggered a cascade of the coverage, including *People* magazine and the *Seattle Post Intelligencer*, and that's what really launched it. It became a pop-culture phenomenon. It just cascaded from there. It was a 3,000-copy first printing, and now there are probably close to a million copies in print, just in the U.S. It was just one of those things where lightning strikes.

Sands: How does a writer get to you? How do you discover a new writer?

Vigliano: A lot of it is referrals, getting to me through somebody who's established. But there is still room for somebody to write a really good query letter that presents themselves in a good way. And if they're a writer, that's what they're supposed to be able to do. In my agency, and in every agency, there are smart, sophisticated, unjaded people. Writers have the opportunity to catch the eye of any of us. It's just persistence and creativity—persistence more than anything else.

Sands: What are your dos and don'ts for writers about making the perfect pitch?

Vigliano: Something original, different, creative in a cover letter really works. Try to present your idea in an interesting way and not be formulaic about it. When something's good, we know it right away. It just shines through. And often everybody else see it, too. When something's good we jump right on it right away, because there are three or four other agents that will also respond.

Sands: What advice do you like to give to writers?

Vigliano: I don't think there's anything better than to keep honing their craft. And really not to be discouraged by rejection. Because in the same way that they're rejected by agents, we're rejected by editors. And you know, I don't personalize the rejection from an editor. And I tell the young agents that work for me that they can't personalize that rejection.

Because it's not about you. It's really about the fit. And it's a personal reaction. Just because I don't respond to what you're writing, it doesn't mean I am the final word. It just means that I didn't respond to it. It doesn't mean I'm right.

So for somebody to take me saying "no" as a judgment on their work is not the right message. I think people have to keep that in mind, not to look at a rejection from an agent as a comment on their work. It's just the agent saying "no" for a myriad of reasons.

Either the agent doesn't get their work, or isn't able to take it on. Not doing that much fiction, being too busy at the time, not sparking to that particular subject. I think too often writers put too much weight on that rejection rather than looking at it objectively. They invest too much emotion in the rejection rather than looking at it as much more of a business-like thing.

For me, it has to be organic. Does this work resonate for me? Everything has to flow from that, in my opinion. That's what this business is.

So think about the business reasons that people say "no." People pass on things and just move on to the next person or the next project.

Sands: What do you see ahead for publishing? Do you think the new technologies are going to change things dramatically?

Vigliano: I do. Somebody is going to develop one of these e-book contraptions that is really going to work. I think that there's going to be a whole new generation of kids and younger people that will get used to reading their books on one of these devices. And that's going to have broad implications for the way books are published. And I'm not sure

WRITERS PUT TOO MUCH WEIGHT ON REJECTION. THINK ABOUT THE BUSINESS REASONS THAT PEOPLE SAY "NO."

exactly what that means, but it's going to have a big affect on the way books are distributed. And I think ultimately it will be a positive thing for writers. But it will be interesting.

Sands: For the writer who might be your client two years from now, how do they enhance their chances of succeeding?

Vigliano: It's really about persistence and it's about staying power and not giving up, in terms of commercial success or getting published that is. It's about maintaining enthusiasm and maintaining a positivity about your work and about the possibilities and not getting discouraged. Because often persistence wins out.

Yes, it's all too easy, even for somebody in my position who's not the artist per se, or an editor, to get discouraged in the business. I know how hard it is for the writer to succumb to the battering that you can feel. But it's really a question of not succumbing to that. There's a real value to not being buffeted by those whims. To just see your vision through to the end. As hard as that may be, that's the key to getting where you want to be in this business.

DAVID VIGLIANO is the owner and founder of Vigliano Associates, a prominent literary agency based in New York City. He was raised in New York and graduated from Hunter College in 1980 before he went on to Harvard Business School. He worked as the director of packaging at Warner Books. After leaving Warner, he started his own agency in 1986. Vigliano Associates represents major bestselling fiction and nonfiction. With a professional background as an editor, David places a great deal of importance upon the editorial process and collaborates with authors on a one-on-one basis.

Many of the books he represents command large advances and often reach the *New York Times* Bestsellers List. In the recent year, four books made it to the #1 position: the Kurt Cobain *Journals*, Bob Greene's *Get with the Program* and *Get with the Program: Guide to Good Eating*, and Dr. Nicholas Perricone's *The Perricone Prescription*.

Vigliano represents a diverse group of high-profile clients including Pope John Paul II, Justin Timberlake, magician David Blaine, former Montgomery County Police Chief Charles Moose, Yogi Berra, Britney Spears, Shaquille O'Neal, and personal trainer Bob Greene. He has also worked professionally as a stand-up comedian.

CHAPTER 24

Booking in L.A.

by Erin Reel

When I graduated from college not so long ago, I was only sure about two things—I wanted to build a career in the business of publishing books, and I wanted to do it in L.A. Why I chose L.A. over New York was partly the romance of Hollywood, partly naiveté about how things really worked out here, and partly bad planning. But what do you expect from a fresh-faced kid from small-town Iowa?

My main fear was simply how I would get along. I had heard so much from the media and political or business leaders about the deficiencies of my generation. You know what they say about Generation X or Y: we're just a bunch of irreverent little bastards, with no grounding, no integrity, no work ethic, yada-yada. But as I worked my way through my internship and my first "real" jobs in the business, I discovered to my amazement and gratification that grounding, ethics, integrity, and professionalism have nothing to do with generations and everything to do with individuals. In fact for a fresh-faced kid from Iowa, raised with copious amounts of each, these seemed like the perfect ingredients on which to found an L.A. literary agency.

Starting Points

Before I jump into specific advice about doing book business in L.A., let's review three important issues to get firmly set in your mind before you ever start to look for representation.

First, spend some serious time researching how agents work—hopefully, that's exactly what you are doing. You need to know all of the who, what, where, when, and why's before you start. Besides this book, there are good literary magazines and websites outlining dangers to look for. Pay attention, take notes, and commit to memory. There are people in this business who look good, sound good, and feel good, but make a living out of exploiting writers. If someone offers you a deal that doesn't seem right, pass it up and wait for one that does. It's one of the toughest things you'll ever have to do, but in the long run, it's always worth the wait.

The second point, very closely tied to the first, is know your worth. Without you, without the work you poured heart and soul into, there would be no publishing business and no agents. You are the life blood of this industry. You deserve respect and compassion. Never forget it. It's the one thing you will have to hold on to when those inevitable rejection letters start rolling in.

Third, recognize that for those involved in the publishing process, this is business and not art. We're involved in the sale of art, not its creation. Don't confuse our job with yours, and don't allow yourself to become your own worst enemy.

Last week, I read a wonderful story that was edgy, clever, and really tight. I was so excited I called the author immediately. Spurred on by my excitement, he started telling me about how much he hated this publisher and that editor, and mentioned that he had "harassed" different people in the industry that hadn't liked his work.

I dropped him so fast I forgot his name before I hung up the phone.

All agents, editors, and publishers want to work with nice people. Wait until you've sold a million books or so before you develop a "Joyce Complex."

The L.A. book business

So, let's get back to my take on doing book business in L.A. The first thing one needs to understand about the Hollywood, Burbank, Beverly Hills, Malibu corridor is that it is all about the movie business. One would expect that in a city this size there would also be a strong publishing community. There is not. There are numerous people who run around and discuss the potential for one. But geography, scarcity of local publishers, and a lack of agents, editors, and writers whose main focus is publishing have kept one from developing.

The second thing to understand about L.A. is that it is a city notorious for exploiting writers—especially new writers. One client of mine, a graduate of the USC Film School, who directs and also writes for film, once told me, "It's like a rite of passage for writers to get screwed in their first L.A. contract. They are so excited to sign anything with anyone, they sign anything, and it almost always comes back to haunt them."

The third thing to understand about L.A. is that a great many "literary" agents here are chiefly interested in selling screenplays; they work books only for the cash flow to feed their movie habit. If you're lucky enough to get your book into William Morris, Creative Artists Agency (CAA), International Creative Management (ICM), or any of the other biggies with offices in New York, you can be relatively sure it will get to people who specialize in publishing and know what they are doing. But if you're shooting from the hip, looking for any L.A. agent under the assumption that he or she might have the inside track on eventually selling the movie rights to your book, you're taking a wrong turn.

This is how the worst of these places operate: Someone wants to get into the movie business, and they begin looking for books or screenplays to sell. Their main goal is finding treatments (screenplay overviews) they can pitch. When they receive a query, they almost always request a manuscript and inform the writer there will be a $20 or more "reading" or "processing fee"—cha-ching, cash-flow. The writer complies, because, "Gee, someone is interested in my work." When these places get your manuscript, because a lot of the staff of these agencies are frustrated artists themselves, they almost always have artistic suggestions—again,

WITHOUT THE WORK YOU POURED HEART AND SOUL INTO, THERE WOULD BE NO PUBLISHING BUSINESS AND NO AGENTS.

looking for ways to work the ideas into a movie, instead of focusing on publishing the author's book.

If the agent thinks he can do something with the work, he makes a big deal of signing the writer and offers him or her a contract. Usually, these documents specify promotional, printing, or phone expenses to be charged to the author. The worst of these documents require the author to pay up-front costs. I've even seen these contracts written with no termination clause, so the writer cannot escape a bad agent unless he or she hires an attorney. (The writer doesn't need to worry much about post-publication charges, because this type of agent rarely gets a book published.) Then, they take the shotgun approach and send copies to publishers without regard to the specialties of editors or the publisher's list. They send the work out to enough publishers to make it look good and then gradually lose interest.

The best indicator of this type of agent is that almost from the beginning, they suggest the new client start working on screenplay treatments while they wait. These treatments provide fodder for what they really spend most of their time on—trying to get a movie made.

Because these abuses seem so obviously heinous, it may be hard to imagine anyone falling into their trap. But the truth is, there are writers lining up to be exploited. They are so excited about the possibility of having a real agent, they look past the obvious. There are many more unscrupulous agents out there than you would expect, some with long track records and seemingly impressive credentials. It isn't as easy to spot them as one would think.

So, how do you really know if an agent fits your purpose? Here's some advice and questions to ask.

1. Be honest with yourself. Just because someone shows some interest in you, don't think your dreams have all come true. Publishing a book is a process of business, not a dream machine. Pay attention to the details.

2. Is there really a connection between yourself and the agent you are considering? Is he or she interested in you and your work? Is there

empathy? Can you work with this person over the long-haul? And is the agent willing to share his or her game plan?

3. If an agent intends to charge you any fees in addition to his or her 10 to 15 percent, think twice before entering into a contract. There are some good agents who pad their margin, but recognize from the start what they are doing.

4. If your agent recommends a professional editor, check his or her track record and research other editors. Ask what the editor has edited which has made it through publication.

5. If an agent insists on a contract, have an attorney go over it for you. Make sure it is clear to you what you are signing.

6. Make sure your agent shares all return correspondence from the publishers he or she has contacted. If more than a few letters come back saying, "This doesn't fit my list," begin to question whether your agent knows what he or she is doing.

7. Understand that a book and a screenplay are two distinctly different art forms. If you want to write books—write books. If you want to write screenplays—write screenplays. But find an agent who specializes in what you want to do.

PUBLISHING IS A PROCESS OF BUSINESS, NOT A DREAM MACHINE. PAY ATTENTION TO THE DETAILS.

The Old School Way

When I started to research starting my own agency, I soon discovered that the best, most respected agents in the business operated on a completely different basis than what I had seen thus far in my career. When I discovered the honesty and integrity in the "Old School" way of doing things, I actually giggled for its simplicity. I decided then and there that I would do business in the "Old School" way, or I would do something else.

This is how I see the Old School method of doing business (and how my agency, ERLA, and many other literary agents operate): We accept submissions only after queries, and then only if we can get excited about the potential of the work. We have no fees that are charged back to the client—no processing fee, no copying fees, no phone fees. No fees. We believe the costs we incur on behalf of our client are the normal overhead of doing business, for which we get paid our 10 to 15 percent.

We also do not expect our clients to sign a contract. When we "sign" a writer, we send them a letter of understanding explaining the details of the process. When a book is accepted for publication, there will be a very detailed contract with the publisher that includes the agent. That is all the legal protection the writer, agent, or publisher needs.

However, the big agencies have always used contracts, and for the multitude of services and specialties they offer, it makes sense for them to spell things out in advance. There are also many very good agents who use contracts, because of, well, the litigious times we live in. There is not necessarily anything sinister about contracts, but I happen to feel a contract between agent and writer is unnecessarily redundant.

No matter whether you're looking for an agent in New York, L.A., Dallas, or Portland, the same sort of things matter. Do your research. Believe in yourself and the quality of your work. Be as careful in the planning of your query as you are in the planning of your art. Look for an agent that fits your purpose, and always be nice. If you do all those things well, you'll be on the right road. Good luck!

ERIN REEL, after spending twenty years in the Midwest, and earning a B.A. in Literature from Iowa State University, moved back to her native Southern California to begin a career in literary agenting. After a start at a boutique agency in West L.A., Erin was hired on at a production/literary management company as a creative executive and literary agent. Eventually, Erin decided to go independent and begin the Erin Reel Literary Agency (ERLA).

Erin is currently working with investigative journalist Suzi Parker, author of *Sex in the South*, on several political/cultural nonfiction projects. ERLA also represents Liz Topp and Dr. Carol Livoti, authors of *Vaginas: An Owner's Manual*; new work by writer, director, and producer Robert Klane, author of *Where's Poppa?* and the comic cult classic, *The Horse is Dead*; and new fiction by writer/director Martin Schenk, author of *A Small Dark Place*.

CHAPTER 25

The Art of the Poetry Pitch

by Amy Holman

Poets are not often encouraged to say what is it they write about, either by individuals in conversation or by the industry (which currently offers more than 50 contests for the publication of poetry books which are judged anonymously). But all books are about something, and here is some advice to teach poets how to summarize their collections.

A poetry query is not anonymous, but all about identity—the poet and her poetry, the publisher and its poets—and how these kinds of identity match. More than any other kind of query, the poetry pitch can clarify for the poet her own artistic quest and put drive in her course towards publication.

A synopsis of a novel feels like a reduction of the book, but a summary of a poetry collection feels like a unification of purpose.

Identifying Your Quest

When writing we are all seeking something or proving something. There is always an over-arching theme or issue that interests us, rattles us, or searches for us. It can be a political agenda, a desire to connect, a need to heal rifts, to define oneself or the world through language, to expose trouble. It can be anything because it comes from the individual writer.

A particular poet's quest will encompass the subjects of individual books or poems. If you look at a few books by one of your favorite poets you will likely be able to identify the quest. Or perhaps, the poet herself will reveal the quest, as has Kathleen Norris with the subtitle of her non-fiction book, *Dakota: A Spiritual Geography*. From the Great Plains to industrial New Jersey, monastery and church to farm kitchen and courthouse, in poetry collections and meditative nonfiction, Norris celebrates and praises inspired places.

From one of her early chapbooks, *Views Without Rooms*, to her most recent full-length collection, *The Cloud of Knowable Things*, Elaine Equi has been figuring herself out through language, from news fragments and the poetry of others to commercial voice-overs and surrealists, the language she likes and does not like shapes her identity. Each book is different, but she returns fresh to certain artists, poets, philosophers, and popular culture.

Once you have identified your quest, it is much easier to define how your current book fits. A book can be a collection of the poems you've been writing lately, a few subjects under a theme, or one subject. It can borrow the format of other genres or be broken into sections. No matter the arrangement, there will be ideas, images, language, emotions, issues and/or themes that connect the poems together.

What is the reason for your title? Why did you arrange the poems the way you did? What imagery do you use? Which subjects or texts inspire your poetry?

For example, Terese Svoboda's recent book, *Treason*, has all sorts of betrayal—familial, political, environmental, bodily—and its sections build to an inevitability. In Edward Hirsch's sixth book, *Lay Back the Darkness*, he descends into middle age and human frailty, and explores everyone's desire to be remembered—his father before Alzheimer's, the children of Terezin through their drawings, Dante in his *Inferno*. Each section is a different kind of darkness.

In Linda Gregg's collection *The Sacraments of Desire*, there are four parts to split between solitude and desire, foreign soil and home. There are no sections, on the other hand, to *Bus Ride to a Blue Movie*, Anne-Marie Levine's second book devoted to sex and sexuality, history and one's own past.

Daniel Nester wrote a poem for every song recorded by the British rock band Queen, whom he idolized in his youth, and then composed his memoir, *God Save My Queen*, by putting the poems in order of the songs on all the albums, from the first album to the last.

Jennifer Michael Hecht, who teaches an undergraduate history course on the ancient world, composed her first poetry collection, *The Next Ancient World*, as a guidebook to understanding our civilization through her life and knowledge of history with the conceit that it would be unearthed by anthropologists in some future civilization.

Yvette Christianse invented texts she then fragmented in her collection, *Castaway*, an epic of exile depicting the transient inhabitants of the uninhabitable St. Helena island off Africa, from Fernao Lopez to Napolean Bonaparte to disguised cabin girls, slaves, and a contemporary black woman.

THERE IS ALWAYS AN OVER-ARCHING THEME OR ISSUE THAT INTERESTS US, RATTLES US, OR SEARCHES FOR US.

The Summary

The book summary will be the second paragraph in your one-page query letter. When writing this, it helps to think of it as having certain metaphors and imagery, and often, an arc of knowledge. Take a look at the way Charlie Smith's *Heroin* is described on the back cover.

> In this haunting collection by one of our most prodigiously gifted poets, heroin serves as a metaphor, both for what's longed for and for desire itself. Sometime past the speaker suffered an irreconcilable loss and he remembers this as it passes away from him over time, remembers it in the form of addiction, of a lover, a wife dead and gone into the desert. He thinks of this under

various guises: where he lived and slept, what he did with his time, how it was when he placed himself closely against the body of a woman he loved, what it was like when he moved away. In these lyrical and moving poems, the narrator prepares himself for something he can't name, something important that is elusive and difficult to see. Slowly and after much time, he comes, if not to understanding, to a sort of peace.

This is a rather lyrical description meant to entice a buyer—perhaps also not to frighten anyone off, by saying that heroin is a metaphor, when it is also the drug that Smith was once addicted to and that killed his first wife.

A query letter, on the other hand, is the introduction of your book and yourself to a particular editor, so your book summary would be in first-person and more personable, and not filled with praise for your ability to write. If we rewrite Smith's back-cover description above to use in a pretend letter, we'd remove "haunting," "prodigiously gifted" and "lyrical and moving." A summary simply tells what the book is, perhaps in this way:

> In *Heroin*, I long for my former wife and to never forget the days before she died. This desire and despair combined is as addictive as the drug that made me a sleepy cattle hand and that killed my wife. Haunted by her presence and absence, how we lived then, and how I've lived since, I've returned to those early days to reach peace in place of understanding.

In this example, I have personalized the approach to describing this book, which has only one subject. As it happens, Smith has been published with W.W. Norton for many years and would not need to sell his book in this manner to a publisher, but the exercise still stands. The title poem, below, offers more details about the subject, and shows how your own poems may give you details to include in your summary.

Heroin

I left messages for my editor to send copies of the contracts
to my new agent,
and then I read a passage about how no one talks
about heroin anymore, and the old life came back to me,
it was early yet, I hadn't used heroin for years,
I was one of the few rural junkies in the nation,
one of the few who tended cattle, there I was
nodding on a rock as the cows, stiff with unendurable shyness,
stumbled up to me. My wife and I would eat mashed potatoes
from the pot and lie out on the porch smoking reefer
until it got too dark to see.

. . .

I loved the graciousness of heroin, the way everything externalized
and obvious in the daylight opened its shirt and revealed its soft pale breasts.
The world slept curled in its own foolhardiness.
And my wife came carefully over the blankets to me and seemed
not to mind who I was. We inserted words
into spaces in the rain. For years I remembered the words
and whispered them to myself, half thinking I might
conjure her back into the world. They never caught us.
We missed them on the way to Mexico, to Puebla,
where eventually the line gave out. We slept on a bench outside a church.
It was two days before she died without regaining consciousness,
as I say in the memoir they are paying me so handsomely for.

from "Heroin"—© Charlie Smith

Your Bio

Your bio will be the third paragraph in your one-page poetry pitch, right
after the book summary. If you've won awards for your writing or received a grant or fellowship, mention that first. If you've published a
book in any genre, mention that. Choose to mention about five magazines from your list of acknowledgments or from others that printed

poems not in the collection. Say what you do for a living, where you studied writing, if you did, and anything that may have bearing on the subject of your book. This is not the place to be shy or modest, but since it is part of a letter, you don't want to condense an entire creative resume. Be personable and use good grammar.

The First Paragraph

You can tell a lot about a publisher by the authors on its list, if you are a good reader. Kathleen Norris' publisher, The University of Pittsburgh Press, has also published Billy Collins (before Random House), Jim Daniels, Jan Beatty, and Toi Derricotte (before Norton). All of these poets write in a direct language and narrative style, mostly, about everyday lives. Daniels and Beatty write about cities or neighborhoods, families and friends, and Derricotte writes about tough issues concerning women, while Collins is often humorous, picking on the minute details of life and enlarging them exponentially.

The first paragraph of your query letter, the pitch paragraph, acknowledges a connection between you and the editor. The best way to do this is with a name. Few poets have the luxury of a referral by an author to his editor, so the best approach is to connect your writing to one or two of the publisher's poets. Every editor likes to hear from readers; using this method proves that you read the books they publish. For instance, Pittsburgh only publishes first books through the Agnes Lynch Starrett Prize, but will read queries from poets about subsequent books. Let's say you had a collection of poems called *City Planning*, about social issues like homelessness and domestic violence; you might take this approach with Ed Ochester, poetry editor at Pittsburgh:

> For years I've admired Toi Derricotte's poems about domestic violence and racism, and Jan Beatty's poems about the hard streets of Pittsburgh, and today, I am querying you about my recent collection, *City Planning*. I have enclosed ten pages from the 52-page manuscript and a list of magazine acknowledgments.

There's no need to mention what the book is about, yet, since I have drawn out the editor with particular, related details from the poets he's published. Also, the book's title makes one think of crowds, conflict, and places of stone, glass, and metal. When I get to the summary, I can write what *City Planning* covers.

Finding Where You Belong

A pitch to a poetry editor is soft, like introducing a friend to someone who may be beneficial to her. It's not about selling a concept or hooking a reader. It's about community, and where you belong.

When you compose a query letter—pitch paragraph, book summary, bio paragraph—you are talking about your book, about yourself. You will enclose with it the list of acknowledgments of magazines and anthologies that first published poems in your collection—proving you have readers—and a ten-page sample of poetry from the collection—revealing your particular voice and style.

This dozen pages will be enough for the editor to decide whether to read your entire manuscript. It is already a better read than you will get by submitting to poetry book contests, where it is said that preliminary readers skim only three to five poems, initially.

At poetry contests, your manuscript is judged anonymously, and no explanation is allowed, as if a point of view or point of origin was verboten. The promise of cash, books in print, and prestige clouds reason, and poets submit to as many poetry contests as they can afford. The cost of photocopying a manuscript of 50-75 poems a dozen or more times, writing checks for $25 each, and paying for priority postage equals several hundred dollars.

Wouldn't you be happier sending to publishers you believed were interested? While you can narrow your selection of contests down to those who would likely publish your kind of book, you still have no identity, an incomplete reading, and a high price to pay for it.

There are editors at small and university presses, independent and large houses who are interested in receiving queries from poets about their books, whether chapbooks or full-length collections, first, second, third, or fourth books. Even presses, like Pittsburgh, that offer contests for first books will read queries about subsequent books. Soft Skull Press (publisher of *God Save My Queen*), Duke University Press (publisher of *Castaway*), Alfred A. Knopf (publisher of *Lay Back the Darkness*), and Graywolf Press (publisher of *The Sacraments of Desire*) do not offer contests. Zoo Press (publisher of *Treason*), Tupelo Press (publisher of *The Next Ancient World*), and Pearl Editions (publisher of *Bus Ride to a Blue Movie*) offer contests and accept queries.

Coffee House Press (publisher of *The Cloud of Knowable Things*) and W.W. Norton (publisher of *Heroin*) participated, at one time or another, in The National Poetry Series, which meant that they published winning volumes. They do not have contests of their own and do accept queries.

It makes sense to be realistic about the poets on a publisher's list before submitting to them, even if you think you are stylistically matched. Very rarely do large publishing houses like Knopf and Norton publish first books.

I believe that the process of identifying your quest makes you feel like you are an artist with vision, not an apprentice in process of learning craft. You are making art and the art of the poetry pitch is to communicate that vision and craft. As a poet, you have chosen a road and just now arrived at one of your destinations by finishing your current book.

It is time to get it settled in a publishing house. Find a good one, ring the bell, introduce yourself, be polite and presentable, charming but not sassy, and you will certainly get an invitation to come back.

AMY HOLMAN, for more than a decade, has been the expert to whom creative writers turn for insightful advice about publishing. She is a contributor to *The Practical Writer* (Penguin) and "The Artist's Toolbox" on the National Endowment for the Arts website, and was the associate editor of *Get Your First Book Published* (Career Press).

Also a poet and fiction writer, she has been published in many print and online journals, thrice nominated for a Pushcart Prize, and is published in the anthologies *And We the Creatures* (Dream Horse Press), *Mercy of Tides: Poems for a Beach House* (Salt Marsh Pottery Press), and *The Best American Poetry 1999* (Scribner). She also founded the Publishing Seminars program at Poets & Writers, Inc. and is author of the forthcoming book *Amy Holman's Tough Love Guide to Publishing*.

CHAPTER 26

Pitching Your Children's Book

by Andrea Brown

My first job in book publishing in the 1970s was at Dell Publishing Company in the "bunny" department. That's short for the children's book department. Within two weeks on the job as an editorial assistant, I was hooked. I loved the children's book business and never left.

Don't be deceived, though, into thinking it is soft and furry and easy. It truly is a bunny-eat-bunny world. Bottom lines abound here, too. Publishers don't pay the big advances they do in the adult trade field, so they expect to make big profits with their children's book departments.

It is rather interesting to note that the wealthiest author in the world is a children's book author—J. K. Rowling. Many agents and editors passed on the first Harry Potter book, so remember that as you get your next rejection letter. About 26 publishers passed on the first Dr. Seuss book, and then that went on to sell around eight million copies.

Numerous times, as an editor and then as an agent, I have seen not-so-talented writers get published through sheer determination, while others with lots of writing talent never get published. Do not shred your manuscript after several rejections. It simply means that you have not found the right editor, at the right house, at the right time.

The tricky part for children's book writers is that they are not writing for themselves, as most writers do. To write successfully for the children's book market, writers must first pass through the gatekeepers—the editors, agents, librarians, booksellers, teachers, parents, and grandparents who must first read and like your book. Then, children's book writers hope it gets into the hands of the children they wrote it for.

Children's book writers have a much tougher job than writers who are writing for their peers. Children's book writers cannot pitch their books to their audience, and children's book agents have the same dilemma.

When I find a manuscript I absolutely love, and am sure that a nine-year-old will also love, I first have to pitch it to editors who think they also know what a typical nine-year-old will love next year. I won't take on a new manuscript unless I can think of at least three editors that are likely to love it as much as I do.

I hate to use the word "rules." But every business has them and every business also breaks them. The children's book rules to follow are:

1. Enclose an SASE (self-addressed stamped envelope) for a response from an editor or agent.

2. Do not say you are writing a book for a child from ages five to eleven. If you have done your homework at all, you already know that a child of five or six will not read the same books as a ten- or eleven-year-old. To sound professional, make sure you know the categories of children's books. Basically, *picture books* are for children under six, *early readers* are for six- and seven-year-olds, *chapter books* for seven- and eight-year-olds, *middle grade* for ages eight to eleven, and *young adult* for twelve and older. The trickiest part of writing for children is first figuring out what age group you really should be writing for from "the child within." If you really remember being five and six, you can write picture books. If you only remember the teen years, write for the teen market and not picture books. Proper voice is everything. Children pick up on a writer's credibility almost immediately.

3. Do not submit art samples drawn by yourself, or that your spouse or child drew. The publishers want to hire their own illustrators for picture books. Editors are trained to match an appropriate artist with your text. And, even if your spouse says it is okay if the publisher does not want his/her art, there will be hurt feelings. Would you rather get published or stay married?

4. Do your homework before pitching any agents. It's a waste of your time (and the agent's) to pitch a book that is not within the "comfort zone" of a particular agent. Use the guides in libraries, in bookstores, and on the Internet that list agents. Find their specialization, and target market your pitches to those agents. Do not say "my children" love this manuscript. Of course, they do. They love you. They also want dinner.

5. The query letter is so important to your pitch. Write several drafts of the letter before sending it out. And keep it brief. All you need is three paragraphs. The first paragraph gives your "Hollywood pitch" —the plot of your story in about three or four lines. Say just enough to whet the reader's appetite and sound fresh at the same time.

   Second, include a bio about yourself—anything relevant to your publishing history. If you have spent twenty years teaching third grade and your book is for third graders, mention that. If you have been a lawyer, now retired and writing, don't mention that. Also list what, if anything at all, you have published.

   The third paragraph may say that you are querying several other agents at the same time. That is fine as long as you say so.

6. For picture books, don't even bother with query letters. Just send a cover letter with your manuscript, properly typed on plain paper and double-spaced. It is impossible to tell from a query letter if a picture book is publishable. It must be read in its entirety. Send up to three different picture book texts, but do not say you have more. It just does not sound professional; it sounds like you haven't taken the time to work on creating one terrific book. After you have some real interest from an agent or editor, you can mention having other manuscripts.

I WON'T TAKE ON A NEW MANUSCRIPT UNLESS I CAN THINK OF AT LEAST THREE EDITORS THAT ARE LIKELY TO LOVE IT AS MUCH AS I DO.

There are two methods of pitching. One is the "spaghetti" method: throwing a manuscript out to many professionals to see what sticks and with whom. It is usually a faster way to get answers on a particular manuscript and may be the best way for a hot, timely subject or for authors who have many projects.

The other is the "exclusive" method whereby an agent chooses one editor who seems like the best editor for a particular project. That editor is offered either an "exclusive look" for a short period of time, or the offer to come in with a silent bid or a pre-emptive bid for the book if the agent thinks there may be an auction. It targets the editor who is the best for the book. Then the agent can go elsewhere if necessary, and usually not that much time is lost.

It's difficult for un-agented writers to do these things, so writers should consider working through agents first. I suggest the "spaghetti" method to look for an agent. All agents are overwhelmed with submissions, and we don't mind writers pitching to others at the same time, as long as you say so upfront.

Publishing is a business. You want to make money. Then your agent makes money. Don't ever pay reading fees while searching for an agent. There are scams for writers cropping up every day. An agent should only make money when you do.

Above all, be professional and courteous at all times, beginning with your pitch. Respect the editor/agent's time constraints, as well as their knowledge of the publishing business. Don't quit after several rejections. Persistence pays off. Remember that often it's just a matter of the right place at the right time.

ANDREA BROWN established her literary agency in 1981, after working as an editor at Alfred A. Knopf and in the editorial departments for Random House and Dell's children's books. Her agency, the first to specialize in both authors and illustrators, has sold about 1,000 books to just about every publisher. The Executive Director of the Big Sur Children's Writing Workshop and former Captain of children's books at the Maui Writers Conference, Brown has published articles and chapters on the children's book field and has been quoted in *Forbes, Good Housekeeping*, and many other places.

CHAPTER 27

Confessions of an Acquisitions Editor

by Phoebe Collins

D id you ever stop to think about that crucial first person who will read your submission? If you're like most writers, the answer is probably not. Your attention is focused upon the agent or editor to whom, after much research, you've taken great care to address your letter. It's understandable that you assume that the name on the envelope equals the hands into which your submission will go. Right?

Not necessarily. There's a "bouncer" to get past. Forget visions of grandeur regarding publishers, *New York Times* book reviews, and Pulitzers. Instead, focus on one goal at this point: getting past the bouncer.

While I'm the last person any self-respecting nightclub owner would hire to guard the door, let alone inspect the line behind the velvet rope—I'd just let in everyone—my ruthless, quick-read analytical skills are prized in other quarters. And, regardless of what you may have heard, my name is not Jennifer and I am not twenty-two! As a card-carrying member of the tribe known as acquisitions editors, I'm the one who reads all those unsolicited submissions (and many of the ones marked "requested") that daily flood the front office of a literary agency. From there, I separate the wheat from the chaff. And by God, it's the former category you want your submission to land in. But how?

Don't be a Philistine at the hedgerow

First of all, an untyped, or ungrammatical, query letter is akin to a polyester leisure-suited yahoo seeking admission to the Four Seasons on Saturday night. Sounds utterly obvious, I know, but you'd be surprised how many people have a misbegotten faith in ignorance. Yes, Rumer Godden's manuscript for the great *Black Narcissus* went to Spencer Curtis in a handwritten bundle. William Faulkner's were littered with cross-outs and such. But friends, those are the exceptions. Times have changed. These days, it's essential to adhere to the rules. It's the only way your work will get any initial consideration at all from me: the acquisitions editor.

Assuming that you've typed up a clear, well-written letter, with a terrific synopsis, further bête noires include the following:

- Sending your entire manuscript. Instead, a query letter, synopsis, and the first one or two chapters (with proper headers on numbered pages) is always sufficient.

- Ten tons of PR and promotional materials, including the big write-up in your local community paper. No, one or two pages will do. Preferably one.

- Gifts. This can be anything from ostrich feather pens, plastic whistles, or pinwheels. Unless it's in a box labeled Cartier, don't bother.

- No SASE!

- International reply coupons. If you're outside the U.S., have a stateside friend send you some U.S. stamps, or order from the United States Post Office online. No one, but no one, has time to stand in line at the Post Office, especially not the nightmare on 34th Street near my office.

No PR overkill

- A first-name salutation. Why push your luck? Relationships grow in their own time.

If it sounds like I'm condemning your creative efforts to some bureaucratic wasteland or conformist hell—throwing cold water on a hot property—think again. These basic editorial formats are ally to both art and commerce, serving both masters equally.

If you're absolutely incapable of thinking like an office professional, fine. Get a grip and engage someone who can. It is essential that your precious submission, no matter how revolutionary or avant garde in content, conforms to a conventional presentation. I won't look at it otherwise, and consequently, neither will anyone else.

And, as any acquisitions editor can attest, it's amazing how many focused, disciplined, and, indeed, talented writers become freewheeling anarchists when it comes to presenting their work.

IT'S AMAZING HOW MANY FOCUSED, DISCIPLINED, AND, INDEED, TALENTED WRITERS BECOME FREEWHEELING ANARCHISTS WHEN IT COMES TO PRESENTING THEIR WORK.

Straight is the gate and narrow the way

Always remember: it isn't just your book you're representing, it's yourself, too. Who wants to work with an unprofessional, uncooperative slob? That's exactly the message conveyed by poor grammar, poor spelling, and incorrectly formatted manuscripts.

If the first two are clear, but the latter a mystery, head to the nearest bookstore or library, or go online, and find the correct format for manuscripts. It will involve numbered pages and specific headers at the top of each and every page, all easily accomplished with a visit to the "Format" menu on any PC or Mac.

Be as creative and unconventional as you want to, within that sacred format. An example of this can be found in a submission we had a few years ago, from an unpublished fiction writer. Before sending us anything, a query letter, a synopsis, anything, she sent postcards. From Paris, Boston, and Los Angeles. Each week, for five weeks, we received a mysterious postcard from one of those cities, with a cryptic note on the back, signed by (I later realized) one of the characters of her novel, briefly describing their predicament within the story.

Well, believe me, when we finally got the query, synopsis, and first chapter—*perfectly formatted*—it went straight to the agent in question who then requested the entire manuscript. This story is a favorite of mine as it illustrates strict adherence to editorial rules without any sacrifice of creativity. Quite the contrary, no?

Home truths

Just imagine my desk. Impossible, as it's constantly obscured by stacks of letters and manuscripts, which also carpet the surrounding floor. Papers that are not instantly identifiable (via proper headers) get permanently lost in the shuffle, including the brilliant page 7 that you spent weeks on. I'm not proud of this, but it's the truth.

Gazing upon an unsolicited, incorrectly formatted proposal for a 500-page manuscript, my heart goes out to you. I'm a writer, too. I know how hard you worked. But guess what? It's going right back like a boomerang if you can't be bothered to put it in proper format. Sad but true!

So, if I were you, I'd conjure up a mental picture of your nastiest teacher from elementary school, your sadistic superior in the armed forces, the uptight misery who fired you for not refilling the stapler, the great aunt who wondered aloud if you'd ever amount to anything . . . in short, the worst hellcat you can think of. That's who your manuscript must get past before it goes to the desk of the agent you've addressed it to. Me, the bouncer! And it virtually all rests with format, including spelling and grammar. With your presentation.

"I found a million-dollar baby . . ."

Your manuscript is your baby. What decent parent would send a child out into the world unprotected? Treat your book the same way and ensure that, before sending it off to your targeted agents, you've checked with each agency regarding their particular requirements. If you're still uncertain, a phone call will clear up any further questions. Then, package your submission accordingly. Write a gripping synopsis that addresses the following questions with wit and succinctness:

- Who needs the book?

- Why are you the person to write it?

- Who is the audience for it?

Then provide the "hook" that no one will be able to resist.

Don't be overwhelmed; if you can dream it, you can do it. I know personally how difficult it is to break down your creative work objectively, into a format that conveys its essence without being long-winded. But, believe me, this sort of submission is a joy to behold, uniting itself with the bouncer as a boon companion, with a viable chance of reaching that next critical leg of the ladder: the agent to whom you addressed it in the first place.

And when that happens, hallelujah! We all want our writing to get the serious attention it deserves, and this is the way.

PHOEBE COLLINS, along with her work as acquisitions editor for several New York literary agents, is a contributing editor at Ambassador Publications. She has worked with Katharine Sands at the Sarah Jane Freymann Literary Agency and with the Jeff Herman Literary Agency, among others, and is co-author of *A Simplified Guide to Creating a Personal Will* (John C. Wiley) and a novel, *The Vantage Ground* (TBA).

CHAPTER 28

Crafting the Nonfiction Proposal

by Elizabeth Zack

My field of expertise is as an acquiring (and developmental) editor for well over a decade at two very well-known publishing houses. Now I run my own business, offering editorial services to aspiring and previously published authors. For all those years as an acquiring editor, however, I was the one who decided what to buy. Sometimes that choice was easy—and sometimes not.

I spent those years selecting mostly nonfiction works, from health to parenting to self-help to spirituality projects. So I can help you understand why nonfiction editors choose one proposal on a given subject over another. Sure, one proposal might be represented by an agent with whom an editor has a particular affinity, or the writing can be stronger in one proposal than another. But usually editors buy a particular proposal based on the presentation and the quality of its components. That's often the reason an "auction"—an event in which several publishers try to outbid other publishers for the rights to a particular project—occurs.

So the cardinal rule to remember is that your job as an author is to make the proposal an easy buy for an editor. You want to minimize the chances that the editor who's interested in your work will have to do some side research to convince the team at the publishing company that there's a reason the company should invest in a particular proposal.

Having the following components in your book proposal make an acquiring editor's job easier:

1. Cover letter.

Recently some of my clients have read advice that says the cover letter is passé. Don't believe it for a second. If you can write a cover letter that in a sentence describes your project and points out what's unique and saleable about it—do so. If you can't describe your project in a sentence, consider that your project needs more focus. Agents sell books, editors buy books, and sales forces sell books to bookstore buyers often based on a single quality sentence.

Now, if you're lucky enough to have a literary agent representing you, it's possible that your agent will come up with this sentence. But if you provide this single quality sentence first, in the initial query letter to the agent, it could be the reason an agent chooses to represent you and your project.

The cover letter should briefly compare your book to one or two other bestselling works—for example, "It's *Where Angels Walk* meets *Finding Time for Serenity*"—while also pointing out why yours is different or better. The cover letter should also provide a bit of information about you, the author, because when it comes to nonfiction, it pays to be an expert in the field about which you're writing.

2. Title page.

Sounds simple, but the title and subtitle of your book can make a huge difference in how the project is perceived, so spend a good amount of time thinking about it. Always be direct and to-the-point in the title—avoid confusion about what the title means.

If you can't figure out what to call your book, err on the side of caution. Be straightforward. Call it *No More Diets* instead of *Choosing to Waist Away*. Make sure that the title offers a promise—*The Seven-Day Pounds-Away Diet* instead of *Thinking about Losing Weight?*

The subtitle should clarify your title even more, pointing out specifics about what's in the book. If the title is *No More Diets*, an appropriate subtitle might be *Making the Pounds Melt Away Through a Unique Two-Week Program*.

And, lastly, make sure that in addition, the title page features your name. If you have professional credentials, be sure to post them after your name, whether you're a Ph.D., M.S.W., or C.D.E.

3. Overview.

In this section, talk for a few paragraphs about your book and what it's going to do. In other words, offer a synopsis of your work.

4. The market.

Here you must identify who is most likely to buy your book, and cite pertinent statistics that prove the size of the specific target audience. For example, if your project is on diabetes, you could cite close to 16 million Americans living with diabetes today, with possibly millions more yet to be diagnosed. Draw relevant statistics from the Internet, magazines, national associations, and/or surveys, identifying your source when possible. The point of this section is to convince the acquiring editor that there is a large market ready to buy your book right now. And if there have been recent news stories in the media that address your topic, make mention of these as well.

5. The competition.

Remember the cardinal rule? Make the proposal an easy buy for the editor. Well, this particular section can really save an editor time and work. He or she will have an easier time of convincing the sales force that a book belongs on the list of a particular publishing house if he or she can prove why it's better than, or different than, other titles on similar topics that are already published. You need to discuss the competition that's already out there, as this competition can do one of two things: (1) convince an editor to buy your work (and an agent to represent you), or (2) provide a reason for an editor to send you a rejection letter (and an agent to say "no, thanks").

Start off citing other books available in the marketplace on the same subject. Every time you mention a particular work, write a sentence or two that explains what this book offers and then go on to explain why yours is better, different, and/or more targeted to today's market. For example: does your book offer new research not yet available in the book marketplace? Are you a credentialed author, whereas a person lacking credentials was the author of the competitive title?

Yes, this step requires you to do a little research. But it will be worth it. You may even realize as a result of your search that you need to re-conceptualize your book, to make sure that it offers new information not available in any other published book. Analyze the results of your search—your agent will, and your editor certainly will. Make sure that you can prove there's a need for your book—even if there's a lot of competition out there, or no competition at all.

IF THERE HAVE BEEN RECENT NEWS STORIES IN THE MEDIA THAT ADDRESS YOUR TOPIC, MAKE MENTION OF THESE.

6. About the author.

This section is exactly what it sounds like. It's very important that you have what's called in the publishing industry a "platform." An acquiring editor will be more interested in your project if you have strong credentials in a field or a website of your own that draws weekly or daily traffic. The editor wants to feel that he or she can really trust in what you have to say. Include information here about your background, education, and career. Mention any awards or special notices, and detail why you are an authority on the subject being presented.

If you're not an authority on a subject? Well, if you've written a book about stopping the progression of Parkinson's disease, but don't have any credentials to back it up . . . you may need to pair up with someone—in this case, a noted Parkinson's researcher who agrees with you and can provide the credentials you will need to get your project sold.

7. Promotion.

In this section, talk about your ideas for how you can help to promote the book effectively. For example, can you provide a mailing list of addresses for the target audience? Do you have close contacts in the media you can call on to write articles on you and your book when it comes out?

This is an appropriate spot to mention sources that you think would be interested in reviewing your book or doing feature articles on it. For example, if you are writing a soy cookbook, mention that it's a natural review choice for *Vegetarian Times*. If there's a specific television show that your book is appropriate for, point it out. (Everyone mentions *Good Morning America* and *Today*, yet the nationals can only feature a limited number of authors. It's more persuasive to suggest other shows that have a particular relevance to your project's focus.) Lastly, mention any local bookstores that would be willing to host a book signing.

8. Table of contents.
Here you'll list the proposed structure for the book. List all the parts (if there are parts or sections) and the chapters. Just as the title of your book should be clear, the same is true of chapter titles.

9. Introduction.
This is a key section to provide. The points to cover include an explanation of what the book will offer, why it is timely, who you are, and why you have the experience and passion to write about the subject matter.

10. Sample chapter (or two).
A sample chapter is a necessity; it allows the book editor to get a strong sense of your writing style and tone. Bear in mind that if your book is prescriptive and offers a program, it's wise to select a chapter that is prescriptive in nature. If it's a cookbook, don't include a chapter only with cooking techniques; choose a chapter that has recipes.

11. Media list.
If you have appeared on radio or television in the past, cite these appearances. If you've been interviewed in the past, attach news clippings or media tapes. (Many authors misplace or never save such tapes/clippings, but they are valuable resources. They can help a publisher get you placed on a national television show, for example.) If you lecture, be sure to include your lecture schedule (recent past, present, and future).

12. Endorsements.

Improve upon the perceived saleability of your project by providing strong endorsement quotes in the actual proposal. Alternatively, it also helps if you simply provide a list of well-respected individuals who would be willing to provide supportive words about your work (but mention only those with whom you have a personal connection; obviously many celebrities/authorities are too busy or unwilling to offer endorsement quotes to all who inquire).

With these elements in your package, it's much easier to convince an editor to buy (or an agent to represent) your work. Then you will have truly crafted . . . the perfect nonfiction proposal.

ELIZABETH ZACK, a 16-year veteran of the publishing industry, founded BookCrafters LLC (www.bookcraftersllc.com), a professional editorial services firm that offers advice to writers on how to perfect their manuscripts and craft commercial, saleable book proposals. Prior to starting her own business, Elizabeth was a Senior Editor for the Ballantine Publishing Group, a division of Random House, Inc., and John Wiley & Sons, Inc.

CHAPTER 29

The Nearly Perfect Proposal

by Robert Shepard

Think of getting a book published as a track-and-field event, with numerous hurdles along the way. You can overcome each individual hurdle with a fair amount of advance planning, research, and hard work. But ignore any of these parts of your "training" regimen, and your book will be in trouble.

One of the nice things about nonfiction books, for authors and agents alike, is that we usually sell them long before the manuscript is written. Maybe that's why forethought is so important. Consider the 200th anniversary of the beginning of the Lewis and Clark expedition in 2004. Many authors rightly saw this as a great topic for a book. Unfortunately, many didn't get around to sending query letters to agents until early in 2003.

"Given the excitement and media attention likely to surround the Lewis & Clark anniversary," explained a query letter I received in January 2003, "it's essential that my book be published in time. . . ."

Too late. This author didn't realize the time period involved in bringing most books to market. True, in the wake of an event of tremendous importance (such as the terrorist attacks of September 11, 2001), publishers can rush "quickie" books to market in weeks. But normally, it takes seven to nine months to crank a book through copyediting and production. Working backwards, if you sell a book in January, it likely will take you the rest of that year to finish writing it—and your publisher most of the following year to edit it and manufacture it. Then it will be shipped it to bookstores.

You can see why advance planning is a good idea. Of course, not every book will be tied to an anniversary; publishers are always on the lookout for books with staying power. But even if the book you're planning to write is designed to be a perennial bestseller, it pays to have your proposal ready to go in the mail the minute an agent says "yes" to your query letter. After sending a well-written query letter, your timely follow-up with a proposal, if requested, is one of the first indications an agent has that you're a dedicated, enthusiastic, organized author: potentially a great client.

Okay—so you *are* a potentially great client. What should you include in your proposal? Here's a list for starters:

- one or two sample chapters (preferably two)

- a table of contents

- an overview of your book (a very important element; more on this below)

- your author profile or (for academics) your c.v.

- any useful background clips: reviews of your other books; articles you've written, especially on the same subject as your book's; maybe articles about you

- a cover letter

- a postage-paid return envelope large enough to enclose whatever you send, without which agents are unlikely to respond at all

That's the basic list, but there's more to it than that. Have you considered what agents and editors are looking for and what's in their minds as they read your proposal? If so, you'll know better how each of these elements should be crafted to give them the best possible impression of you and your work.

The proposal's mission

Proposals vary. But the mission is always the same: The proposal not only has to paint an accurate, attractive picture of your book, it also has to sell the work to agents and acquisitions editors. Some authors don't like to think of the "selling" part; they prefer to see writing as a creative endeavor, a collegial process in which authors, agents, and acquisitions editors alike instantly agree on the vision and validity of a book.

The reality is quite different. Publishing houses are businesses. They're on the lookout for great, even artistic writing, but they know this is only one of several qualities a book must have to be successful. So you should think of your book proposal as a business document, almost like the plan you'd write if you were starting a new company. You wouldn't start a business without thinking about its mission, its objectives, the product or service it will sell, the consumers it wants to reach, and the competition it wants to beat, would you? Books are the same way, and your proposal must start with defining the mission of the book—the key lessons you want your readers to carry away from reading it.

Those lessons also vary from book to book. A how-to book about home improvement will probably have well-defined objectives: to show readers new, simpler ways to conquer painting, wiring, woodworking, and gardening. A book about politics might have very different objectives: to change the way readers think about the election process, or even about a particular candidate. But no matter what the subject, it's essential for an author to think about the book's objectives, and express those in the proposal.

Remember, your proposal is aimed at a very small audience—agents first, but also, by extension, the editors to whom your agent may one day pitch your book, and in turn some of their colleagues. Agents and editors are intellectually curious people, but they aren't experts on everything. They're relying on your proposal to introduce them to your topic and convince them that you're about to write a really terrific book that will find a large audience and sell well.

As you craft your overview and outline and select your sample chapters, place yourself in an acquisitions editor's shoes. Ask yourself, "If I were an editor, what kinds of questions would I want this proposal to answer?"

Putting yourself in an editor's shoes

SHOULD THIS REALLY BE A BOOK AT ALL, OR DOES YOUR PROPOSAL SEEM TO DESCRIBE A LONG MAGAZINE ARTICLE?

Here are some of the questions to consider:

- How is this author's approach different from that of other authors who have written on the same topic?

- If this author isn't very famous (yet), what kinds of things is he or she prepared to do to help us market the book more effectively? Is the author well-connected? Does this person appear regularly in the media, or lecture widely to people who might be eager to buy this book?

- Why will the subject matter be of interest to a wide audience, and not just to other experts?

- If this is an autobiographical work, does it really speak to readers who know nothing about the author, or does it seem more like a self-indulgent exercise?

- Does the author seem prepared to dig into the subject, raising and answering some surprising questions or, perhaps, answering the usual questions in surprising ways?

- Should this really be a book at all, or does this proposal seem to describe a long magazine article instead?

- How will I sell my colleagues on the idea of acquiring this book, when they'd rather spend my house's acquisition dollars on their own projects? Will the marketing and sales people see this project's potential?

While you're putting yourself in the editor's shoes, editors are putting themselves in the reader's shoes. They'll wonder whether, as readers, they'd buy your book if they happened to see it in a bookstore. Are there already too many books like this to bother with another one? They'll ask themselves, if I were a consumer, would I choose to spend $20 or $30 on this book? Or would I go to the movies, log on to the Internet, watch TV, or buy some other book?"

And as noted, they'll also be thinking about their colleagues. An editor's decision to acquire your book—and even to pay you a larger or a smaller advance—is usually made in a group. Your agent knows this, and when deciding whether to represent your book, has an eye on that future editorial board meeting. These days, publishers acquire only those books they think have a very high likelihood of paying their way—"earning out" the advance paid to the author and remaining popular with bookstores and readers for a long time.

The review board that will make this decision includes marketing and sales people, who are natural-born skeptics. A publicist will not be convinced that Oprah will want you to be a guest. A sales manager may report that major bookstore chains haven't had much success with books on your topic lately. And other editors on the board may be worried that spending $100,000 (or $50,000, or even $5,000) on your book might doom their own pet projects.

I'll never forget a bizarre rejection letter I received from an editor many years ago, when I was starting out as an agent. I knew that this editor had been been very excited about the book and felt confident about convincing her colleagues. And yet she rejected it. Here's what her letter said:

Dear Robert:

Thank you very much for sending me [this proposal]. As you know, this is one of my favorite subjects, and I think [the author] has impeccable credentials. We all agreed that the writing was superb, and this is one of the most complete, best-presented proposals we've seen in a very long time.

And then:

> And yet, sometimes we just don't get what we want.

IF I WERE A CONSUMER, WOULD I CHOOSE TO SPEND $20-$30 ON THIS BOOK?

What happened? The proposal got to the editorial committee, and the publicity department was overwhelmed with other projects that season—and remembered having difficulty marketing a similar book a few years before. The editor tried but couldn't overcome their objections. That was enough to doom the project.

I don't mean to be harsh to publicists. Most of them do a good job of making books stand out amid all the clutter of the daily news—and competing books, movies, CDs, DVDs, and all the forms of entertainment that compete for our time and money. But 60,000 books are published in the U.S. every year. Marketing people know that all of them can't possibly be hits.

The nearly perfect book proposal

So, how can you write a convincing book proposal? After 20 years in the book business, I don't know if I've seen the perfect one, but I've seen many that came close. They all incorporated hard work, creativity, a bit of salesmanship, and usually the fruits of other people's good advice.

That's right: it's important not to work in a vacuum. Share your work, including your proposal, with trusted friends or colleagues who will give you meaningful feedback, not just pat you on the back. Once you have an agent, he or she will also join this process. This is one of the most important parts of the partnership I have with my clients, which goes far beyond selling their books and negotiating their contracts. Editors will see your proposal only once; it's important to make it as close to perfect as a proposal can be. Here are some elements that can help:

A convincing overview

The overview is a crucial piece: an essay, typically around 15 pages long, in which you introduce the book and everything that's key about it. Use your overview to answer every question that might occur to an agent or editor. Why did you decide to write this book? What credentials do you have to do so?

Who is in your intended audience, and how large is that audience?

What are the major lessons you want your readers to carry away from the book?

Why do you know that people will be interested?

What kind of experience do you have as an author and with the media, and how might you be able to assist a publisher in marketing your book?

Why is the book unlike anything else that's out there? Why does this topic lend itself to a book, and not just an article?

It may help to keep this question in mind: "How does my book add up to more than just the sum of its parts?"

Give your overview a boost by knowing your book's competition. That means going to real bookstores and scanning the shelves, not just running a search online. Agents and editors know that there is always competition.

A strong proposal will mention perhaps a half dozen other works, pointing out similarities and differences. Throw in one or two bestselling books that are different enough from yours not to be directly competitive, then point out why yours is similar in some ways.

The right sample chapters

Choose your sample chapters carefully. They must place the quality of your writing front and center, yet also reinforce the idea that the book will be fresh, intriguing, and a worthwhile read in every way. Choose chapters that will "grab" agents and editors and make them want to read more.

It may be easiest to submit your book's Introduction, but does that chapter really show off your writing to the fullest, and reflect the "voice" you'll be using in the rest of the book? Does it allow you to capture the level of detail or the balance of information and anecdote that you'll use in the other chapters?

If you submit more than one chapter, you'll have the flexibility to present a wide variety of your book's best qualities. Put yourself in Herman Melville's place. If he were submitting sample chapters for *Moby Dick* and selected only the ones dealing with harpoon designs, no editor would see his work as a cosmic, American transcendentalist rumination on humanity, nature, and obsession. It would seem like a book about harpoons. Who wants to buy that?

On the other hand, to sell a nonfiction book, you don't need to submit an entire manuscript, either. Agents and editors will get the point after a couple of chapters.

KEEP THIS QUESTION IN MIND: "HOW DOES MY BOOK ADD UP TO MORE THAN JUST THE SUM OF ITS PARTS?"

Annotated table of contents

Outline the work by drafting a table of contents. This is not cast in stone; it can change later on. But it's essential to include as representative an outline as possible with your proposal, with at least a few lines (maybe a paragraph) about what will appear in each chapter.

Your planned table of contents shows agents and editors that you've thought about what should and shouldn't be included in the book—how you'll develop a narrative "thread" and characters (if it's literary nonfiction) or provide all essential information without being boring (if it's a more practical work).

Are all of your chapters meaty enough, or should some be combined? Are some of your chapters too overloaded with information and in need of being divided? Should you move some chapters up (as more important) and others back in the outline?

You may find that your first idea of how to organize the book isn't the very best idea. But it's your book: you can change it! Creating this table of contents may be the most important thing you can do to avoid the "agony of defeat" once you submit your proposal to agents.

Getting what we want

Here's the good news: sometimes we really do get what we want. Nothing is more thrilling to an author or an agent than selling a book—maybe one that didn't seem like such a slam-dunk at first—to an editor who's really enthusiastic about publishing it. The subjectivity of this process is a double-edged sword: It allows people to say no, sometimes, for purely subjective reasons.

But if you and your agent really do your homework, the same subjectivity can work to your advantage. A really great proposal can convince an entire editorial board to overcome their hesitancy and get downright excited about acquiring your book.

Then you will find yourself sailing over all the potential hurdles. And your agent will be cheering you on like the most crazed fan in the stadium, as you both realize that all those training laps were worth it.

ROBERT SHEPARD, a publishing professional for two decades, founded the Robert E. Shepard Agency in Berkeley, California, in 1994. He represents literary and genre-specific nonfiction only, with emphasis on history, current affairs, science, popular culture, sports, business, and finance. He seeks works that can change the way people look at the world around them and books by recognized experts in their fields.

His list has included bestsellers *Word Freak*, Stefan Fatsis' book about Scrabble players; *Wine & War*, a history of the French wine industry during World War II, by Don and Petie Kladstrup; and *Coal: A Human History*, by Barbara Freese.

Prior to becoming an agent, Mr. Shepard worked on the editorial staff and as a sales manager at Addison-Wesley Publishing Company. A graduate of the University of Pennsylvania, Mr. Shepard teaches classes on nonfiction writing and publishing, and serves on the faculty of a number of writers' conferences. Visit his agency's website at www.shepardagency.com.

CHAPTER 30

The Telling Detail

An Interview with John Ware

by Katharine Sands

Sands: If writers want to pitch work to you, how can they best express what their book idea or characters or setting are about?

Ware: A query letter has to be succinct. You have to provide an agent, or any reader of that letter, with just the general idea of what your book is and then, by way of illustration, a telling detail or two.

Not just detail upon detail. But an important focal detail or two. That's what gets people's attention.

We love a one-page letter. And I mean *one,* not two.

It's the writer's job, in the query letter, in one page, to give a general idea of what the book's about and what their point of view is, or what they are trying to accomplish in the book.

And then the detail. Never use a generic if you can use a particular, because particulars are what light us up, reach us as individuals. If someone in your work is having a cocktail, specify what they're drinking. The specificity provides a greater literal picture for the mind than any generalization.

So the agent reads a letter like that and, one hopes, gets a sense of delight for the writer's feel of particulars, for detail. You also get a look in a letter at the writer's eye and ear.

Don't give the whole plot. Do give a little taste. Because that's what's pleasing, and even teasing, in a positive way.

Sands: What do you see writers do wrong when they pitch?

Ware: Writers should spare us all the propaganda. Other than maybe a simple statement of emotion that says, "I am excited about this project because . . ." I don't think salesmanship should color the prose. Just be forthright and descriptive.

Say to the agent, "This is what I have. This is the rundown, this is what it's about in general, here's a little flavor and some telling details.

I hope you want to consider it.

Thank you for reading the letter." (Courtesy counts.)

No propaganda. The writers should not say, "I'm writing you because of this wonderful suspense novel I've just completed." Better to say, "I'm writing you about a suspense novel I've just completed." A little lightheartedness helps too.

Sands: What hooks you? What compels you when reading a query letter?

Ware: Well, that's a little more mysterious. Two writers, as an exercise, could write up a query letter or a description of the novel *The House of Seven Gables*, and one could be really exciting and one of them less so.

That's of course the wonderful mystery of writing. Somehow, the way one of them strung the words together affected you.

But in a query letter, as in a book, economy is key. However good a letter is, a writer should go back and say with each sentence, do I need that word? Do I even need that sentence?

That economy should be a major focus. There's no point in having anything unneeded for other people to read.

Sands: Can you tell a discovery story, a story of a letter that worked?

Ware: This was a nonfiction work, one of those rare queries where before you even read the second paragraph you're dialing the phone. I have had that happen only about three times in my whole career.

It was the memoir of a Chicago bicycle messenger named Travis Culley. And I was captivated by the way he described his work and his background and also, and this was very important, his urban philosophy. His view of what makes for optimum city life.

It was just such an incredible combination of the whimsy of a young 25-year-old guy riding his bike, making his rent as a messenger, but with a vision, like a Jane Jacobs or Lewis Mumford, without portfolio. He could have been an educated urban planner from his comments on city life.

It was a combination of his exuberance and his insight. So I indeed dialed his number before I had even finished the letter. And he sent me his proposal, and I sold the book to Villard. It was a Barnes & Noble Discovery Book, selling almost 20,000 copies. It's a wonderful success story, I think.

Sands: You mention in your bio your interest in a "bird's-eye view" of phenomena. How is that different from popular culture or hot-button topics?

Ware: Well, it actually covers all "categories." I phrase it that way because, whether it's a rare memoir or an expert's book on whatever subject, I've always enjoyed individuals giving their takes on their worlds.

I enjoy going inside worlds that I don't happen to know much about, to learn the small details of those worlds and what makes the participant in them succeed and have pleasure and joy.

It's looking for expertise, even if the expertise is as subjective as one person's happiness with their occupation, their little view inside their

I DON'T THINK SALESMANSHIP SHOULD COLOR THE PROSE. JUST BE FORTH-RIGHT AND DESCRIPTIVE. SAY TO THE AGENT, "THIS IS WHAT I HAVE."

world. It can be a large canvas, or it can be someone like Travis, a bike messenger who tells you about that special world.

Sands: What advice do you give writers in general about growing as writers?

Ware: A developing writer, I think, needs to have complete and utter respect for every word that he or she writes down. Because every word writers write down is going to be read by others. So they should work hard, I think, on economy, on clarity.

And they have to be pleased by their writing's effect. Its affect. Both. I think that their own excitement is key.

But beyond the passion there is the hard, hard work of sitting down, and looking at every sentence you write and saying: What is it now? A certain rigor has to be there. And an openness of mind, in receiving both their own ideas, which perhaps contradict what they first wrote down, and those of their agents, their editors, a friend they trust, whomever it is.

Writers have to be careful and patient. Sometimes good pieces of sustained writing do come out in a rush, quickly. But in the end, to finish the book—to really wrap it with the kind of care I'm talking about—that cannot be an impatient process.

I find myself frequently saying a little litany to writers: care beats speed every time.

I think there's such an eagerness to get to market. To get done with it. To get on to the next book for which they may have an idea.

But I think that writers need that combination of open-mindedness about the perfectibility of their work, care in reaching it, and the patience to go through that process.

Sands: How would you advise writers to cope with the commercial needs of the marketplace or writing business?

Ware: Well, this may shock you, but I don't think they should worry about those needs. That's our worry. And editors' worries. I feel bad for writers at a conference who ask something like, what should I be working on? Or what are the trends?

My answer is always to ignore all this.

Ignore all statements about what kinds of books are "coming back" or "on the decline." Do what pleases you. Work hard on it, but do what is your passion.

And if what you turn out is the 14th book on Lewis and Clark, if it's a good book, it doesn't matter. There will be a place for it.

JOHN WARE, after an B.A. in Philosophy from Cornell and graduate work in English at Northwestern, worked as an editor at Doubleday for eight years. During that period, for five years, he also taught the industry-wide editorial workshop at New York University. After a year as a literary agent with James Brown Associates/Curtis Brown, Ltd., he began his own agency in 1978, representing nonfiction and fiction. Jon Krakauer, Jennifer Niven, Stephen E. Ambrose, and Elise Blackwell are among the writers he has represented.

CHAPTER 31

It Has to Be Cutting-Edge Work

by Peter Rubie

The truth is, editors and agents are always looking for good, original material. The frightening thing is how difficult it is to find. Lots of writers are pretty competent and do decent enough jobs with their proposals, but I constantly ask myself when I see submissions: Do we really need yet another cozy mystery? Or hardboiled Mickey Spillane regurgitation? Is this another Tolkien fantasy rip-off? Another "literary novel" about dysfunctional families, divorces, or the death of a spouse or child—by someone with few credentials in the writing arena who thinks they stack up to Zadie Smith, Annie Proux, or John Updike?

Does all that sound harsh? Sorry. No one deserves to be published just because they work hard at their craft. What we're all looking for is that new voice, those fresh eyes on something we thought we knew that causes us to re-examine who we are, where we live, and why we do things.

It's all well and good taking justifiable pride in your mastery of technique, but if that technique is not slave to a good idea then you're emphasizing form over content. The fact is that publishing is a business;

and editors are under a stunning pressure these days to find new, original, and well-written material. The vague—or the same-old same-old—just isn't going to cut it. It has to be cutting edge.

What's cutting edge? A cutting-edge work is something that is more than just "relevant" to a contemporary audience. It should appeal to a wide audience, while at the same time present a unique voice or new take on a familiar subject.

Obviously, this gives talented young writers, and those from cultures other than the mainstream, a slight edge when it comes to writing about or viewing the mainstream. If you can come up with this kind of angle, use it in your pitch.

For example, many editors are looking for an epic Latino novel in the tradition of *Gone With the Wind* (though not necessarily about the American Civil War). Or consider what is understood or taken for granted in the world of a 13-year-old today as opposed to a 13-year-old in 1925, 1945, or 1960, for example.

We Americans, in particular, reinvent ourselves at an alarming rate. And in the act of reinvention, talented and imaginative writers can show us how to view anew things that are familiar to us. This is not a matter only of age or ethnicity, but of flexibility of thought. (For example, Sid Ceasar is as funny now as he was in the 1950s because his humor was based on acute perceptions of humanity.)

It's a mistake to think that writing is about putting down words on paper. That's technique. Writing is about thinking. So when we speak of finding a fresh new voice, we are talking about a writer who can not only think originally and commercially, but who can also capture that in elegant, sexy language on the page. There's nothing we long for more.

Publishing professionals primarily stay in the industry because we have an enduring love affair not just with books, but with ideas. It's a heady thought, but the publishing industry is really a marketplace for ideas, especially those with strong emotional impact.

So what has all this to do with pitching your book? The answer is that well-conceived content is what publishers are looking for these days. That is why books that aren't that well-written often get published (because they had interesting premises if not particularly well-executed).

And why wonderfully written ones sometimes languish in manuscript form on a shelf (because the idea is overly familiar, if well executed).

As my old boss at Walker & Company used to say when I tried to acquire a well-written book for the company, "And . . . ?"

"But he won half a dozen awards for writing," I would persist.

"And . . . ?" came back the answer.

Define your audience. Not sure who the audience is for your book? Do some research, online and at the local library and bookstore. Don't be vague, be precise and informed. Use the information in your pitch. Science-fiction romances that are also mysteries won't sell because they have no audience. The sci-fi people don't read romances, the romance fans don't particularly care for mysteries, the mystery fans often hate sci-fi. You're not tripling your audience (as you might think), but decimating the one audience you might be able to appeal to.

Pick a genre (read: marketing handle) and make sure it's going to appeal to that genre's readership. People who want a cat as a pet aren't interested in a gerbil that purrs like a tiger and looks like Chihuahua. They want a cat. Genre, of course, is a guide to a reader's expectations. Approaching your book from the perspective of your audience forces you to become more objective. That in turn helps you re-examine, reshape, and, if necessary, restructure your idea. Write with a mental image of your ideal reader in mind.

Learn to objectively compare your idea against what is already published in this area. When pitching your book, be prepared to let editors and agents know what your book adds to the field you want to write about. If it's only your thoughts and philosophies—unless you're an expert whose opinion is sought after by colleagues in the field—it's likely that your book will be a tough sell. If, however, you know your subject well enough that you realize there's a "hole" (i.e., something that hasn't been written about much yet), you're probably onto a good thing.

Ask yourself this: "Do I honestly believe that 10,000 people will buy a trade paperback version of my book?" If the answer is "No," then this is either a small press book, or a magazine article. If it's "Yes," then make a detailed, practical case as to why you think this number of books will be sold. Does the subject matter you're interested in writing about have a fan base? Is there a magazine devoted to it? Are columns written about it in national or regional magazines?

Start reading magazines and newspapers that cover your area of interest. If you see a lot of articles about new trends in the subject, perhaps there might be a corresponding interest in a new book on the topic. Let your passion for a topic drive you, but also be objective about its sales potential.

The next thing to do is size up the competition. Go online to Amazon.com or Barnes&Noble.com to check out the category or subject. Are there other books on your topic? And if so, how many? And how successful have they been?

Visit your local bookstores and browse the shelves. Has anyone written something like your book and published it recently? What are the names of the publishers who publish books like the one you propose? Who are the big-selling authors in this genre, and what are the titles of their latest and/or most successful books?

Go to the library and check out *Books in Print*. Then, with your *Books in Print* list in hand, start browsing the shelves of your local bookstores. See if any editors or agents names are mentioned on the acknowledgment pages of the books you've got stacked beside you. Make a note of the individual and the book you found their name in as well. You may want to pitch your book to them.

Do the books that have been published already on the subject fit a pattern? Can you fit into or manipulate that pattern to your own advantage? For example, could there be room for a cheap paperback that would appeal to a large mass of people?

When pitching your proposal, emphasize your ability to sell copies yourself. From the moment the editor reads your proposal, the question everyone asks is: "Does this author have a platform?" Let potential editors know if you have a regular newspaper or magazine column, or a constituency of any kind. Do you teach a course or hold a seminar on the topic you're writing about? Anything that helps book sales is looked upon with enthusiasm.

When preparing your pitch, call publishing houses and ask for their latest catalogs. You can find the numbers in *Literary Market Place*

(LMP), *Writer's Market*, or *Jeff Herman's Guide to Book Publishers, Editors, and Literary Agents*. Publishers are usually happy to send prospective authors free catalogs. Once you get the catalogs study them carefully. They'll tell you what the publishers intend to publish in the upcoming season, with details of how each book is being pitched by the publishing company to the sales reps and bookstores.

Five things to know about pitching an idea

1. Make sure your idea is a fresh idea. If you've seen or read it elsewhere, don't try to rewrite it in order to get published. You need to look at the world and see it with fresh eyes. Difficult? Who said that writing publishable material was easy?

2. Make sure what you send in is well written. Don't use "fiction novel" and other equally redundant phrases. Learn to use words gracefully and well. They are your tools, so become comfortable with them and know how to use them effectively. Write plainly in simple Anglo Saxon, not in flowery language that boasts your erudition.

3. Be professional. If you don't know what this means, read lots of books about publishing until you figure out what editors and agents like and expect from the authors they deal with.

4. Be able and willing to communicate clearly and effectively with the editor or agent you're submitting to.

5. Be willing and able to promote your work.

PETER RUBIE is the author of *Telling the Story: How to Write and Sell Narrative Nonfiction* (HarperCollins) and *The Elements of Storytelling: How to Write Compelling Fiction* (John Wiley & Sons). He is also co-editor of *Hispanics in Hollywood* (Garland Press/iFilm/Random House Espanol).

He is the president of the Peter Rubie Literary Agency and has been involved in the publishing industry for over fifteen years. He regularly lectures and writes about writing and publishing and is on the faculty for the Center for Publishing of New York University.

CHAPTER 32

How I Learned to Sell Sex, Death, and Rock 'n' Roll

by Lori Perkins

When I attend writers' conferences, many of the new writers are shocked when I inform them that everyone in publishing has to specialize these days. Then I explain the numbers: 55,000 books are published in the U.S. every year, sold by about 1,000 literary agents. (Publishers no longer read unsolicited manuscripts as a result of 9/11.) So to stand out, every agent today must have a niche.

Then I'm asked how an agent knows what kind of books she'll sell well. And I explain that those who truly excel have picked a few things that they know better than anyone else and staked their territory. We are known as "boutique agencies."

After nearly two decades in publishing, I realized that I know how to sell sex, death, and rock 'n' roll like nobody's business.

I didn't start out this way. I have a nice respectable degree in art history and journalism from an extremely prestigious New York institution of higher learning, so when I became an agent I thought I would sell books about art, hard-hitting works of investigative reporting, and the occasional great American novel. But life conspired against me.

I trained as an agent in a well-rounded agency, where one day the head of the agency asked if any of us had every read "this guy, Stephen King," because he had multiple books on the bestseller list. Though I always lied and said I was reading the latest Updike, Oates, or Roth, if truth be told, I usually had a King, Koontz, or Rice in my bag for subway reading. So I meekly mentioned that I was familiar with his work. "Poof," the head of the agency said, as if throwing some magic dust on me, "you're now the horror agent." And just like that, I was.

I sold four horror first novels in one month, because I was so well read in the genre. It had taken me two years to sell my first literary novel (and for a fraction of the three-book deal I got for my first horror novel). I still sell the occasional literary novel, but the themes are all quite dark, so I tell people that I represent "dark fiction."

As an outgrowth of the horror novels, I started doing a lot of non-fiction about sci-fi, dark fantasy, and horror, which often meant books about death and dismemberment. In one year, I had sold a travel book on celebrity tombstones and morbid tales about cemeteries, and one agent I know said to me, "So, you do death."

The rock 'n' roll part came from selling pop culture. Many of the rockers from my teens were writing now. Since I knew how to help someone get a first novel published, I figured it might be worth it to work with some of my idols. So I represent the horror novels of Greg Kihn and the first novel of Ray Manzarek of the Doors. I'm working with other rock stars on their first novels as well.

Selling books about sex was also a result of selling pop culture. I've always been fascinated by unique communities—the trekkies, couponers, and the S&M world—so I sold a book by a dominatrix. This led to a book by a fetish photographer, which lead to a dream book by a sex therapist, which lead to representing Vivid Entertainment, the leading studio of adult films in the country, which lead to representing Jenna Jameson, America's reigning porn queen. I found it was a niche that no one seemed to have claimed. So I made it my own, but with what I hope is a combination of wit and style and even post-feminism.

Writers who understand that agents and editors work in very specific markets will always have a better chance of connecting with someone who is really interested in their niche. When I call editors who know my taste and say something is exceptional—that I think I've found a young Stephen King or the new Anais Nin—they'll pay attention. In the same way, a writer who knows his market, and his place in it, will be taken that much more seriously by a prospective agent.

Finding the right agent will take some research. Of course, first you have to know what kind of book you've written. Don't fool yourself, because you're not fooling anybody else. If the main character is a vampire, it is a horror novel, not a literary novel, no matter how wonderful the metaphor or language. It can be a literate horror novel, but when it's published in paperback it'll say "horror" on the spine.

Next, you'll need to find agents who represent horror. There are several wonderful annual guides that will give you the information you need, such as Jeff Herman's annual guide to agents and editors. Once you've gone through these books, make a list of agents who seem appropriate. Then write a query letter that tells them how you found them. The fact that you've done some work and research will impress an agent.

You can also get a list of appropriate agents by contacting the genre organization for your kind of writing, such as the Science Fiction and Fantasy Writers of America, or the Romance Writers of America, to ask if they can provide a list of agents specializing in the field. Again, mention to the agents you contact that this was how you got their name.

You can also search the web for agents specializing in the kind of books you are writing. Try searching for word like "agents horror." Again, if you have gotten someone's name this way, let them know you've done some research.

As an agent, I have learned that good solid information is one of my most important sales tools. Take the time to research your field. You'll find that your chances of attracting the right agent are greatly increased.

LORI PERKINS is a New York literary agent with 20 years experience. She is the author of three books including *The Insider's Guide to Getting an Agent* (Writer's Digest Books) and has taught a graduate class on being an agent at New York University.

WRITERS WHO UNDERSTAND THAT AGENTS AND EDITORS WORK IN VERY SPECIFIC MARKETS WILL ALWAYS HAVE A BETTER CHANCE.

CHAPTER 33

Pitchcraft, the Zen of, and the Secrets of the Galaxy

by Patrick LoBrutto

Three things to start. First, it is wise that we define our terms. *The New Shorter Oxford English Dictionary*, 1993, has more than a full page of definitions for the word "pitch." Some of the many definitions are: "the act of plunging head foremost . . . ; (Baseball) the action or an act of pitching the ball to the batter . . . ; behaviour or speech intended to influence or persuade . . . ; a net set for catching fish . . . ; (Cricket) the place where wickets are pitched . . . ; [to] plant, implant, stick, fasten . . . ; [to] put together, construct by fastening the parts together . . . ; [to] prepare a battle or battlefield; draw up troops in array."

The word "craft" similarly includes among its many definitions the following: "skill, art, ability in planning or constructing, ingenuity, dexterity . . . ; an art, trade or profession requiring special skill or knowledge . . . ; scholarship, learning . . . ; [to] make or construct skillfully . . ."

Zen has but one definition: "a school of Mahayana Buddhism emphasizing meditation and personal awareness."

Well, obviously, the intelligent reader need look no further. Everything you need to know about Pitchcraft can be found in the *OED*. This is a common occurrence. So many of the World's problems could be neatly disposed of if only more of the World's leaders were to read the *OED* . . . but I digress.

Second, for the purposes of this article, I will not be discussing non-fiction. Because I'm so taken with stories—with lies, if you will—I will concentrate on Fiction.

Third, Baseball, Life, and Writing are all intertwined; many of the same rules hold true across all three. All the great philosophers say so. . . . Okay, so maybe they don't, but they would if they knew about Baseball. It should come as no surprise, then, dear writer, if, in an article about "pitching," I occasionally use Baseball lore to illustrate some of my points about Writing.

> "Groves was a thrower until he hurt his arm. Then he learned to pitch."
>
> —Connie Mack on Robert Moses "Lefty" Grove
> (Mack called his star pitcher "Groves")

Lefty Grove was one of the most talented ballplayers in the history of baseball. Despite his success, he wasted a tremendous amount of time and effort fighting with everyone around him and refusing to learn how to use his enormous talents until later in his career.

The lesson here is obvious: Don't just be a "thrower." Be smart, use your advantages to understand the other players, the field, and the game. Don't waste your strength and time by just "throwing" the manuscript at a publisher. Make sure it's in the strike zone; the more strikes you throw, the more chance you'll have. Even more important, make sure you're in the zone where your book lives.

"What a pitcher he was! The greatest that ever lived. He had almost perfect control. There was never a time when he couldn't throw the ball over the plate if he wanted to."
—Chief Meyers on Christy Mathewson
(who was, by the way, a graduate of Bucknell, president of his class, and member of two literary societies.)

In a whole book of telling you how to pitch your project, should I waste your time and mine by talking about the obvious? Should I talk to you about organizing your selling points and comparing yourself to other successful projects, and telling the editor your track record (if any) and the quotes and reviews (if any) and awards (if any) your previous books (if any) have received?

You should, of course, know this valuable information. My wise and experienced colleagues in this voluminous volume will cover the mechanics thoroughly. Listen to them or face doom, defeat, and despair.

By all means, you should learn the rules of grammar and punctuation, the basics of coherent writing. This is a given. It is knowledge that can be obtained from many sources. A writer ignores the basics at his/her own risk. A writer must learn technique, must understand how to construct a well-made story. This, indeed, can be taught; it is knowledge that can be acquired. Acquire it.

"Game after game he'd pitch in an hour and a half. No fussing around out there, no wasted motions."
—Rube Bressler on Grover Cleveland Alexander

Know who you're pitching to. This is the one piece of the "Mechanics" of the Pitch that I want to spend some time discussing. In truth, it is related to knowing your book and being in its zone, for you must sniff out those who have the best chance of understanding your book.

Do your homework.

A simple rule, but too many writers skip this part. If you are pitching to an agent (and you should, Heaven knows, since it's so difficult to be published from what is so elegantly termed the Slushpile), another digression follows. Here it comes. . . .

The Slushpile is composed of those manuscripts that are sent in to a publisher unagented, that are not directed to a particular editor. These manuscripts are piled up on the floor outside offices, perhaps, or are put in a closet; a dark, dank, lonely closet that no one visits except to pitch another victim onto the pile. And then, the editorial assistants are herded into a conference room for an afternoon, pizza and sodas are brought in, the manuscripts brought into their Place de Greve, and this group of assistants—unhappy and feeling put upon—are directed to make the pile go away. They are *not* directed to find good books. Each manuscript will get, if lucky, a 10-page read. Of these manuscripts, 99.9% are returned with a form rejection slip. After all, the pile must disappear.

Once in a periwinkle-colored moon, a manuscript will be published from the Slushpile. I, myself, have done so a number of times and so have many other editors. Frankly, however, the odds suck. Avoid this at all costs. Get an agent. Failing that, do the homework and send a manuscript to a particular editor.

Here's what I mean by homework: You go to the biggest bookstore you can find, search the Internet bookstores as well. You look for books that are similar to yours. For example: You've written a Science Fiction novel, one that deals with Alternate History. Look through the SF novels, and even general fiction, for those publishers who are publishing SF and, in particular, Alternate History novels. In this particular case, it's a good bet that all of the houses publishing SF will look at Alternate History. But first I'd try the ones that have a current book out.

Look in the Acknowledgements Page of the Alternate History titles you've found to see if the author credited his editor. Check the *LMP* (*Literary Market Place*) to get a list of that publisher's editors; double-check by calling the publishing house and getting the names and titles of the editors who handle SF. You can do that one better by calling the editor her/himself.

If you do get to talk to the editor, do yourself a big favor: tell him/her your credits and give them the synopsis in 30 words or less, be quick.

KNOW WHO YOU'RE PITCHING TO. YOU MUST SNIFF OUT THOSE WHO HAVE THE BEST CHANCE OF UNDERSTANDING YOUR BOOK.

I would suggest that you ask if they'd like to see a synopsis and the first 50 pages (a nice size for a quick read and one that doesn't scare an already overworked editor). Do that one better by attending conferences to meet that editor or an SF convention.

> "You win a few, you lose a few. Some get rained out. But you got to dress for all of them."
> —Leroy "Satchel" Paige

First, write the book. Beginning to end. Polish. Rethink. Rework. Polish. Rework. Until it is the best book it can be. You have to get up every day and do the job, what Stephen Sondheim calls "Finishing the Hat" in *Sundays in the Park with George*. Creating a book, writing a novel, is no easy job. It will most likely be the most heart-wrenchingly difficult fun you will ever have, remember that while you read all that follows. "A writer is somebody for whom writing is more difficult than it is for other people." This is a quote from no less than Thomas Mann, novelist and Nobel laureate, so you should pay heed.

There is no roadmap. There are helpful tips; some of these tips will help you, some will not. It's up to you to learn which is which. Despite the difficulties, it has to be a thing that you must do; you are obsessed with telling the story that you have in your head. If you do it correctly, you will become one with the journey, the quest for the story only you can tell, with the descent into places in your mind and heart that you never imagined could exist.

> "Vance could throw a cream puff through a battleship."
> —Johnny Frederick, on Dazzy Vance

This must be the "Zen" part.

Bottom-line basics: You need to convey why your book is so good, so compelling; you must tell the editor why he needs this book (to paraphrase Maxwell Perkins), why it will be successful on his list. Simple as that. But you can't do that until you, the author, are convinced. There are smart, efficient methods of conveying this in a cover letter, proposal, and synopsis. But. The most important part of your pitch, the only part that really means anything, is the work itself. Always and everywhere, it is the story . . . and the reader, the listener . . . for the business of a story cannot go on without a reader. You are the first reader.

How do you throw a cream puff through a battleship? The same way you put an entire three-dimensional world of time and place and people onto a one-dimensional page with words thrown at a faraway reader: through a process of intense meditation and personal awareness.

> "Mother always told me, if you tell a lie, always rehearse it. If
> it don't sound good to you, it won't sound good to no one else."
>
> —Leroy "Satchel" Paige

If you come away from this with one piece of knowledge, let it be this: A complete, well-crafted story is the pitch, and the pitch is you. Without the story and the characters and the voice, there is no pitch. Believe in your work. You have a vision. Get it on paper, do it, make it happen on the page, let the reader, whoever that may be, live in your story. This, of course, means that *you* must live in your story. For that to happen, the story must come from you, from your heart.

Do not attempt to write like someone else, do not attempt to be someone else; you will not ever, cannot ever, be John Updike, or Michael Crichton, or Stephen King, or Nikos Kazantzakis. You must be entirely and without reservation yourself. The very act of attempting to tell stories, to entertain, educate, or inspire through fiction, is Big Mojo (yes, it is in the *OED*; as Casey Stengel says, "You could look it up.")

To show the deep variations in human emotion and experience, to try to make the reader understand the incredibly feelingful difficulty and wonder of being human, to stand up and testify your dreams and hopes, is to be in the vanguard of the forces that deny chaos and loneliness, defies isolation and ignorance. This cannot be done by faking any part of it. Only by lying. We live a life that is pregnant with meanings, rich in danger and pleasure; we live a life that is interesting in the fullest sense. We do this with the people in our stories, with our lies, for we are

> "A WRITER IS
> SOMEBODY
> FOR WHOM
> WRITING IS
> MORE DIFFICULT
> THAN IT IS FOR
> OTHER PEOPLE."
> — THOMAS
> MANN

making this all up. We do this with the language that we use, the words that we choose, the combinations of images we create, the moments in the lives of our characters. We must somehow, inexplicably, mix and measure the blazing fires in our hearts with the cold place in our center to create a reality that would have no existence without us.

That sounds like Zen to me.

Work diligently on your pitch. Work harder on your novel.

Lastly. The Secret of the Universe? Brush your teeth. Wash everywhere everyday. Work hard. Be kind. Act justly. Walk humbly.

Or if you feel there is no Meaning to Life, no Secret to the Universe . . . make one up. You're a writer, for Pete's sake. Make up a nice one, it shouldn't be mean spirited (you don't want you should come back in the next life as Roy Cohn's sitz-bath), and an interesting one, it shouldn't be boring.

Finito, we're done. Go now, do what you were meant to do. Write your story.

PATRICK LOBRUTTO currently lectures at writers' conferences and works as a book doctor and writing coach for authors, as an acquiring editor for Tor/Forge and Quill Driver Books/Word Dancer Press, and as a scout for the Trident Media Group. His website (Patrick LoBrutto Editorial Services) is www.patricklobrutto.com.

He has been an editor, author, and anthologist for over 30 years, working in all areas of fiction and nonfiction, especially science fiction, fantasy and horror, thrillers, historical fiction, westerns, military history, and mysteries.

His career in publishing began while in Graduate School for Urban Planning; he took a summer job in the mailroom of Ace Books and discovered there were people who would pay him to read. He never looked back. He has worked for Ace Books, Doubleday, M. Evans, Random House, Kensington, Stealth Press, and Bantam. He has held the position of Editor, Senior Editor, and Editor-in-Chief, working with authors Isaac Asimov, Stephen King, Eric Van Lustbader, Walter Tevis, the Louis L'Amour Estate, the Star Wars novelizations, Don Coldsmith, F. Paul Wilson, Joe R. Lansdale, and the Dune Novels of Brian Herbert and Kevin Anderson.

He received the World Fantasy Award for editing in 1986.

CHAPTER 34

The Perfect Pitch: Low and Inside

by Andrew Zack

Ah, the perfect pitch. I've always been a fan of slightly low and inside. It makes the batter really bend from the waist and cuts the power of the swing, and still can be a strike if they choose not to swing.

Oh, wait, not *that* kind of pitch?! A book pitch? Well, there's not a lot of difference. I still like low and inside. By low and inside, I mean I like books with *low* common denominators, i.e., books that will appeal to a wide readership, and *inside* information or knowledge, like military novels written by ex-soldiers or science thrillers written by scientists or nonfiction works by established experts in their fields.

After all, being a parent doesn't actually qualify you to write a book on parenting! But being a child psychologist, with numerous published papers and years of experience in treating children, probably does.

So, low and inside. Be it baseball or books, it works.

The most common way I'm pitched is with a query letter. And few things trip up authors more than the simple query letter. I get several dozen a week. The worst one I ever got went something like this:

"I am writing a fantasy trilogy [remember, that's three books!]. I have completed ten sample pages and an outline and am in search of an agent. Are you interested?"

My response? Without a complete manuscript in hand, I couldn't help this author. Many authors feel the secret to a good query letter is being able to "hook" an agent. And that's certainly true. But remember, there has to be a payoff also.

I've received dozens of queries for novels that exist only as three chapters or, as in the case above, only ten pages. In today's marketplace, editors are far less willing to buy partial fiction manuscripts than ever before. Certainly, they are not going to buy a partial *first* novel, not when there are thousands of completed novels out there. Finished manuscripts involve far less risk; we already know how they turn out. Therefore, I never take on a first novel unless it's complete.

What do I look for in a query letter? Well, besides "low" (wide readership) and "inside" (knowledgeable), I like query letters that show an awareness that the book will have to be sold someday to a chain or independent bookstore buyer who is really only looking at a cover and a description of the book.

Authors have to remember that books are judged by their covers every day, including the cover copy. So I like query letters that have that kind of spin.

More importantly, query letters should probably be a bit like the "tip" or "title information" sheets publishers' sales representatives are given. After all, no sales rep can read every book he or she is selling, so the tip sheet is a sort of "CliffsNotes" version for the rep's use.

Here's an example based upon a book I represent:

[Sample publisher's tip sheet:]

Distant Valor
by C. X. Moreau

In the tradition of James Webb's *New York Times*-bestselling novel, *Fields of Fire*, comes a powerful novel of the United States Marines Corps.

"*Distant Valor* . . . is as authentic as they come, heartrending and true, exciting and brutally tragic. It is a worthy monument to heroes cast aside."—Ralph Peters, *New York Times*-bestselling author of *The War in 2020*.

Out of the crucible of war has come a long list of best-selling, award-winning, and long-remembered novels: *The Red Badge of Courage, All Quiet on the Western Front, The Caine Mutiny*, and *The Thirteenth Valley*. Until now, none has captured the power and drama of the United States Marine Corps' ill-fated 1983 mission to end the war for southern Lebanon, which culminated in the barracks bombing that killed almost 300 Marines. For Sergeant David Griffin, a "peacetime" Marine, Beirut was the chance to prove himself capable to the generation of Marines that had been blooded in the Vietnam War. For Corporal Steven Downs, Beirut was a struggle to separate the civilian from the Marine, and to meet not only the expectations of his sergeant, Griffin, but also his own. Faced with Griffin's court-martial for engaging the enemy against orders, these two young men find themselves questioning their faith in themselves, their commanders, and eventually that which above all else they must have faith in, the Corps. With the insight that only a Marine Corps veteran could have, C. X. Moreau portrays the men who fought and died in Beirut with a skill and ability that brings home to the reader the true meaning of *Semper Fi*.

"With his first book, *Distant Valor*, C. X. Moreau, joins the company of top-rank military novelists. He shows the reader what it really means to be a Marine."—W.E.B. Griffin, *New York Times*-bestselling author of *The Corps* series.

QUERY LETTERS SHOULD BE A BIT LIKE THE "TIP" SHEETS THAT PUBLISHERS' SALES REPS ARE GIVEN.

"Outstanding! A classic in, yet above and beyond, the war genre."—John M. Del Vecchio, *New York Times*-bestselling author of *The Thirteenth Valley*.

C. X. Moreau is a former Marine NCO and veteran of the Lebanon deployments of 1982-1984. A native of Virginia, he currently resides in Charlotte, NC. **Distant Valor** is his first novel.

Selling Points:
* The first major novel set during the Marines' peacekeeping mission in Lebanon.
* W.E.B. Griffin's series, *The Corps*, has consistently made bestseller lists.
* Over 173,000 Marines are on active duty today; millions are retired.
* Recent operations by the U.S. military remind readers of the tragic fate suffered by hundreds of Marines in Lebanon.
* Compare to titles such as David Poyer's *The Med* and *The Gulf*; Tim O'Brien's *The Things They Carried*; James Webb's *Fields of Fire*; and John Del Vecchio's *The Thirteenth Valley*.
* Special markets to consider are military bases, especially naval and Marine, and the towns surrounding them, e.g., San Diego, Norfolk, Washington, D.C.
* Audio rights have been sold to Brilliance, which will publish simultaneously with the hardcover in both abridged and unabridged audio formats.
* Major marketing in *Army/Navy Times, Book Page*, and Baker & Taylor *Forecast*.

It's from tip sheets like this one that pretty much every book is sold. Now, here's how your query letter can be like a tip sheet, even without quotes from bestselling authors.

Dear Mr. Zack:

As a veteran of the Marine peacekeeping mission to Beirut, I have always been disappointed by the absence of a major work of fiction addressing that difficult and tragic time in our history. This led me to write *Distant Valor*, a first novel of approximately 120,000 words that captures the Marine experience in Beirut in a manner similar to the way Jim Webb's *Fields of Fire* captured the Vietnam experience.

As recent history has shown, U.S. military personnel, civilian and government facilities remain vulnerable to attack by those determined enough to either risk or sacrifice their lives in the process. Over 300 Marine and navy personnel perished when a determined terrorist drove a truck full of explosives into the Marine barracks in Lebanon. That event continues to haunt the almost 200,000 Marines on active duty today, and the millions of vets living throughout the world.

Distant Valor tells the story of the mission, and ultimately the bombing, through the eyes of two soldiers. For Sergeant David Griffin, a "peacetime" Marine, Beirut was the chance to prove himself capable to the generation of Marines that had been blooded in the Vietnam War. For Corporal Steven Downs, Beirut was a struggle to separate the civilian from the Marine, and to meet not only the expectations of his sergeant, Griffin, but also his own.

Faced with Griffin's court-martial for engaging the enemy against orders, these two young men find themselves questioning their faith in themselves, their commanders, and eventually that which above all else they *must* have faith in, the Corps. I would be happy to send you the completed manuscript, or a synopsis and chapters. For your convenience, an SASE is enclosed.

Notice what this letter does: It tells me the author was actually there, so he knows about his subject, he's got an *inside* viewpoint. It gives me a well-known comparison title to put it into focus. It mentions a nonfiction "hook" in recent history; this can be very important in selling fiction (for instance, increased tension between the U.S.S.R. and the U.S. did wonderful things to help build Tom Clancy's career). It tells me there is a built-in marketplace for the book, a low common denominator.

It gives me a short and concise description of the book that doesn't give the entire story away, i.e., that intrigues me. The author offers to send the completed manuscript (so I know it is done and not still being worked on) or chapters and synopsis, with an SASE (so I know this author is a pro who probably also knows the standard submission formats). Without a doubt, I would ask to read this manuscript.

In the end, if your query has those low and inside qualities, provides a professional presentation, and is well written, chances are you've got the perfect pitch . . . for your book, that is!

ANDREW ZACK started out on the retail side in his hometown's independent bookstore, attended the Radcliffe Publishing Course at Harvard, and has worked in various capacities for several different houses. He's reviewed for *Kirkus*, been a reader for the Book-of-the-Month Club, and acquired and/or edited titles for Warner Books, Donald I. Fine, the Berkley Publishing Group, Avon Books, Dell, and Tom Doherty Associates.

As an agent, Zack started at Scovil Chichak Galen Literary Agency, then left to start his own firm, the Zack Company, Inc., in 1996. His clients include acclaimed oral historian Patrick O'Donnell, crime writer John Clarkson, bestselling fantasy authors Ed Greenwood and Peter David, and bestselling golf author Bill Kroen. More information about the agency and his clients can be found by visiting www.zackcompany.com.

CHAPTER 35

Intelligence and Imagination

An Interview with Ellen Levine

by Katharine Sands

Sands: How does a writer communicate their story in a way that will get you to ask for 50 pages?

Levine: Too many fiction writers spend a lot of their letter describing the whole plot. Or talking about a character in the book—the protagonist is this and this—in a way that the character becomes a stock figure. It makes me think that they haven't really experienced the character; that it's going to be formula writing.

Sometimes the shortest, most articulate, pointed few paragraphs, that show the writer's intelligence and what's behind the book, convey what it's about in a very brief way. Those few paragraphs convey that the book deals with things that I might want to learn about. And the letter is written beautifully and very concisely.

And my eye goes to the bottom of the page—and I hope it is only one or two pages—where it states publication credits, even very small ones, or a writing program that somebody's gone to, or a prize that might have been won. And perhaps a quote of praise for the writer or the work. So that I know that this is somebody who's been out there, setting the stage for later publication. Those things catch my eye.

In terms of nonfiction, obviously it's concept-driven. It needs to be a subject I'm interested in, presented intelligently, and in an area that I think that is marketable. And again, credits.

I get many letters that describe projects that are very publishable, but they are just not something that I'm interested in exploring.

Sands: If someone hasn't won a prize or hasn't been to an M.F.A. program, what can they do?

Levine: Well, those first few paragraphs, if they're written the way I've described them, I might just be so intrigued by the writing in them—the expression, the articulateness of the person writing, or the depth of what that person is exploring in the novel. Or maybe there's a concept that really interests me. If it's very well-written, that might interest me. And in that case, I might ask for 50 pages.

Sands: Do you like high concept lines in query letters? Do you like it when writers say this will be *The Player* meets . . .

Levine: Not when it's forced. I'd rather have the writer just say what this book is about—why it would be of interest and what it deals with. But if somebody absolutely knows that, say, this is in the vein of *Cold Mountain*, set in the Civil War, then it's useful.

Sands: Tell me a good discovery story, something you just spotted from the query letter.

Levine: One writer, someone I hadn't heard of, just wrote me cold. His name is Joseph Garber, and the book was called *Vertical Run*. It was pretty high concept. It took place in a high-rise building. The hero was a corporate executive, and somebody was after him. He knew that they were trying to kill him. And he had to figure out why—what he had done in his life—so he had to go back and think about what it was. And it sort of unfolded in the telling of the story.

It had a lot of suspense, a lot of intrigue. Was he going to make it? There was a love interest. Then you found out what really had happened earlier. You just kept turning the pages. In the description, he laid this all out, and it sounded intriguing. That, plus the fact that he had one book published by a smaller press, made me interested in seeing it.

Sands: Who does the reading at your firm, initially?

Levine: I have an outside reader, who used to be an editor, and I will give her some manuscripts. I will also give my very bright assistant manuscripts. And some things I'll just take home and read myself, without having a first reading, if I'm so excited to get it.

Sands: Editor Michaela Hamilton said something wonderful about how everyone in publishing is still a cockeyed optimist because every envelope holds promise.

Levine: That's right, you don't know what you're going to find. I will never forget reading the great novel *Housekeeping*, which is a classic by Marilynne Robinson. She was an unpublished author, but it was recommended to me by another writer. From what he told me, I thought I wanted to read it myself. So I took the manuscript home, and I was just blown way.

It's a classic to this day, in my opinion one of the best novels ever written. It's taught in schools everywhere. It won the PEN Hemingway Award and other prizes, and was made into a film with Christine Lahti.

Anyway, the thing is, you just open each box and start reading, hoping to make a great discovery.

Sands: What lights you up about being an agent?

Levine: First of all, having the privilege of handling some incredible writers and being the midwife to their work. I just feel really blessed to have these incredible, talented people in my life that I can help.

And it's also the joy of discovery. It's the joy of taking something that you really believe in and are absolutely committed to . . . and finding

> MY EYE GOES TO THE BOTTOM OF THE PAGE— AND I HOPE IT IS ONLY ONE OR TWO PAGES— [TO SEE] THAT THIS IS SOMEBODY WHO'S BEEN OUT THERE.

other people who feel the same way and delivering it into the world and making the whole process happen. I love finding really great first novels. And starting careers and watching them develop.

And in terms of nonfiction, it's a real treat to be able to get into so many different worlds. To be constantly learning.

And I have some wonderful, very close relationships with my clients, and these are very rich experiences. I enjoy taking care of business and making the right match, working to make the right sale, getting things to happen in the right way. Seeing the book get out into the world, and making sure that it's dealt with the way it deserves to be dealt with.

Sands: What do writers do wrong in their querying? How do they misfire?

Levine: Trying to get the agent on the phone, to pitch on the phone. Particularly unpublished authors—they really shouldn't do that. They should put it in writing. That's what they are: writers.

So that's how to catch the attention of the agent, with your writing.

Sands: Do you like it when writers try to hook you by either using dialogue or an excerpt from the novel right in the query.

Levine: I don't really care for that. Other people might.

Sands: What advice do you have about the first paragraph in a query? What needs to be there?

Levine: Give me something surprising, arresting, in that first paragraph. It shouldn't be too prosaic, not "I'm writing a book about a woman who lives in a small town who goes to school. . . ." I don't want that kind of recitation. I want something that shows some imagination and intelligence.

Sands: Some agents like whimsy, or gimmicks. Does either work for you?

Levine: Whimsy could.

Sands: What is going through your mind when you first look at someone's query.

Levine: If it's nonfiction, did the writer really think about how she is going to research her subject? Why are you the person to do that particular book? Writers need some credentials in the field they're working in, something to offer besides coming cold to the subject. Background? Magazine articles? Just try to get some credits going. That's really important for journalists.

For writers of literary fiction, they should try to get short stories published in little magazines, if they are story writers.

Sands: What advice do you like to give writers about the craft of writing—about growing and developing as writers?

Levine: Don't be afraid to revise. Writing isn't just getting it all done in one whoosh. It's going back in. Writing is rewriting.

Sometimes it's better to leave a little space between finishing the book and going back into it. Think about things like, where does the story really start? Well, it starts from the characters. But who are these characters? Are these real people? Or are you just trying to construct somebody to represent a particular point of view, rather than somebody who's really alive?

Do you know your character as a living and breathing person? If so, who is he or she? For me, so many good books come from the characters.

Yes, you need your story, but where does it start? Whose story is this, and why should we care about this person?

Sands: Any examples of characters that jump out at you that you've read recently or in recent months?

Levine: A book that came in one day and I fell so in love with the character. It's a first novel that just arrived one afternoon. I really connected with this character named Bean, this wonderful young woman who's had a lot of trouble in her life. She's just a funny, brave, wry young woman who's very warm.

I LOVE FINDING REALLY GREAT FIRST NOVELS. AND STARTING CAREERS AND WATCHING THEM DEVELOP.

But she's had a lot of difficulty in her life and you don't really know everything that had happened.

She meets this wonderful guy, they get married, and very early in the book he is killed in a climbing accident. So we're watching her deal with this new tragedy in her life. How is she going to come to terms with it? What does she have to do? But she's funny as well. She's got spunk and spirit, and your heart goes out to her. You admire her. You're in there rooting for her. She's so alive. Anyway, you can tell I'm in love with this!

Create a character like that.

Sands: What would you like writers to understand about how you do your job, based on what they give you?

Levine: For nonfiction, they should learn how to write the proposal—a selling proposal. There's a real technique to that. You have to really go into more detail than some people do. Why will anybody want to read this book? What's the structure? What are the chapters? How is this book going to unfold?

And what kind of things will you deal with in each chapter? You need to get the scaffolding for the book.

And know your market. Who's going to read this book? Yes, you can compare it to other books. If it's an environmental book, is it going to be the new *Silent Spring*? If it's a book about motherhood, how is it going to be different from other books on the subject?

Why is there a need for this book? Those are important things to put in your proposal.

Sands: How did Russell Banks come to you?

Levine: I wrote him. This goes way back. I read some terrific work of his in a little magazine. And he's stayed such a great guy too. It was wonderful that he could give up his teaching and write full time.

Sands: He was a fabulous teacher. I'm sitting here today in part because of him. He opened my mind so utterly to the love of writing and the written word and the literary world. He had a roundtable atmosphere, and was such an equal with his students. He would show us things like how he would keep a folder of names for characters. Or news items that inspired him. He invited everyone to be wherever they were, to do whatever they were doing with such respect, and he created such an atmosphere of exploration. He was a terrific inspiration.

Levine: I'm not surprised. Because he still approaches and connects to people that way. It was a long road that we took together before anything happened for him. And he's earned every bit of his success.

Sands: So you're passionately committed to finding new writers?

Levine: If I read something and I love it, yes.

I'm never too jaded to see what's in that basket. I've been eyeing that basket for two days saying, gee, I wonder what gem might be in there?

I have to go thumb through those letters, to see if there's anything I need to pull out. I don't want them to sit too long, because if I don't respond pretty soon, somebody else might get the book.

And you never know what's in that basket.

ELLEN LEVINE began her career with two publishers, New American Library and Harper & Row (now HarperCollins). She then worked at two agencies before forming her own company, the Ellen Levine Literary Agency, in 1980. In 2002, her agency merged with Trident Media Group. Ellen continues to represent her strong client list and appears on many publishing panels and at many writers' conferences.

She represents a wide array of authors of literary fiction, including Russell Banks, Michael Ondaatje, Cristina Garcia, and Marilynne Robinson; popular women's fiction writer Jane Heller; thriller writer Joseph R. Garber; biographers Christopher Andersen and Brenda Maddox; journalists Todd Gitlin and Mark Hertsgaard; children's literature author Louis Sachar; and professors Dolores Hayden and Carolyn Heilbrun. Her clients have won major awards including the National Book Award, the Booker Prize, the L.A. Times Book Award, and the Asian American Writer's Award.

CHAPTER 36

Publishing as a Circus

by Elizabeth Pomada

Someone once asked me what I sell the most of. My response was "Hope." And it's still true. Agents do sell hope to writers and to publishers. Agents, like editors, are optimists. Every day, when the mail hits the desk in our mailroom, we sort through it with hope. Yes, we hope for big checks. But we also hope for salable books, for authors who will deliver wonderful books every year that continue to sell every year.

And every time we look at a piece of mail, whether it's simply a query letter, a proposal, the first ten pages of a novel, or a complete manuscript that we've asked to see on an exclusive basis, we always start with hope.

We try to meet author's pitches half way. We love exciting new ideas. We'll read your pitch with a third eye, the eye that sees what's not there, what your book can be with my editorial suggestions.

And we will hope, as much as you do, that your pitch will light the fire of enthusiasm, that your book and all of the books that follow it will enable you to receive your due—and us to pay our mortgage and keep us in business.

You may ask, "What will it take for my pitch to work? What is it that keeps you turning the pages of my book? That makes you call with the news I live to hear?"

I love fiction. I'm looking for novels that make me forget I'm an agent and make me feel that I'm just a reader who can't put the book down. Talent will out. When I start reading a wonderful book, the hairs on the back of my neck stand up, I get more and more excited, read faster and faster, and tell my partner, Michael Larsen, "This is a book! A real book!"

How do you get to that point? It takes talent. It takes craft. It takes attention to detail. Here's what works for me: Love that conquers/ vanquishes all doubt. It has taken me as long as ten years to sell a first novel. So unless I fall in love with a book, I can't handle it, because I won't have the *passion* I will need to sell it, however long it takes.

I'm not just interested in literary fiction. I adore romance, and am eager to find mysteries and thrillers of all kinds. If I respond to your work the way you want your readers to, if I am swept away by your writing and can't stop turning the pages, then we're a match for an enduring working marriage.

A cartoon shows a room full of bullet holes, and cowering on the floor in a corner is a hostage. Standing next to him is a bearded young revolutionary standing in front of an open window holding a rifle in one hand and shouting into a megaphone: ". . . $500,000 in tens and twenties, a plane ride to Cuba, and a good literary agent!"

It's been said that an agent is like a bank loan—you can only get one if you can prove you don't need it. But I believe if you have a salable book, it's easy to get an agent, and it's easy to sell it. The more salable a book is, either because of its literary or commercial value, the easier these challenges are. What's really hard is making a book sell once it's published.

You find an agent the same way an agent finds a publisher: by having something salable to sell and being professional when you approach them. The moment you have a complete novel or a proposal for a non-fiction book that is 100 percent as well conceived and crafted as you can make it, agents will be glad to hear from you.

> WHEN I START READING A WONDERFUL BOOK, I GET MORE AND MORE EXCITED, READ FASTER AND FASTER, AND TELL MY PARTNER, "THIS IS A BOOK! A REAL BOOK!"

In today's increasingly demanding market, a first novel has to be finished and polished. Until you've completed a novel, you can't prove that you can sustain plot, character, and setting for the length of a novel.

Random House Executive Director Kate Medina warns writers to beware of "premature emission." I've sold second or third books on as little as a sentence or a concept, but first-timers have to prove themselves to themselves as well as to agents, editors and their readers.

Craft counts. Nothing turns an agent off faster than bad writing. I was once reading a partial, and at the top of page two, the hero walks through a door, turns to his friend and says, "Walla!" That stopped me. It took three tries for me to figure out that what he meant was "Voila!" I circled the word, noted that "Here's where I stopped reading," and returned it.

That writer made two mistakes. First, he didn't make sure that every word he used was the right word. And he didn't even have readers to help him make sure his work was ready to submit.

I also regularly reject people who depend on a spellchecker to get the words right. *Its* or *it's* may be right or wrong, but a spellchecker can't tell you that. Obvious mistakes make it look like nobody read the work and the covering letter before submitting them.

Use your networks to get feedback on your work. Or go to a freelance editor or anyone who can offer an objective critique. Your manuscript should be 100 percent before you share it with a professional.

Although I sometimes wish that we could do away with query letters and just receive the first pages of a novel, I do think writers should send cover letters with the beginning of their books. Some agents prefer just a query letter as your initial pitch.

Make sure that your query and cover letters put your best foot forward. Three paragraphs: one to interest us in the book, one to tell a bit more about it, and one to tell us about yourself.

Include everything that will convince us that your book will succeed, such as other writing achievements, your media experience and contacts, and the name of a nationally known opinion-makers who will give you a foreword and cover quotes.

Here are two query letters that self-destructed on sight:

"Not that I compare myself with Shakespeare's *Hamlet* but ..."

"Dear sir:
I have completed two novels. One is fiction. One is nonfiction."

I ask for a two-page synopsis that, among other things, will be used to solicit interest in Hollywood, where people don't read books.

When Pat Conroy's hefty bestseller *The Prince of Tides* was being sold to the movies, one of the producer's assistants said to Conroy: "I read it last night and it brought tears to my eyes."

Pleased but surprised, Conroy asked: "You read my book last night?"

"No," said the assistant, "I read the two-page treatment."

As other contributors have noted, relating your book to a similar, successful book will convey what your book is and the market for it immediately. If, for example, your novel is a Spanish *Joy Luck Club* or *The Da Vinci Code* meets *Charlie's Angels*, I'll know what to expect.

Your letter is a sample of your writing. Spelling or grammatical errors or awkward, flat prose will guarantee your letter an immediate nonstop flight to the circular file. Write nothing that sounds self-serving. Let the facts prove your points.

Regard a query letter as a piece of professional writing, since that's the business the agent is in and the one you are aspiring to be a part of. As agent Marcia Amsterdam has remarked: "If they can't write a letter, they couldn't write a book."

Agents are used to receiving simultaneous query letters, although we do begin to wonder when we get a query addressed to "Occupant." (Just kidding.) Thanks to computers, we receive queries that have the wrong address or that start: "Michael Larsen/Elizabeth Pomada," followed by a salutation that reads: "Dear Ruth . . ."

You know the adage: You never get a second chance to make a first impression. Many agents will not read past "Dear Agent" or "Dear Sir/Madam"—let alone "To Whom It May Concern." And I've been known to reply, "I am no gentleman!" when returning a note addressed to "Gentlemen"!

Be sure that we handle your kind of book. Sending us something we're not interested in wastes time for both of us. Research agents through their websites and in directories. If you e-mail me a query, and I tell you what to send and ask you to read our website, your reply asking for my address won't help your cause!

Remember the lesson agents relearn every day: The more professional the writer, the better the book. A writer once lamented: "Sometimes, it feels like I'm submitting boomerangs instead of manuscripts." To help avoid having agents bounce your work back to you, submit your manuscript properly.

One of our favorite William Hamilton cartoons shows an ambitious-looking young writer confiding to a lady friend over a glass of wine: "I haven't actually been published or produced yet, but I have had some things professionally typed."

Make your manuscript a document that looks like it's worth the advance you want for it. Although some agents accept material on diskettes and queries through e-mail, I prefer hard copy: double-spaced, on good 8½-by-11-inch paper, a readable typeface like Courier or Times Roman, in black, not right-justified (i.e., the right margin is ragged, not justified). Use 1½-inch margins, and 250 words per numbered, unbound page. Use your last name and the first important word in your title as a header.

And you can't be sure of getting a reply unless you include a stamped, self-addressed #10 envelope.

The more professional the writer, the better the book. The appearance of your material reflects the professionalism with which you are approaching the agent, the subject, and your career.

When I give talks, I wear my publishing necklace, which shows two trapeze artists in midair trying to keep their balance—as we all do in publishing. The woman represents the author, the person with the vision and idea. The man represents the publisher and the marketplace.

They're both reaching for the brass ring of success, and they're held together by the gold ring, the agent.

Please pitch your manuscript my way—and let's grab that brass ring of success together.

ELIZABETH POMADA co-founded the Michael Larsen–Elizabeth Pomada Literary Agency in San Francisco in 1970 after working at Holt, David McKay, and Dial Press. She is also a freelance journalist and the author or co-author of nine books including six *Painted Ladies* books and the 30th anniversary edition of *Fun Places to Go With Children in Northern California*.

She represents adult book-length fiction, narrative nonfiction, and non-fiction for women. You may reach Elizabeth via the agency's website at www.larsen-pomada.com.

CHAPTER 37

This Pen for Hire

Pitching Collaborative Projects

by Tonianne Robino

I f you love to write, have a passion for learning, and enjoy meeting and talking with interesting people, you have the first three requirements to make it as a professional writer.

Thousands of people need writers. Celebrities, politicians, professional speakers, researchers, and experts in every field employ ghostwriters, collaborators, and editors. Whether you yearn for a footloose life of travel and adventure or dream of a quiet sanctuary in the heart of nature, with today's technology a writer can live and work almost anywhere. And that means you can begin working as a professional writer wherever you live right now. By following the ten steps provided below, you can establish yourself as a professional and reap the rewards of the writer's life.

Step 1: Make your Topic List

Begin by making a list of the topics you would love to write about. Use the following questions to assist you in making your Topic List.

1. What do you like to talk about?

2. What are you most curious about?

3. What have you always wanted to learn or explore?

4. What do you want to teach others?

5. What types of articles and books do you enjoy reading?

Step 2: Make your Prospect List

A significant amount of your success as a professional writer depends on your ability to find the right experts for the topics you want to write about. I suggest that you make a list of experts for each subject on your Topic List. If you are well-versed in a particular subject, begin your Prospect List by writing down the names of the experts associated with the subject.

It's a good idea to list at least three experts for each of your topics. I generally begin with an Internet search. Go to your favorite search engine and type in the key words for your topic, plus the word expert. With the names of experts in a particular field, you'll find details on each expert's background, education, affiliations, and previous publications. It's amazing how much is available on line, so take advantage of this fast, efficient method of identifying experts and learning more about them. You might find out that some of the best and brightest experts for your chosen topics are located in your own back yard.

Next, consider who would be the most interesting, informative, and enjoyable. Rank your experts on a scale of ten, with one being the least desirable and ten being the most desirable. You will be pleased to know that some of the world's leading authorities are much easier to approach than you might imagine. Many of them are delighted that a professional writer is impressed or intrigued by their work and wants to write about it. Some of them have been thinking of writing a speech, article, or book for years, but have never found the time to do it.

But don't contact any of your prospects yet. Put your lists aside until you have completed the next few steps.

Step 3: Prepare your Pitch Package

Create a promotional package to let your prospects know who you are and what you do. This package should represent the best of your best; in many cases it will determine whether a prospect is willing to set up an appointment with you or not.

Your Promotional Package should include:

- A resume or autobiographical sketch, highlighting your skills, talents, and experience.

- Description of the writing and editorial services you offer.

- Writing samples showing different styles and topics. (If you've been published, include copies of three or four of your best clips.)

- Testimonials from people who attest to your abilities, talents, and professional integrity.

Although these packages are traditionally printed on high-quality paper and enclosed in slick folders, you can create the same package online with a website. If you can afford to create both printed and online versions, better yet. While some potential clients will be completely comfortable with checking you out in cyberspace, others will prefer good old-fashioned ink on paper.

Step 4: Calculate your Professional Rates

Setting your rates can be one of the most confusing and challenging aspects of successfully running a writing business. It's tricky for two reasons. First, many writers either underestimate or overestimate their value. Second, many writers don't know how long it actually takes for them to complete a piece of work.

Although I don't recommend including a "rate sheet" in your promotional package, it's imperative to create one for your own reference. It will serve as your financial guide when you're deciding what to charge a client.

The first step in setting your rates is to determine your current value as a writer. Begin by educating yourself about the editorial marketplace so you know the average price ranges for various services. Then, based on your experience and background, determine if you are at the high, middle, or low end of each range. Be brutally honest with yourself. For example, if you are pitching yourself as a ghostwriter for a nonfiction book, but you have not had anything published, you will need to begin on the low end of the scale. On the other hand, if you have been writing professionally for a company or organization, you may have enough expertise and experience to be paid in the middle range. In most cases, only writers who have publishing credits can garner the high-end fees for book-writing, although there *are* exceptions.

Keep in mind that your clients are not buying your writing services. They are buying what your writing services will do for them. In business lingo, they are not buying the product, they are buying the product of the product. Each of your clients will have different values linked to the writing and publication of their articles and books. Some will be seeking fame and fortune. Others will be seeking increased credibility, or will simply be burning with knowledge they want to share with others. For some, a speech, presentation, or book is a tool to carve out a unique niche in a particular marketplace.

This means that the same work can be worth $1,000 to one client and $10,000 to another. Every project is different, so don't commit to a price until you estimate how much time and money you will need to do the job well.

One key to setting appropriate rates is to know how long it takes you to produce final copy. The Hourly Rate Exercise below will give you a realistic idea of how long it takes to produce a final draft. While you may speed through a first draft, the project isn't finished until you've edited, polished, and proofread.

Hourly Rate Exercise

How fast you create final copy? Keep track of the actual minutes and hours spent writing, editing, and proofreading an article or sample chapter. When the piece is completed, follow this formula:

(Total number of words in final copy)
divided by (Total number of hours to complete final copy)
= Your average speed per hour

In addition to estimating your writing speed, calculate time for research, interviews, and meetings with the author. Estimate the amount of postage, phone charges, faxes, audio tapes, transcription services, and anything else that will be money out of your pocket.

Step 5: Write your Pitch Letter

It's time to start pitching! Begin by writing a personalized pitch letter to the first few experts you want to contact. Take the time and do the research to write the most enticing letters that you have ever written. Edit, crystallize, and refine these letters to make them as short and concise as possible.

Each Pitch Letter should briefly address the following points:

- Why readers and publishers will be interested in the book you are proposing.

- Why this expert is in the perfect position to author this book.

- How this book can support the expert in achieving his or her professional goals.

- Why you are the perfect person to write or collaborate with on this book.

Close your letter by telling the expert that you will contact him or her within a few days to explore the possibilities of working together.

Step 6: The Windup (to score an appointment)

Phone the expert. When you get ahold of him, don't launch into the book discussion right off the bat. Introduce yourself and ask if he has a few minutes later in the week to discuss the package that you sent to him regarding a speech, article, or book you would like to help him write. If he sounds hesitant, reassure him by saying something like, "I know how busy you must be, but I really admire your work and I'd like to help you to get your message out to others. It would be great to have a few minutes with you just to explore the possibilities."

If the expert says that he already has a writer—or that he is absolutely not interested in working on a book at this time—thank him and ask him to keep your materials in the event he changes his mind in the future.

Step 7: The Pitch!

During your follow-up appointment, be prepared to pitch your idea with the same level of enthusiasm and certainty that you feel in your heart. At the same time, remember that selling is all about asking the right questions. Steer the conversation toward learning what your potential client finds most valuable about the project you are proposing. Ask questions that will help you to determine what she sees as the ultimate product or outcome of this writing project. Listen carefully to what she says and what she doesn't say. It may be that she's not interested in authoring the book *you* have in mind, but might have her own ideas for a book.

While not all experts are interested in authoring a book or hiring a professional writer, many of them are. So don't let the rejections get you down. Persistence pays off. Move to the next expert on your list and throw another pitch.

Step 8: Close the Deal

When you connect with an expert who wants to work with you, take the necessary steps to close the deal and move the project forward. Verbally negotiate a price, the terms of payment, and a deadline schedule. And then put what you and your client have agreed upon into writing.

Within 48 hours of reaching a verbal agreement with your client, review your notes or your tape and create a "letter of agreement." This letter, typed on your letterhead, details the services you are providing, your fee and/or percentage of royalties, the date of delivery, terms of payment, and any other considerations that should be put into writing. You and your client should sign this document. It will help to prevent incorrect assumptions or other misunderstandings concerning your business agreement.

Step 9: Ask for Testimonials and Referrals

After you have completed a project to a client's satisfaction, ask her to write a testimonial that will help other experts to see the value in working with you. These testimonials are critical selling points in your promotional package. They will carry more weight than what you say about yourself.

Also ask your satisfied clients to tell their colleagues and associates about you and your services. I have found that referrals tend to result in the best working relationships. Although this is not always true, the referrals I receive often turn out to be ideal clients. If you've delivered the goods with flying colors, your clients will be happy to introduce their friends and colleagues to you and your talents.

Step 10: Keep the Door Open

When the manuscript has been delivered to the publisher or printing press, the author will be busy with promotional plans and getting back to his regular business. You will be focusing on other projects. But, keep in mind that repeat business is easier and more cost effective than winning the heart of a new client, so make a conscious and planned effort to keep the door open for every one of your clients.

Make it a point to connect with them every few months. Send a card or handwritten note to let them you know you're thinking of them and wondering how they are doing. Mail them a newspaper article, book, or magazine that contains information of interest to them professionally or personally. Celebrate their birthdays by sending gifts; recognize anniversaries by buying them dinner for two at their favorite restaurant.

The idea is to let your clients know that you appreciate them and are willing to go the extra mile to express your gratitude. Hearing from you from time to time will keep the door open to future projects and increase the likelihood of receiving referrals.

Supplementing your income by working as a professional writer is fantastic way to strengthen your organizational and writing skills, polish your talents, and learn about a wide assortment of different subjects. If you are currently among the ranks of writers who protest, "I couldn't possibly work on more than one project at a time!" you may want to reconsider.

TESTIMONIALS ARE CRITICAL SELLING POINTS IN YOUR PROMOTIONAL PACKAGE.

I have discovered that I'm much happier and more inspired when I'm researching and writing about several different topics simultaneously. My mind clicks faster and so do my fingers on the keyboard. I am able to access a variety of information to assist readers in understanding the points I am trying to make and the concepts I am illustrating.

My writing is sharper, more rhythmic, and more interesting when I'm juggling a variety of subjects. And perhaps most importantly, when I work this way, I have a lot more fun.

TONIANNE ROBINO has co-authored and ghostwritten many books and edited countless manuscripts. She is the co-author of *The Pregnant Couple's Guide to Sex, Romance and Intimacy* (Citadel Press) and *Inspiring Breakthrough Secrets to Live Your Dreams* (Aviva Publishing). Other publications include *Change Management Transition: The Next Step* with Jim Canterucci; *Make Up, Don't Break Up* with Dr. Bonnie Eaker Weil; *Count Your Blessings: The Healing Power of Gratitude and Love* by Dr. John F.Demartini; and *Athena Starwoman's Zodiac* by Athena Starwoman.

She has written articles on ghostwriting and collaboration for *Jeff Herman's Guide to Book Publishers, Editors & Literary Agents*, and is frequently quoted in *The Writer* and other periodicals.She also teaches writing seminars on getting published, ghostwriting, writing book proposals, and manuscript editing, and co-teaches The Writing Experience workshop with bestselling author Sophy Burnham.

She founded the company With Flying Colours in 1991 to provide writing, coaching, and editing support for new writers and established authors.

CHAPTER 38

Pitch Perfect

In Three or Four Easy Steps

by Jandy Nelson

Years ago, I received a query letter that began:

> I am a Vietnamese American man, a witness to the
> Fall of Saigon, a prisoner of war, an escapee, a first-generation
> immigrant, and an eternal refugee. After my sister committed
> suicide, I quit my job, sold all my possessions and embarked on
> a year-long bicycle journey, back to the land of my birth, to the
> memories of my sister and the battlefields of my own psyche.
> *Catfish & Mandala* is my story.

I called for this manuscript immediately—and so did every other
agent to whom Andrew X. Pham had sent his letter. His query was
"pitch perfect." It simply and elegantly revealed story, style, and most
importantly his authentic narrative voice.

So the love affair with your work begins with the pitch. And despite the fact that at Manus & Associates Literary Agency, we get over one thousand submissions a week, we are still looking to fall in love, to be swept off our feet by the promise of a terrific project.

As an agent, I spend a great deal of my time writing pitch letters to editors so I understand how difficult it can be to encapsulate an epic novel, to reveal the essence of great literary fiction, to determine the audience for prescriptive nonfiction, to do a competitive study of all the other similar books on the shelves. Editors like agents are inundated with submissions and I know my pitch letters need to intrigue, excite, and evoke in the editor the passion that I feel for a project. And so do your letters for us.

An effective pitch goes a long way. If I like your pitch and use it to then pitch your book to editors, those editors will then use it with their editorial boards and sales/marketing departments to stir up in-house enthusiasm for the project. And then, if the editor buys the book, that same pitch could be used to inspire the sales force who in turn uses it with book buyers across the country.

K. M. Soehnlein sent me a query letter years ago for his novel *The World of Normal Boys*. It began:

> When all the kids around him were coming of age, Robin MacKenzie was coming undone.

What a great set-up! I was immediately gripped. When I then turned around and pitched the novel to editors, I used the same opening in my letter. When his editor then took on the book and began pitching the novel in-house to marketing and publicity people, he used it as well. And now if you look on the book jacket, the flap copy begins with that same wonderful pitch. Your pitches to agents can be the beginning of a very long train of enthusiasm, so it really is worth it to take the same time and care with them as you did in writing your book or proposal.

While there really are no simple rules to follow to write the perfect pitch letter, I am going to give you some brass tacks that might help you get started.

ALTHOUGH WE GET OVER ONE THOUSAND SUBMISSIONS A WEEK, WE ARE STILL LOOKING TO BE SWEPT OFF OUR FEET BY THE PROMISE OF A TERRIFIC PROJECT.

Pitching nonfiction

Fiction and nonfiction pitch very differently (although narrative nonfiction pitches like fiction). Nonfiction pitches need to cover four important elements:

1. What is the concept of the book?

2. Who is the audience and why do they need this book?

3. Why are you an authority? What credentials do you have that make you an expert in this field?

4. What differentiates this book from all other books on the topic?

In addition to these four elements, you will also want to reveal in your nonfiction pitch if you have an author platform. This is an existing audience for your proposed book that comes from your visibility or access to readers. Do you have a lecture circuit? Run workshops? Have a radio show? Do you have additional venues where you can sell your book?

Also, very important in the nonfiction pitch is a great title. I always think of the movie *Shakespeare in Love* where they joked that *Romeo & Juliet* was originally called *Ethel, the Pirate's Daughter*. Definitely don't pitch your project to agents with *Ethel, the Pirate's Daughter* as a title; brainstorm with everyone you know until you find your *Romeo & Juliet*.

Here is an example of a strong nonfiction pitch I received:

> *Hot Flashes, Warm Bottles: A Guide for First Time Moms Over Forty* is the first prescriptive guidebook for the multitudes of women who make up the growing ranks of midlife mothers. [Answers: What is the book and who is the audience?] The concerns of these women are unique; they are as different from the concerns of young mothers as they are from older mothers with grown children. [Answers: Why does the audience need this book?] *Hot Flashes* combines the candid and often hilarious anecdotes from the women in Nancy's support groups with field-tested and mother approved advice. [Answers: Is the author an authority in the field?] *Hot Flashes* promises to be the bible for this growing

demographic of women whose concerns are not yet addressed elsewhere—and who are actively seeking resources. [Answers: Are there other competitive titles?]

I asked to see the proposal right away. This simple, straightforward pitch revealed what the book was, who the audience was, why the book was so important, so topical and so needed within the targeted community. It revealed the author's expertise and how the book differed from all the other parenting books on the market. All that in four sentences!

VERY IMPORTANT IN THE NONFICTION PITCH IS A GREAT TITLE.

Pitching fiction

Pitching fiction (and narrative nonfiction) is trickier. It is less about convincing us there is a market or of your expertise, and more about the quality of your writing and storytelling ability. That said, there are ways more effective than others to pitch fiction.

The biggest mistake I see is writers who confuse a pitch with a synopsis. When pitching your novel, you do not want to give a detailed breakdown of the plot, character motivations, scene descriptions, etc. I know it's daunting to think of breaking down your 400-page masterpiece into a few sentences, but it is imperative. Remember how many queries we pass on in a week!

Many novels can be broken down this way:

1. Set Up (sets the stage: Who are the characters, where are they, what has been happening to them of late?); Act 1

2. Hook (a turn of events that is compelling, pivotal in the plot, something which changes the course of the narrative); Act 2

3. Resolution (a wrap-up that doesn't give away your ending); Act 3

Here is an example of a fiction pitch for *The World of Normal Boys* by K. M. Soehnlein:

In a time when the teenagers around him are coming of age, Robin Mackenzie is coming undone. [*Set Up*] A terrible accident has jarringly awakened the Mackenzie family from the middle-American dream they have been living and suddenly each member of the family is spinning out of control. [*Hook*] Through the impeccably authentic narrative voice of thirteen-year-old Robin Mackenzie, Soehnlein tramples over the perfectly mowed lawn of Surburbia in the late 1970s to reveal the emotional complexities that bind and unbind one family. [*Resolution*]

For *Dream of the Walled City* by Lisa Huang Fleischman:

The daughter of the chief magistrate, Jade Virtue spends the first 10 years of her childhood without ever stepping outside the walls of the family's great mansion. [*Set Up*] But after the mysterious death of her father, she and her family must embark on a new life in a rapidly changing China. [*Hook*] With exquisite prose, **Dream of the Walled City** recounts the tumultuous life of Jade Virtue as she is swept into the torrent of historical events that mark early twentieth-century China. [*Resolution*]

Sometimes when pitching fiction or narrative nonfiction, it helps to do a comparative pitch. Lisa Fleischman's *Dream of the Walled City* could be pitched as a Chinese *One Hundred Years of Solitude*, or *The World of Normal Boys* as a gay *The Ice Storm*. But when using a comparative pitch, make sure to be accurate. Don't say you are writing an Irish *Joy Luck Club* when you are writing about a Scottish expedition up Everest. And don't baffle us with an impossible pitch like "my book is *Chicken Soup for the Soul* meets *The Great Gatsby*."

While the author biography is essential for nonfiction pitches, fiction pitch letters are not the place for modesty. Do mention if you've had stories published in magazines, have received an M.F.A., or if you have some experience that gives you an inside look into a particular arena.

For instance, a client of mine, Laurie Lynn Drummond, wrote a collection of short stories, *Anything You Say Can and Will be Used Against You*, about women cops in Baton Rouge. The fact that she was a cop in

Baton Rouge is an essential part of the pitch for her book even though it is fiction.

These are just some pointers. Ultimately, you need to take the care, the innovation, and the passion with which you wrote your book to write your pitch letter. Your letter can be simple. It can be funny. It can be persuasive. It can be enthusiastic or quirky. It should be whatever works best to introduce your work to the world. Every day, when I go through my mail, I hope there will be a letter that will make my heart beat a little faster.

I am not sure what it is exactly that makes me pick up the phone and call an author in a fit of enthusiasm to see their work, but it happens every day and it happens because of the strength of their letter. I hope tomorrow it will be your letter that does it!

FICTION PITCH LETTERS ARE NOT THE PLACE FOR MODESTY.

JANDY NELSON is a literary agent with Manus and Associates Literary Agency, Inc., representing authors for over 20 years from offices in New York City and the San Francisco Bay Area. Jandy has a varied list that includes narrative nonfiction, memoirs, self-help, health, and fiction (from literary fiction to multicultural fiction to thrillers). She regularly sells clients' work into the television and feature film markets.

Reflecting a commitment to new writers, her client list includes Andrew X. Pham, author of *Catfish & Mandala*; Karl M. Soehnlein, author of *The World of Normal Boys*; Joelle Fraser, author of *The Territory of Men: A Memoir* (Random House); Laurie Drummond, author of the short-story collection *Anything You Say Can and Will Be Used Against You* (HarperCollins); Terry Tarnoff, author of *The Bone Man of Benares* (St Martin's); and Tom Dolby, author of *The Trouble Boy* (Kensington). Other nonfiction titles include *Geisha, A Life* (Atria/Simon & Schuster) by Mineko Iwasaki with Rande Brown; and *Lily Dale: The Town That Talks to the Dead* (HarperCollins) by Christine Wicker.

Her list also includes serious health and self-help books, including *Breast Cancer: Beyond Convention: The World's Foremost Authorities on Alternative and Complementary Therapies* (Atira/Simon & Schuster), and *Hot Flashes, Warm Bottles: First-time Moms Over 40* (10 Speed Press) by Nancy London.

Jandy has a background in theater and film and has taught creative writing at Brown University where she did her graduate work. An award-winning poet herself, she is often actively involved in the development and marketing of clients' work.

CHAPTER 39

Pitch and Catch

Building a Relationship

by Jeff Herman

In publishing, the importance of pitching is contingent upon the extent of any pre-existing relationship between the pitcher and the catcher. If a publisher already admires a certain writer, for instance, the editor may be "pre-sold" on virtually anything that the writer comes up with next. So an elaborate pitching process is simply unnecessary.

It is a fact that positive and mutually fulfilling relationships are the most crucial ingredient in most ongoing endeavors, including the world of publishing. Any writer who wishes to progressively sustain herself for years to come will want to work towards building rich relationships, to the point where she is in a sense "branded" in the minds of the players within her genre. Once this is achieved, her name is the pitch.

Of course, "What have you done for me lately?" is never unimportant.

But everyone must begin somewhere. Let's assume you don't know anyone in publishing and that nobody knows you. The first question to ask is: "Why would they want to know me?" Well, they probably don't want to know you unless they think they perhaps need you. Why would they need you? Because they have to publish acceptable material on a continuing basis, and they need people who can reliably generate it.

Can you do that? If yes, then there should be a basis for a mutually beneficial relationship.

But it's not as simple or straightforward as it sounds. As you have been aware, I'm sure, there are too many wannabes chasing too few opportunities. This means you have to compete.

However, the competition won't only be about the alleged quality of your written product. In fact, that's sometimes a secondary consideration. The real competition often is simply about getting attention; getting noticed; making sure that someone with the power to issue a contract actually senses that you're out there and maybe opens the door just enough for you to slip in for a brief moment.

How do you get this door to open?

That's where pitching comes into play.

THE REAL COMPETITION OFTEN IS SIMPLY ABOUT GETTING ATTENTION.

Pitches that fail

It's so much easier to talk about why people fail at pitching than why they succeed. The magic of failure is so abundantly obvious to everyone but the "doer," whereas the alchemy of success is seemingly elusive and intangible. If it were any other way, we would all succeed all the time. How incredibly boring that would be.

Let me be very frank. Most of the pitches I see and hear suck. The usual reason is that most are painfully boring.

Most pitches are self-centered, unending diatribes about something. It can be really painful to have to sit down and read a few dozen of them at a time. Yes, on occasion we affirmatively respond even to one of the bad ones, because the germ of a good project sometimes peeks through even a poorly constructed pitch letter. But in general, the worst pitch letters are like reading the instructions for how to put together a garbage disposal, or the limited warranty on your new electric can-opener.

It's amazing how many pitches start out telling me how many other agents and editors have already rejected the work in question. Or how many years they have been unsuccessfully peddling it. Is there an assumption that some of us are so co-dependent that we will feel compelled to help this poor miscreant loser by agreeing to do what hundreds of professional have already decided not to do?

This is not good salesmanship. If you tell me you're a loser, I'll believe you. If you choose to portray yourself as a loser, what are you trying to sell? What kind of reaction can you rationally expect?

If you tell me you're a winner, I'll at least consider the possibility that you are. Fake it until you make it.

I get angry pitch letters. The writer is incensed that they have to belittle themselves writing letters to sell themselves to complete jerks. If your pitch letter comes across like a complaint letter, you're wasting your time.

I get long letters with long paragraphs that hide the lead. The point of your pitch must come through immediately. Each paragraph should support and reaffirm that primary thesis, while doing as little harm as possible to the reader's dedication to her career.

Then there are those packages that are just too bizarre. Someone once sent me an illegal street drug. I quickly flushed it down the toilet and listened for sirens. The homemade confections are as routinely discarded. I've received reading glasses. There was something that involved beach sand that got all over the place and took a long time to disappear. All the assorted weird stuff over the years is a blur. Do any of these enhance the writers' odds? No.

Sometimes writers will have an opportunity to verbally pitch their works. Oh boy. Since we live in a hard-copy world, the verbal presentation is of dubious value. You may be an eloquent speaker, but that in itself does not mean that you actually wrote anything sellable yet or ever will.

As listeners, we are conditioned to politely listen to what's being said to us. But this process is often poorly used, sometimes abused. In the worst scenario, the pitcher just keeps talking, but there's no connection between us. I don't really know what's being said, and the pitcher is not assessing whether I am participating as a bona fide listener. The pitcher enters an obsessive stage of jawboning; they just can't stop talking about their project. It's not a conversation. It's dumping; it's acting out. And it can be misery for the listener.

READ YOUR JUNK MAIL AND LEARN FROM IT. THERE IS NO WASTED SPACE OR WORDING.

Pitches that succeed:

Why isn't there mouse-flavored cat food?

Now that's a provocative opening.

Why is the man who invests all your money called a broker?

No need to answer the above questions. But did it make you start thinking? Of course it's totally out of context, but if it got your attention, it did something that few pitches manage to do.

Read your junk mail. I'm serious. Read it and learn from it. Billions of dollars have been spent to perfect the art of writing and presenting junk mail. The paragraphs are short. There is no wasted space or wording. Everything is meant to be easy on the eyes and easy on the brains. Every sentence and paragraph reinforces the primary concept of the product or service, and several compelling "calls to action" are built in throughout the draft.

Always be conscious, then, of the following:

- Do not bore.

- Do not confuse.

- Be clear.

- Give reasons why your letter should be read and acted upon in an affirmative way.

- Be sure your concept doesn't get lost or forgotten.

- Be sure your concept can be easily stated and comprehended.

- Be sensitive to the fact that it is part of the reader's job to read pitch letters.

- Understand that nobody is required to like your pitch letter, or to even read your letter.

Like any veteran agent, I receive too many pitches every week. It's not wrong to assume that your pitch may not get read for a long time.

How do you improve the odds that yours will be read sooner? In my office, everyday a stack of envelopes is rubberbanded and put in a pile to wait for their turn to be eye-balled. It's very low tech. However, a fraction of people e-mail their queries. As I download my daily e-mails, I tend to scan everything briefly.

Guess what? The e-mailed tend to bypass the rubberbanded pile.

Let's accept the truth that everyone can be manipulated to do things that might not make any sense, at least to some of us. What does this have to do with pitching? People are powerfully affected by physical and emotional stimuli, which has nothing to do with the quality or quantity of cerebral cells.

In my case, I'm more likely to be impressed by nice-looking business-quality letterhead and envelopes, while inexpensive stationery that you can get at any drug store strikes me as more of the same before I ever open it and read it. For sure, it's better to have a good pitch presented on crappy letterhead than a crappy pitch on beautiful letterhead.

But beauty laid upon beauty is more likely to breed more beauty.

So be clear and provocative—and full of style and concept—and maybe we'll have the start of a positive and mutually fulfilling relationship.

JEFF HERMAN founded the Jeff Herman Literary Agency, LLC, in 1987 while still in his twenties. The agency has expanded rapidly and more than 500 titles have been sold. He is one of the most innovative agents in the business, and his agency has established a strong presence in general adult nonfiction, including business, general reference, commercial, self-help, computers, recovery/healing, and spiritual subjects.

He is the author of the often-recommended directory, *Jeff Herman's Guide to Book Publishers, Editors, and Literary Agents* (The Writer Books), and co-author of *Write the Perfect Book Proposal: 10 Proposals That Sold and Why!* (John Wiley), and *You Can Make It Big Writing Books* (Prima). The titles, among the best tools available to writers, have sold hundreds of thousands of copies.

Herman speaks throughout the country about how to get published and be successful as an author. He's been written about in many periodicals, including *Success, Entrepreneur, Publishers Weekly, Forbes*, and *The New Yorker*, and has been interviewed on many television and radio shows.

Previously, Herman worked for a New York public-relations firm where he designed and coordinated national consumer marketing campaigns for Nabisco Brands and AT&T. Prior to that, he was a publicist at Schoken Books, where he promoted the bestseller *When Bad Things Happen to Good People*. He graduated from Syracuse University with a degree in consumer economics.

CHAPTER 40

Selected Resources

How To Find & Contact an Agent

by Katharine Sands

Do you really need an agent? Why would you want a complete stranger (who may not even sound very nice!) to take 15% of the monies you might generate as an author?

Let's say you know the name of a huge publishing company, such as HarperCollins. How could you know the many imprints—the many publishers—under the HarperCollins corporate umbrella, including Ecco, Cliff Street Books, William Morrow, ReganBooks among others?

How could you possibly know which editor at each of these imprints would want to acquire and publish your book? Only agents know this, learning—lunch by lunch, call by call—which editor is looking for which kind of book, who does not want to acquire certain categories, and how each editor's personal taste and house "personality" affects who gets published.

But, if you need convincing, try this test: call a major publishing house yourself and see what happens. Chances are a civilian would spend a frustrating time and never get out of voice mail. If you do manage to get a live person on the phone, it will probably be an editorial assistant, who will tell you to get an agent. Agents are, in effect, a screening service for publishers. Editors want agents to do the representing, and to bring them writers whose works fit their publishing program.

Describing what she does as a literary agent, Sarah Jane Freymann says: "I'm a treasure hunter constantly in search of hidden gems and undiscovered talent. I'm an editor who helps clients shape their manuscripts and proposals. I'm a matchmaker, a deal-maker and a negotiator. And finally, I'm a believer with the conviction that books (in whatever form they're published) are still our most powerful magic."

When reading through query submissions, I see myself as a book dowser—a literary version of the water witch who starts to throb when she finds water in the desert. As an agent, I do the same thing: seeking the source of new writing talent with an internal divining rod that starts to hum when I come across an author-to-be.

I hope this book you hold in your hands has helped you develop your perfect pitch—which you are now ready to use to win over the perfect agent who will be your treasure-hunting, deal-savvy matchmaker and literary dowser. Here, then, are some places you can look to find agents.

IF YOU NEED CONVINCING THAT YOU NEED AN AGENT, TRY THIS TEST: CALL A MAJOR PUBLISHING HOUSE YOURSELF AND SEE WHAT HAPPENS.

Acknowledgements

Most published books have a page listing credits and thanks to all who made the book possible. You can pluck agent names from these pages.

Associations

Association of Authors Representatives (AAR)
For a list of AAR members, visit their website or send a check or money order for $7 (include an SASE with $.99 cents postage).

Association of Authors Representatives
P.O. Box 237 at 201 Ansonia Station
New York, NY 10023
www.aar-online.org
(212) 252-3695

The National Writers Union (NWU)

NWU is the trade union for writers of all genres. Members have access to several databases, including the Agent Database (listing names of agents). Members also receive copies of resource materials such as "Understanding the Agent-Author Relationship."

> The National Writers Union
> 113 University Place
> New York, NY 10003
> www.igc.apc.org/nwu
> 212-254-0279
> E-mail: nwu@nwu.org

Genre associations

Professional associations for mystery writers, science-fiction and fantasy writers, romance writers, and other genres often maintain and make available lists of agents interested in representing work for that field.

Books (Directories)

Literary Market Place

For a comprehensive list of agents, submission guidelines, and interests consult *LMP*, a phonebook-sized resource guide available at your local library.

The Writer's Handbook

Edited by Elfrieda Abbe and published by The Writer Books, this is "a premier compendium of writing techniques, inspiration and advice." The annual directory's resources include agents, organizations, conferences, writer's markets, with a 50-page section focused on the special needs of new writers.

Jeff Herman's Guide to Book Publishers, Editors, and Literary Agents
Updated annually, this 800-pound gorilla of writing advice gives how-to tips and profiles of literary agents. Features hundreds of agents and details their likes and dislikes, along with descriptions of their clients from hell and dream clients.

The Watson-Guptill Guide to Writers Conferences
Compiled by David Emblidge and Barbara Zheutlin, this is a resource guide to workshops, conferences, artists' colonies, and academic programs. You will find agents' names in brochures and websites when you check the state-by-state listings.

The New York Writer's Guide
"From the tables at Elaine's to the bar at the Cedar Tavern, from the desks of the Writers Room on Astor Place to the therapy couches of the Washington Square Institute, New York is the writer's town, literary Ground Zero," says author J.B. Miller. Profiling everything from classes to cyber cafés, *The New York Writer's Guide* (www.iuniverse.com) describes organizations, guilds, unions, centers, societies, colonies, grants, fellowships, workshops, bookshops, open-mikes, reading series, writing courses, and boot camps for the writer, all of which offer agency events.

Books (by other agents)

Not only will you get a strong sense of these agent-authors, you can also comb through the text for other agents whose names are featured in anecdotes.

A few recommended titles include:

- *Literary Agents: What They Do, How They Do It, and How to Find and Work With the Right One for You* (John Wiley & Sons), by Michael Larsen

- *The Complete Idiot's Guide to Getting Published* (Alpha Books), by Sheree Bykofsky and Jennifer Basye Sander

- *The Insider's Guide to Getting an Agent* (Writer's Digest Books), by Lori Perkins

ASSOCIATIONS.

DIRECTORIES.

OTHER BOOKS.

Educational Programs

University programs and continuing education centers offer courses on writing and publishing topics taught by agents. Literary agent names and biographies will be listed along with the courses they teach in the catalogues and on websites.

New York University

7 East 12th Street
New York, NY 10003
(212) 995-3656
www.sce.nyu.edu

92nd Street Y Unterberg Poetry Center

Offers literary seminars, as well as a lecture series, called "Biographers & Brunch," featuring writers talking about their subjects, followed by a light lunch. The catalogue also offers seminars and panels taught by literary agents. Call (212) 996-1100 for more information.

Learning Annex

Offers many agent-taught classes in U.S. and Canadian cities such as New York, Chicago, Los Angeles, San Francisco, Vancouver, and many others. For more information, see www.learningannex.com

Writers' Conferences

Agents have sparkling bios in writing conference brochures and on conference websites. These conferenceniks attend writers' conferences to source new clients, plug their books, and travel as invited guests to interesting destinations.

Magazines

Poets & Writers

Published by Poets & Writers, Inc., a nonprofit organization founded in 1970, this writing magazine answers writers' top questions and offers many resources for further information. The organization also runs workshop programs featuring agents.

> 72 Spring Street, Suite 301
> New York, NY 10012.
> (212) 226-3586
> www.pw.org

Publishers Weekly

The magazine, known as the bookselling bible for the industry, recently started listing agent names at the bottom of book reviews in its book review section, "Forecasts." This section features pithy reviews of upcoming books and is used by booksellers and publishers alike to get the buzz on forthcoming books.

The Writer

This monthly magazine offers articles and interviews that focus on the process of writing. How-to pieces, marketing ideas, publishing trends, profiles, book reviews, and market listings are featured in each issue.

> *The Writer* magazine
> www.writermag.com

Newsletters

Publisher's Lunch

This free daily e-mail newsletter covers the business of the publishing industry, focusing especially on recent book deals. To sign up, visit the website: www.publisherslunch.com.

About agents and their listings

In fact, you already have a literary representative . . . you! . . . until you find a literary agent to represent you. And like the search for true love, you have to believe the right one is out there.

Agent Lori Perkins agrees: "Think of the process of finding an agent as like dating. You are embarking on a matchmaking experience . . . what you really want is someone who is not only going to tell you that you are brilliant, but someone who truly understands your work and your vision for how you want to grow as a writer."

Agents are always looking for good writers. Anna Ghosh of Scovil Chichak Galen points out in particular that "Young agents are eager to build their list; in fact, as eager to find good writers as writers are to find agents." New associate agents are always springing up at agencies. While an agency traditionally may not handle mysteries or chick lit, maybe a new associate is interested in developing these areas.

Also, agents may choose to vary what they do intentionally. For example, an agent who has had success with several spiritual journey books may not want to agent another. S/he may be "over-inventoried" in the category. Or perhaps s/he wants a new challenge, or wishes to avoid cannibalizing sales for existing clients' sales, or may simply not want to be typecast or overspecialized. (For example, I've agented many books for gay readers, but I'm not actually gay!)

So don't take agency listings as gospel. Innovations in our fast-changing industry are not always reflected in resources listing agents. New agents, editor/publicist-turned agent, assistant-promoted-to-agent may be terrific representation for you. New agents are hungry, open, and more available than the mega-über-agents (who are likely to farm newer writers to junior associates anyway).

You cannot know who will be receptive, so cast your net as widely as possible, like any other job application process. There is no reliable predictor of how you will find the right agent for you.

Last tips & reminders

Every agent says don't phone, don't phone, don't phone. But . . . shhhh, this tip is a secret . . . if I were a writer looking for an agent, I might phone and take a chance. If so, I would call either very early or very late in the day—after working hours when the assistant whose job is to say "next" has gone home. (Not to dismiss assistants; they can be a wonderful source of information and might be starting to take on clients.)

NEW AGENTS ARE HUNGRY, OPEN, AND MORE AVAILABLE.

If you call, make sure your phone pitch is sharp, has panache, and is well rehearsed. When you first get an agent on the phone, s/he may not be welcoming or friendly, but if you make the perfect pitch in the briefest possible manner, and if s/he invite you to go ahead and submit a full query or sample chapters, then you can use the golden word "requested" on the outside of your package. Then, it goes straight to the agent's requested pile. Yes, you've skirted the slush pile and the plethora of proposed books from the "Other Side."

However, if the agent is not encouraging or doesn't want to hear a brief pitch, end the conversation quickly and prepare to send in your materials in the traditional manner.

And whatever you do, don't lie. The industry has a lot of gossip and channels of communication, and fabricating stories will too soon be brought to light. There's a famous story, according to Lori Perkins, agent and author of the book, *The Insider's Guide to Getting an Agent* by Lori Perkins, an author who made up a quote from a bestselling writer, which his agent then used in selling said book for a six-figure deal. When an article about the sale appeared, the published author called *The New York Times* to complain that he had never read the book. The publisher rescinded his offer quite publicly.

In another book, *The Complete Idiot's Guide to Getting Published* by agent Sheree Bykofsky and Jennifer Basye Sander, they offer several useful tips of things to avoid at all costs, including: misspelled agents' names, packages with postage due, queries that say, "All of my friends think this is a great idea," proposals that smell like cigarette smoke, and queries that mention the minimum advance the writer will accept.

According to J.B. Miller, author of *The New York Writer's Guide*, "Make sure the work is immaculate. That is, no typos, no spellos, no grammos. Submit typed work, double-spaced, with wide margins. Make sure the pages are numbered, and your name and address . . . are clearly marked on your title page. Obvious stuff, right? But you'd be surprised how sloppy some writers get. Your apartment can be a junk heap, but your typescripts should be immaculate. Make it as easy, as painless, as possible for the agent to read your work. After a long day slogging through pages, the agent will want any excuse to pass over—that is, not read—a manuscript. Make sure that doesn't happen to yours."

Tonianne Robino, associate literary agent with the Jeff Herman Literary Agency, says she is surprised by how many people include gifts or gimmicks with their submissions. "We've received lottery tickets, bubble bath, CDs, baseball tickets, and a homemade voodoo doll. It makes opening the envelope more entertaining, but it doesn't encourage us to represent the book on its merit." It generally has the opposite effect, making an agent leery of getting involved at all, as it confuses the core issue of whether the work is worthy and the author reliable and professional.

When you are sending in unpublished work, your material is called a "submission" or a "manuscript." When publishing rights to that work are "acquired" by a publishing house, then it's called an "acquisition." It doesn't technically become a "book" until it's published. If you tell an agent you have "written a book," she or he will assume you mean a book that's been published. This can ensure an Abbott and Costello "who's-on-first" routine when the agent asks you who published your book.

Before publication—before copyright is obtained in your name with an ISBN number from the Library of Congress—to be accurate, you should tell agents that you have written a manuscript for a book, a manuscript for a novel. You can also refer to it as the work, or, in the case of nonfiction work, the project.

Of course, when you refer to future marketing efforts, as you look ahead to the time when the manuscript has (you hope) indeed been published, then it makes sense to call it a "book"—and you can logically discuss what you can do to help publicize the "book" in the section where you present your marketing platform.

Finally, all submissions should be accompanied by an SASE (Self-Addressed Stamped Envelope) so that an agent can respond or return material easily.

Good luck!

INDEX

The Writer

The Writer was founded in 1887 by two reporters from the *Boston Globe.* Their mission was to create a publication that would be "helpful, interesting, and instructive to all literary workers." The magazine soon became an essential resource for writers, publishing articles in the first half of the 20th century by literary luminaries such as William Carlos Williams, Wallace Stegner, Sinclair Lewis, William Saroyan, Daphne du Maurier, and many others.

After a long editorial tenure into the latter half of the 20th century by A. S. Burack and then Sylvia K. Burack, in the year 2000 Kalmbach Publishing Co. purchased the magazine, along with its affiliated line of books on writing fiction and nonfiction, and moved the editorial operations from Boston to Waukesha, Wisconsin (a suburb of Milwaukee).

Continuing its long heritage of more than 110 years of service, *The Writer* continues to be an essential resource for writers into the 21st century, providing advice from our most prominent writers, featuring informative articles about the art and the business of writing.

It is dedicated to helping and inspiring writers to succeed in their endeavors and to fostering a sense of community among writers everywhere.

More information on *The Writer,* with current articles and other resources, can be found online at the magazine's Web site, http://www.writermag.com.

—Elfrieda Abbe, Editor
The Writer